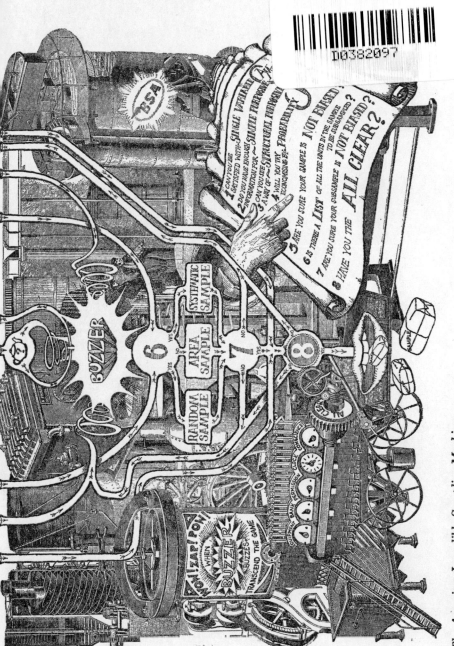

The Amazing, Incredible Sampling Machine

Paradigms and Fairy Tales

'*Their equipment, though marvellously fashioned, was quite unfamiliar*'

Paradigms and Fairy Tales

An Introduction to the Science of Meanings

Volume 2

Julienne Ford
*Department of Sociology,
Middlesex Polytechnic*

Routledge & Kegan Paul
London and Boston

First published in 1975
by Routledge & Kegan Paul Ltd
Broadway House, 68–74 Carter Lane,
London EC4V 5EL and
9 Park Street,
Boston, Mass. 02108, USA
Illustrations by Martin Davis and Sally Cutting
Set in Monotype Imprint
and printed in Great Britain by
Western Printing Services Ltd, Bristol
© Julienne Ford 1975
ISBN 0 7100 8215 0 (c)
ISBN 0 7100 8249 5 (p)
ISBN 0 7100 8216 9 (c) THE SET
ISBN 0 7100 8250 9 (p) THE SET

Contents

Volume 2

10	The Light is Above	219
11	A Short Cut from A to B	224
12	Rabbit on the Shopping List	235
13	Will You Join the Dance?	241
14	A Most Unlikely Story	263
15	The Amazing, Incredible Sampling Machine	293
16	A Box of My Own Invention	322
17	Uncertain Measures	343
18	Coder Coda	383
19	Statistricks!	396
20	What You Will!	424
	Notes	439
	Glossary of Fairy-Tale Words	463
	Index of Names	465
	Index of Subjects	471

Chapter 10

The Light is Above

Alice was not a bit hurt, and she jumped up on to her feet in a moment: she looked up, but it was all dark overhead: before her was another long passage, and the White Rabbit was still in sight, hurrying down it. Away went Alice like the wind, and she was just in time to hear it say, as it turned a corner, 'Oh my ears and whiskers, how late it's getting!' She was close behind it when she turned the corner, but the Rabbit was no longer to be seen: she found herself in a long, low hall, which was lit up by a row of lamps hanging from the roof.

There were doors all round the hall, but they were all locked; and when Alice had been all the way down one side and up the other, trying every door, she walked sadly down the middle, wondering how she was ever to get out again.

Like Alice, we have been here more than once before. The spiralling MOUNTAIN corridors have brought us again and again to what seems like the same cloister in the midst of an unbroken series of hermeneutic circles. Each time we have felt trapped within a ring of meanings from which there was no obvious escape – and each time we have paused to wonder how we were *ever to get out again.*

How can the sociologist successfully extricate himself? How can he return to the real worlds of everyday appearances without taking off his GOLD-STAR BADGE?

The RABBITS have taught us many things about science and we have learned from them that good FAIRY TALES can be made to come true$_4$ if the proper rituals are correctly observed. And, like all serious magicians, the GOLD-STAR RABBITS have warned us against the dangers of performing the rituals in an inappropriate frame of mind. A genuinely *falsificationist attitude* towards theoretical preconceptions, PLUS a healthy respect for the ever-punctual wisdom of common sense are, as we now know, essential prerequisites for the successful establishment of those truths$_4$ which may be universally regarded as worth-knowing-about.

But now suppose that *you* are a sociologist. By virtue of that supposition you cast yourself as an acceptor of the basic metatheoretical perspective which is available to any RABBIT who is bold enough to clamber up onto the shoulders of giants like Marx, Durkheim, Simmel, and Weber. Now you want to find some simple rules for sociological research. What you want is a clear route from theoretical to hypothetical, to operational, and then to factual judgments.

But where do you begin? The White Rabbit is no longer to be seen. And where is Alice?

Suddenly she came upon a little three-legged table, all made of solid glass: there was nothing on it but a tiny golden key. . . .

The key you require is, of course, an *IMPLICIT THEORY*. The second-order happenings which crowd upon your sociological consciousness when you adopt the role of a real stranger in a real social world are meaningless phantoms until *you* bestow meaning upon them by sociological theorizing. Not until you have some second-order theoretical conceptions, albeit vague ones, do you have a starting-point for research. And, though many sociological RABBITS have tried to reduce the activity of second-order theorizing to a set of routinized procedures, none denies the importance of pure *imagination* in the initial conception of theory.

Certainly there are some funny bunnies who, like Glaser and Strauss,[1] will try to seduce you into a Tiggiwinkle world of dirty smalls. These furry fellows believe unflinchingly in liberated LAUNDRY; so much so that they keep flaunting their theory-construction procedures before you. Indeed, they even attempt to lure you into that steamy backroom of the mind where they spend many sweaty hours chanting the four principal modes of John Stuart Mill's inductive methodology:[2]

1. THE METHOD OF AGREEMENT
If two or more instances of the phenomenon under investigation have only one circumstance in common, the circumstance in which alone all instances agree is the cause of the given phenomenon.

2. THE METHOD OF DIFFERENCE
If an instance in which the phenomenon under investigation occurs, and an instance in which it does not occur, have every circumstance in common save one, that one occurring in the former, the circumstances in which alone the two instances differ is the effect, or the cause, or an indispensable part of the cause, of the phenomenon.

3. THE METHOD OF CONCOMITANT VARIATIONS
Whatever phenomenon varies in any manner, whenever another phenomenon varies in some particular manner, is either a cause or an

effect of that phenomenon, or is connected with it through some fact of causation.

4. THE METHOD OF RESIDUES
Subduct from any phenomenon such part as is known by previous inductions to be the effect of certain antecedents, and the residue of the phenomenon is the effect of the remaining antecedents.

These strategies for theory construction are still to be found in most textbooks on sociological methodology. But you have my personal guarantee that, if you try to emulate them you will get nothing but hot and sticky. For not only do these procedures rest upon a number of unacceptably positivistic assumptions – such as the implicit belief that all ¿relevant? variables are available to the theorist in the form of observables – but, far from stimulating the imagination, they tend to stifle it. And it is not until the intervention of imagination that theory-work can truly begin.

So do not be bamboozled into the steam-room of routinized induction! No one can show you where to find your theory. Though the stock of knowledge-kept-as-sociology, may be regarded as a three-legged glass table it is still up to you to pick up your own golden key.

And, once you have the key, it remains for you to fit it in the right lock! For, like keys, theories are created for a specific purpose. Theories are no more use without puzzles than are keys without locks: though both may be works of great craftsmanship they have only formal value. It is *curiosity* which is the starting-point for theorizing, and theorizing which, as we have seen, is the first stage of scientific investigation.

Curiosity and *imagination*! These are the secret tokens which decide the final outcomes of research rituals, for, without these two, the elaborate procedures and techniques of research will yield only boredom and sterile statistics.

Let me now assume that you have both lock and key. From a multitude of appearances you have abstracted a puzzle and you have invented (or at least borrowed) a causal story which has, for the moment, a certain plausibility, at least as a second-order construction of meanings.

Now look *above*! You will see that you are standing underneath an illuminated sign, and a little further on down the low warren is another such sign. The signs seem to extend in sequence down the length of this dark hall, a hall remarkably like that in which you last saw the comforting figure of the White Rabbit. But that GOLD-STARRED gentleman is certainly not here now, and there are not even any of his ordinary run-of-the-mill colleagues to guide you. No. Unless you know another way out, your only guide from now on is the book in your hand. (See the illustration on page 222.)

If you look at that illustration you will notice that it bears a striking

Lights Above

similarity to the pattern of the illuminated signs on the roof above. The first part of the plan is probably clear to you already.

It seems that you have already made one move down the dark warren which leads from this FAIRY-TALE place to the lands of reality outside. You have moved from your starting position under the sign *PUZZLE* to a part illuminated by the *IMPLICIT THEORY*. The next stage is to turn your vague FAIRY TALE into a more formal causal model; because only when your second-order construction of meanings can be stated as a formal pattern of causes and effects – of INDEPENDENT, INTER-VENING and DEPENDENT variables – will it be genuinely open to the critical scrutiny of the community of RABBITS whom you have chosen to adopt as peers.

In the next chapter you will find some hints on theory formalization which may be of guidance to you. You will find that, if you are to move away from this dimly lit and muddy part of the passage and on to the firm, dry part, illuminated by the much brighter lamp which lights the sign *ANALYTICAL THEORY*, then you will need to take four steps.

Chapter 11

A Short Cut from A to B

If you accepted the GOLD-STAR version of the methodology of science, you will agree that, from the point of view of preparation for the rituals of scientific research, the ideal way to present a theory is as a deductive nomological explanation (D.N.E.). That is to say that, *ceteris paribus*, it is desirable to formalize one's theory as a *'logical' pattern of intrinsically connected judgments about causal relationships between variables, where at least some of those variables are specifiable as actual or potential appearances*. But – as I once learned to my cost in a school chemistry laboratory – *ceteris* rarely are *paribus*.

There are many reasons why it may be impractical to formalize an *EXPLANATORY THEORY* before proceeding to testing rituals. One very good reason is that that sort of formal theory-work takes a long time, and the normal run-of-the-mill RABBIT is generally impatient to state his theoretical fabrications ('Oh my ears and whiskers, how late it's getting!'). And, as we have seen, the retroductive process of theorizing often involves the 'premature' testing of hypotheses – a theorist may well wish to test part of his theory before risking placing the whole delicate edifice on a few caryatidic hypotheses.

It is for these reasons that so many theorists choose to draw up their ideas in the form of causal models or *ANALYTICAL THEORIES* rather than going the whole GOLD-STAR hog. Of course, an *ANALYTI-CAL THEORY* is less precise as a structure of ideas than is an *EX-PLANATORY THEORY* and the former cannot be so readily checked for errors of reasoning as can the latter. Yet even a two-dimensional model is to be preferred to a rambling verbal description. For, in a well-presented *ANALYTICAL THEORY*, much of the causal framework which the theorist has constructed is clearly open to scrutiny by other scientists, while an *IMPLICIT THEORY* remains an essentially covert set of judgments.

Do you remember when our erstwhile rabbity guide suggested a short cut through the MOUNTAIN?[1] Well, I think that we would do well to take that short cut now. Let's not dally in the warrens of esoteric formalism but proceed by the quickest and most practical route.

The quickest and most practical way that I have found[2] for drawing up a causal model is as follows (and you will have to read to pages 256–8 to understand the numbering!):

Devising an analytical theory

II, 1. Take a large piece of paper and divide it into three sections (see Figure 12).

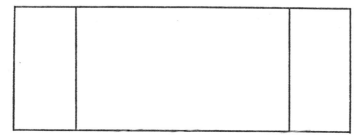

FIGURE 12

II, 2. Now label the sections of your page from left to right, thus:

| INDEPENDENT VARIABLES | INTERVENING VARIABLES | DEPENDENT VARIABLE |

The DEPENDENT VARIABLE is the event or phenomenon – the happening – whose variance you wish to explain, it is the variable which you would have named as the subject of the *explanandum* if you had decided to draw your theory up as a deductive nomological explanation. The other side of your page you have a space for the INDEPENDENT VARIABLE(S), that is for that (those) happening(s) which you have decided to treat as (a) given factor(s) whose variance is to be taken-for-granted. Another way of describing INDEPENDENT and DEPENDENT VARIABLES is, of course, in terms of 'causes' and 'effects'. Anything that you place in the first column on the left is to be regarded by you as a 'cause', while whatever appears in the right-hand column is to be taken as an 'effect'.

In the centre column you list all those variables which you consider to 'intervene' between the 'causes' and the 'effects'. These are those fictions which you have invented (or borrowed from other theorists) as part of your explanation of the relationship between the INDEPENDENT and DEPENDENT variables.

For example, suppose that you wish to compose a causal story to explain some puzzling aspect of the variance in *educational qualifications* in England and Wales. You posit *social class* as an independent causal factor, and, in order to link this with your dependent variable, *educational qualifications*, you introduce a number of other notions which can be placed in the middle box. These INTERVENING VARIABLES are concepts which, like the dependent and independent variables, are believed to have equivalents in appearances which, if not directly observable, are at least indirectly so. Thus, for example, notions like *socialization practices, intelligence,* and, say, *teachers' attitudes* may appear in your middle box. Each of these is a theoretical fiction which can, none the less, be linked arbitrarily with the world of appearances via certain measuring operations: intelligence, for example, may eventually come to be replaced in your thoughts by *IQ scores, teachers' attitudes* by *the-answers-certain-teachers-give-to-certain-of-your-questions,* and so on.

Your page should be beginning to look like a rather scruffy shopping list, thus:

INDEPENDENT VARIABLE	INTERVENING VARIABLES	DEPENDENT VARIABLE
social class	socialization practices intelligence teachers' attitudes	educational qualifications

II, 3. Once you have sorted the variables-which-have-already-occurred-to-you into these three boxes you can begin to arrange them in some sort of pattern. You will find that, as you do this, you are both elaborating and clarifying your ideas about the causal sequences involved in your original implicit theory.

In my view it is easiest to use the simple arrangement of boxes and arrows which I suggested in chapter 7. For instance, the example suggested above might be rearranged as in Figure 13.

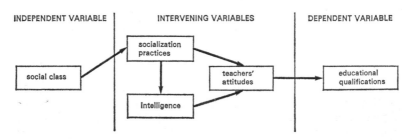

FIGURE 13

Looking at this rearrangement (Fig. 13) it becomes apparent immediately that there is still a great deal of work to do before *this* theory looks adequate as an explanation of the relationship between *social class* and *educational qualifications*. Certainly there are a host of other INTERVENING VARIABLES begging for inclusion. What about the *parents' attitudes towards education?* What about the child's own *self-conception of ability?* How are these two causally related? And how do *school selection routines* enter into the picture? What part do *informal friendships at school* play in the story? And so on, and so on.

EXERCISE
Play around with this FAIRY TALE until you are satisfied that you have a plausible *ANALYTICAL THEORY.*

Eventually you will find an arrangement that seems to make reasonable sense as a construction of sociological ideas. Remember, though, that, however impressive your diagram may look, it *is* nothing more than a FAIRY TALE. Even the classification of variables into boxes is entirely dependent upon your theoretical whim. Thus the 'same' variable may appear as a DEPENDENT VARIABLE in one theory, an INDEPENDENT one in another, and an INTERVENING one in yet another. For example, *political values* may be taken as happenings-to-be-explained in a theory which postulates *social class, education* and a number of other variables in a causal sequence. However, a different theorist might take *political values* as the INDEPENDENT VARIABLE, say in a theory about *propensity to support industrial militancy*. And still another theorist might place *political values* between *social class* and *propensity to support industrial militancy*, as an INTERVENING VARIABLE.

So, from the standpoint of other theories, your model may not only be rearranged, but certain other variables might be included or even used to replace some of those which *you* had chosen. For example, a critic of your theory of the relationship between *social class* and *educational qualifications* might suggest an alternative. He might suggest that the relationship is due to the differential distribution of *educational facilities in the home*. Behind this suggestion might be an implicit theory based upon the idea that educational qualifications reflect the *standard of schoolwork* which a child has achieved throughout his school life. A quiet room to do homework, plenty of books, and the ability of parents to help with homework and suggest further lines of study, might be decisive factors.

Major INTERVENING VARIABLES in this theory are therefore

educational facilities in the home and *standard of schoolwork*, but from the point of view of *your* theory these are EXTRANEOUS VARIABLES.

Of course, these two (equally unsatisfactory) theories can be put together in one diagram (Fig. 14). The solid lines describe the original story and the broken lines the causal links posited by our imaginary critic.

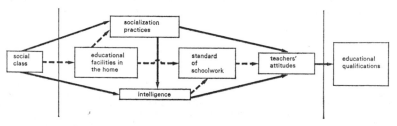

FIGURE 14

In order for you to put your theory at risk properly it is necessary for you to be fully aware that a wide range of EXTRANEOUS VARIABLES might be suggested by critics of your view, and to consider the ways in which at least some[3] of these EXTRANEOUS VARIABLES might interact with those in which you are interested.

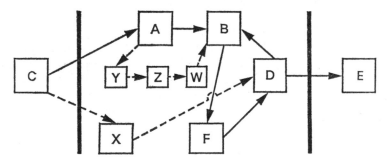

FIGURE 15

II, 4. So the next step is to take a different coloured pen and sketch into your diagram all those EXTRANEOUS VARIABLES which, as it seems to you, could be posited from the viewpoint afforded by rival theories. Consider carefully the ways in which these additions affect your original story. Do they simplify it, complicate it, or even render it absurd? Your page should now look something like Figure 15.

Here three EXTRANEOUS VARIABLES, W, X, Y and Z, have been added to an original story which had been written in terms of the six variables A, B, C, D, E and F. If you look at this model of an amended theory you will see that one of the new EXTRANEOUS

VARIABLES, X, provides a *short circuit*; it posits a more simple causal connection between the INDEPENDENT VARIABLE, C, and the last INTERVENING VARIABLE, D. On the other hand, consideration of rival FAIRY TALES has led to an *elaboration* of the tale at another point: the link between A and B has been spelt out more fully by the intervention of Y, Z and W.

Now, perhaps it has occurred to you that some of these EXTRANEOUS VARIABLES won't fit on your page! This is because they are variables which, from another point of view, might be posited as causes of your original INDEPENDENT VARIABLE. In the examples we have considered so far all the EXTRANEOUS VARIABLES suggested by rival theories could be included in the middle boxes of the original theories as INTERVENING VARIABLES. But suppose that a critic suggests (or you anticipate one suggesting) that there may be some factor(s) ANTECEDENT to your *whole story*. Suppose he puts forward a theory suggesting variable(s) which may be taken as causally independent of your own INDEPENDENT VARIABLE(S), the latter thus taking the status of mere INTERVENING or DEPENDENT VARIABLE(S) with respect to that new factor.

In order to assess the ways in which such ANTECEDENT VARIABLES could affect your own analytical theory you would need a larger piece of paper! Your original sketch could then be incorporated into a 'bigger' picture by simply including the first within the framework of the second. In this manner you would be *transcending* one analytical theory with a more general or 'roomier' one.

For example, suppose that you have a model which looks like Figure 16.

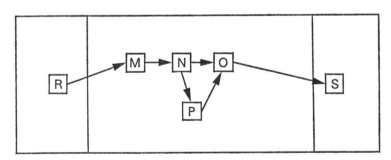

FIGURE 16

Now suppose that someone suggests that your INDEPENDENT VARIABLE, R, is itself an effect of an ANTECEDENT, Q. You can simply sketch the two theories together in a 'larger' diagram, as in Figure 17.

The left-hand section of your original diagram has now been demoted to the status of a mere part of the middle section in the new theory. But notice also that the causal sequences posited by your original FAIRY TALE remain unchanged within the 'bigger' story. In these circumstances then, you would be quite justified in retorting to your critic, 'so what?'. For his criticism is irrelevant to your task of devising an adequate set of tests for your theory: though it generates an *additional* proposition, regarding the effects of Q on R, it does not lead to any judgments which *conflict* with those of your original theory. There would, then, be no reason at all for you to consider changing your level of analysis as a result of this criticism.

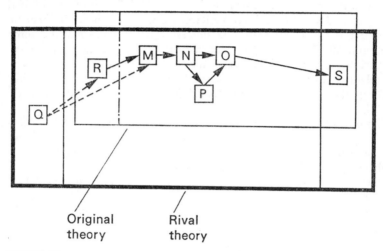

Original   Rival
theory   theory

FIGURE 17

But now consider the case as shown in Figure 18.

Here the second FAIRY TALE does not merely *add to* but actually *contradicts* the original one in some respects. The second theory states,

$$Q \rightarrow R \ and \ Q \rightarrow M$$

That is to say that the new ANTECEDENT is treated as a factor causing variance in both the original INDEPENDENT and one of the original INTERVENING variables. This means that, from the standpoint of the second theory, the original proposition,

$$R \rightarrow M$$

is regarded as spurious.

Obviously there are quite a number of different ways in which conflicting stories can fit together, some of these involve transcending levels

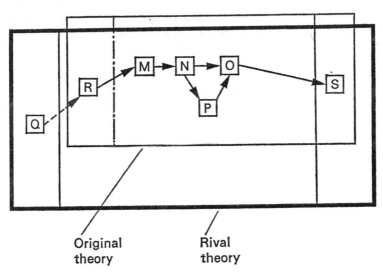

Original theory

Rival theory

FIGURE 18

of analysis and some do not. In Figure 19 two stories are represented which, though not involving any change in the level of analysis, none the less provide quite mutually exclusive explanations of the relationship between an INDEPENDENT and a DEPENDENT variable.

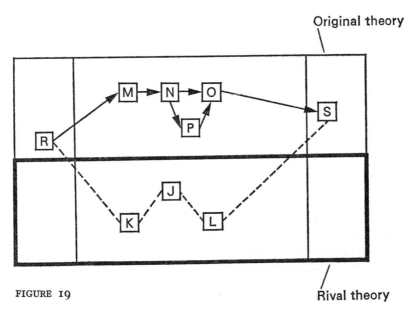

Original theory

FIGURE 19   Rival theory

And in Figure 20 there is a more complicated example where a change in the level of analysis results in a quite different story which, none the less, collides with the first at certain points.

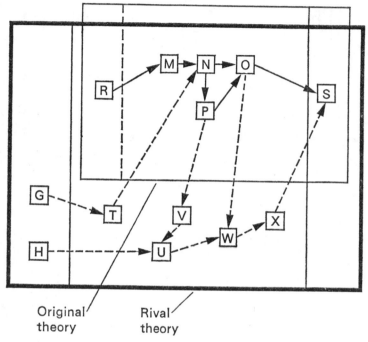

Original   Rival
theory   theory

FIGURE 20

You will also notice that in Figure 20 the second theory, unlike any we have considered so far, makes use of more than one INDEPENDENT VARIABLE. Of course there is only a practical limit to the number of INDEPENDENT VARIABLES which a theorist can put forward in connection with a single DEPENDENT one. Indeed theories as elementary as the examples I have sketched so far, theories woven around the influence(s) of a single independent causal factor, are, as we saw in chapter 7, as rare in sociology as they are in any other scientific discipline.

Now it is only when you have succeeded in formalizing your theoretical ideas in some manner that you will be in any position to plan a research programme designed to throw some light on the truth$_4$ or falsity$_4$ of your explanation of the puzzle in question. This is not to say that there is never any point in research undertaken in an investigatory rather than an overtly theory-testing frame of mind. But you should now recognize that what is generally termed 'exploratory research' is not to be regarded as a genuine voyage of discovery. No research is ever undertaken in the absence of *any* second-order theoretical assumptions, and programmes which masquerade as such are actually based on assumptions which, being hidden, are not open to inspection by others. I suggest therefore that, if you *do* wish to commence investigations before you feel able to formalize your theoretical ideas in some way, you should regard this research as a mere preliminary to theory construction and theory-directed research. Eventually you *must* face the rather daunting prospect of structuring your theory as a sequence of causal notions.

The advantages of the paper-and-pencil method I have suggested here are twofold. The act of drawing up your theory as a two-dimensional model helps you to clarify, and in so doing perhaps to revise, your own ideas. At the same time it exposes the structure of your causal FAIRY TALE to the critical scrutiny of others. In both these ways the ideal of *collective falsificationism* is more nearly approached than it would have been if you had left your theory in the untidy state that characterizes an *IMPLICIT THEORY*.

On the other hand, if you go in for this sort of *ANALYTICAL THEORIZING* you must not forget that even this is only a poor substitute for GOLD-STAR theory-work, for *EXPLANATORY THEORIZING*. In a proper deductive nomological explanation hypotheses are logically deduced from the higher order generalizations according to rules of reasoning which are universally respected by RABBITS. Any critic applying these rules can readily determine whether or not you have committed logical errors or falsehoods$_3$. And, since the whole logical structure must stand or fall upon the results of testing rituals whose outcome decides the truth$_4$ or falsity$_4$ of the testable hypotheses, those hypotheses enjoy the status of *categorical causality* with respect to the theory.

Of course, the sort of *ANALYTICAL THEORIZING* outlined above does not come up to this GOLD-STAR standard. Since the models are produced directly from *IMPLICIT THEORIZING* rather than serving as shorthand versions of completed *EXPLANATORY THEORIES*, they cannot generate *categorically causal* hypotheses. This means that the whole theory is never really being put to test, for, even if *every* hypothesis were to be falsified in the course of the testing rituals, it would still be possible for you to defend the plausibility of your basic theoretical approach. And, more important, it means that *failure* to falsify your hypotheses says very little about the truth$_4$ of the model itself.

However, if you have produced a clear *ANALYTICAL THEORY* and carefully considered the ways in which rival theoretical notions may be brought to bear upon it, you can at least maximize risk-taking in your research by drawing up a list of hypotheses for testing which, though only casually causal, do as far as possible permit judgments to be made about the relative truth$_4$ of your theory *vis-à-vis* rival theories which have come to your notice.

This degree of falsificationist rigour is obviously better than no rigour at all, for it clearly enables a comparative examination of the empirical plausibility of a number of rival explanations of the puzzle in question. What this method of elimination does not permit, however, is the disposal of any other theories which, though equally able to save the same appearances, have never entered into your head!

Chapter 12

Rabbit on
the Shopping List

Once you have formalized your theory the next step is to draw your hypotheses from it. If you have a proper *EXPLANATORY THEORY* this will, of course, be a matter of logical deduction. But if you have employed the method of *ANALYTICAL THEORIZING* suggested above there is an easy way of compiling an exhaustive list of the hypotheses entailed by your theory.

Every pictorial link in your diagram represents a hypothesis. This means that, if you have used the simple arrangement of boxes-and-arrows, then each arrow refers to a hypothesized relationship, thus, for example,

A ————▶ B

can be translated into words as 'B will vary as A varies', or 'As A increases (or decreases) in value B will increase (or decrease) in value', or 'A and B are positively (or negatively) correlated', or some other equivalent verbal expression. (Of course, you may also have followed my suggestion in chapter 7 and invented other sorts of diagrammatic expressions such as

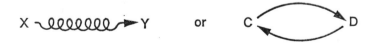

in which case you will no doubt be in a better position to translate them into words than I am!)

IV, 1. Clearly, then, the next thing to do is to compile an exhaustive list of all the hypotheses involved in your own theory.

Here, by way of example, is a list of hypotheses drawn from the theory presented on p. 231 above.

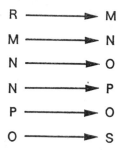

R ⟶ M

M ⟶ N

N ⟶ O

N ⟶ P

P ⟶ O

O ⟶ S

Notice that I have not bothered to translate these hypotheses back into words, nor have I used a shorthand form with which you may be familiar, namely:

$$D \propto E, \text{ or } F \propto \frac{1}{G}$$

This is because, so long as you retain the arrows, you will be less likely to forget that causal relationships, unlike mathematical functions, are asymmetric, irreversible, or ¿*directional?*.[1]

When you have listed *your own hypotheses* you can proceed to draw up an inventory of those *rival hypotheses* which you have been considering.

IV, 2. Make a list of hypotheses deriving from alternative theories. Here is a list of all the rival hypotheses examined on pp. 231–2.

Q ---→ R
Q ---→ M
R ---→ K
K ---→ J
J ---→ L
L ---→ S
G ---→ T
T ---→ N
P ---→ V
V ---→ U
H ---→ U
U ---→ W
O ---→ W
W ---→ X
X ---→ S

Now there are a number of reasons why you may not wish to test every one of the hypotheses you have listed. In the first place some of the statements in your theory (particularly some of those in the middle section involving the INTERVENING VARIABLES) may not be regarded as having equivalents which are realistically observable. As we saw in chapter 7, many scientific theories have at their core a number of judgments about relationships which are held to obtain between entities of *such* a fictional nature that attempts to pin them down to representative appearances would be absurd. Second, some of the relationships you – or indeed your critics – have suggested may have already been subjected to testing rituals by other scientists. In this case you may be prepared to accept the outcomes of these previous tests, though, of course, you are not by any means bound to do so. There may also be other hypotheses which, though testable in principle, seem to you at this stage to be outside your practical research means. But if you do choose to exclude certain hypotheses from your research programme you must make it quite clear *why* you are doing this and remember that, in so far as some of your hypothetical links (or those of your critics) remain untested, your research will be even less adequate as an arbiter of the truth₄ of your theory than it would otherwise have been.

IV, 3. Now, strike from your lists those hypotheses which you do not intend to test and *clearly record your reasons* for doing this. You will find that it is essential to keep a record of your reasons for this (and later) research decisions. For, by the time you come to write up the results of your research you will almost certainly have forgotten them.

At last it is time for you to start to think about what you are actually going to measure. For *which* variables will you wish to find measurable representatives in the real world(s)?

V, 1. Well, I suggest that you now take another piece of paper (or turn another page in your brand new research notebook!) and divide it into two sections, headed like this:

Inventory of variables to be measured

EXPERIMENTAL VARIABLES	UNCONTROLLED CONFOUNDING VARIABLES

V, 2. In the left-hand column simply list all the variables remaining in your abridged list of your own hypotheses. Like this:

EXPERIMENTAL VARIABLES	UNCONTROLLED CONFOUNDING VARIABLES
R, M, N, S, etc.	

That was easy enough wasn't it? But now comes the difficult bit!

In order to complete the list on the right-hand side of the page you will need to apply a rather complex formula.[2]

V, 3. Take your abridged list of EXTRANEOUS VARIABLES and prepare to classify these into three groups. You will first sort out

A. *Those you can control by selection,*
and B. *Those you can treat as random errors.* All the remaining variables then fall into the third group,
C. UNCONTROLLED CONFOUNDING VARIABLES, and will be listed on the right-hand side of your page.

If you remember the discussion in chapter 6 you will follow the rationale for this classification. What you are trying to do is to separate the effects of your EXPERIMENTAL VARIABLES from those of the EXTRANEOUS VARIABLES. In order to do this you have to try to hold the EXTRANEOUS VARIABLES *constant* – keep them 'still' – in some way, so that you can examine the relationships between your EXPERIMENTAL VARIABLES without becoming confused by the influence of these nuisance factors.

One method of controlling EXTRANEOUS VARIABLES is by *selection.* For example, suppose that you have a theory connecting an INDEPENDENT VARIABLE, *social class,* with a DEPENDENT VARIABLE, *law-violating behaviour,* via a complex of INTERVENING VARIABLES such as *values, perceptions,* and *opportunities,* etc. A critic might suggest that the relationship in question may be explained by a different theory which posits *poverty* as the crucial INTERVENING factor. This EXTRANEOUS VARIABLE poses a real threat to your theory because it might be shown to correlate with both *social class* and *law-violating behaviour.* You could, however, control this variable by selecting a sample of individuals for your research who did not vary amongst themselves in this respect. For instance, if you chose to limit your research to a universe of individuals with limited means (or, for that matter, a universe of people with more-than-adequate, or adequate means) you could be sure that any relationships holding between *law-violating behaviour* and *social class* in your sample could not be attributed to the variance of the EXTRANEOUS factor, poverty, simply because that factor had not been left free to vary.[3]

Another way of disposing of EXTRANEOUS VARIABLES is, of course, by *randomization.* Again this involves special sampling procedures: if you can select a sample of individuals for which you feel entitled to make the assumption that a particular EXTRANEOUS VARIABLE is randomly distributed, then you can safely ignore its effects. Suppose that it is suggested that *slightness of stature* and *nimbleness of limb* may be determinants of *law-violating behaviour* ('He who thieves and gets away is free to thieve another day!'). Then, so long as you can be sure that these factors are randomly distributed throughout the social class structure (a dubious assumption as a matter of fact!), you can forget all about them. And, for the moment, we shall continue to pretend, as did the RABBITS in chapter 6, that the assumption of randomization may also make a nice quieting illusion with which to deamplify the unimaginable squeaks of those EXTRANEOUS VARIABLES which are missing from your Inventory.

Of course a great many EXTRANEOUS VARIABLES which you or your critics have dreamt up cannot be controlled by randomization. After all, they have been suggested as rivals to your own EXPERI-MENTAL VARIABLES precisely *because* their influence cannot be assumed to be irrelevant. It is just because they *could* plausibly correlate with some of your own variables, particularly your DEPENDENT, and/or INDEPENDENT VARIABLES, that they *have* been brought to your notice!

At the same time it is often impractical to control an EXTRANEOUS VARIABLE by selection. For in many cases you cannot select a sample which is constant on a certain factor without actually *measuring* that factor yourself. Though lists may have been compiled by certain agencies which would enable you to pick a sample of, say, teetotallers (via Alcoholics Anonymous and the Temperance Society), or, say, members of the Elvis Presley fan club (via the secretary), no such lists exist of groups like Arsenal supporters, fatties, or cannabis habitués. So in order to get samples which were constant on factors like these you would have to draw larger samples, measure those factors, and then chuck away all the people you had sampled who had the 'wrong' values on those variables – a rather time-consuming and wasteful procedure to say the least! After all, if you are going to have to measure a variable *anyway* then why not *treat* it as a variable rather than trying to turn it into a constant? In that way you could not only compare, say, 'fatties' with 'non-fatties' in relation to your own variables, but also make finer comparisons, perhaps like this:

1	2	3	4	5
skinnies	yogis	straights	plump-straights	fatties

and all that fun would cost you very little extra effort!

V, 4. Now, all the EXTRANEOUS VARIABLES which cannot plausibly be treated as random factors, nor economically controlled by selection, must be regarded as UNCONTROLLED CONFOUND-ING VARIABLES. So, once you have made a clear record of the variables you have classified as 'A. *Variables to be controlled by selection*' and 'B. *Variables to be treated as random errors*', and carefully noted your reasons for doing so, you can simply strike these off your already-abridged list of EXTRANEOUS VARIABLES. Everything left on that list is now transferred into the right-hand column of your *Inventory of Variables to be Measured*.

Now, like our intrepid furry friends, you are ready to try to make a break for it across the perilous bridge that divides the FAIRY-TALE world of second-order theorizing from the real worlds outside. Like the RABBITS too, you already have two essential pieces of equipment in addition to your bait,[4] you have your shopping list (your *Inventory of Variables to be Measured*) in your pocket, and your theory in your head. Without these you won't stand any chance out there. But you will need something else if you are to get through the SPIDERS and safely to the other side. You will also need a well-considered plan. In the next chapter some useful stratagems are suggested which may help you to devise such a plan.

Chapter 13

Will You Join the Dance?

So there you stand, trembling at the brink of the BRIDGE, clutching your bait firmly in your hand and occasionally muttering phrases from your theory – just to make sure that you haven't forgotten it already. You put your hand in your pocket and draw out the scruffy shopping list. Though the ink is fading fast, the heading at the top can still be read plainly enough: '*Inventory of Variables to be Measured*'. 'That's easy enough then,' you catch yourself saying aloud. 'All I've got to do now is to *find* them.' But at that very moment two strange characters appear before you. They seem to be SPIDERS dressed in RABBITS' clothing. Yet over his phoney fur each sports a dashing striped suit. Boaters with striped bands and glossy dancing pumps complete the odd apparel.

FIRST FELLOW:	'Oh no oh no oh no oh no oh no!'
SECOND FELLOW:	'Oh no oh no oh no oh no oh NO!'
YOU:	(*Catching on fast*) 'Oh no oh no oh no oh no oh no WHAT?'
FIRST FELLOW:	'You can't *measure* variables.'
SECOND FELLOW:	'*You* can't measure variables.'
YOU:	'I can't measure *variables*?'
FIRST FELLOW:	'You can't.'
SECOND FELLOW:	'You certainly can't!'
FIRST FELLOW:	'Oh no oh no oh no oh no oh no!'
SECOND FELLOW:	'Oh no oh no oh no oh no oh NO!'
YOU:	'What can I measure then?'
FIRST FELLOW:	'Indicators.'
SECOND FELLOW:	'*Indicators!*'
FIRST FELLOW:	'INDICATORS!'
YOU:	'What's an indicator?'
FIRST FELLOW:	'Oh dear oh dear oh dear oh dear oh dear!'
SECOND FELLOW:	'Oh dear oh dear oh dear oh dear OH DEAR!'

FIRST FELLOW: 'Indicators are deputies. . . .'
SECOND FELLOW: (Nodding) 'Stand-ins.'
FIRST FELLOW: (Continuing despite interruption) 'selected by
                 fiat.'
SECOND FELLOW: (Breaking into song as sixteen little feet start to
                 tap) 'Quite arbitrareeeee, Do you seeeee?'
YOU: 'Something to do with Campanella and the
                 Pope?'
FIRST FELLOW: 'You've got it!'
SECOND FELLOW: 'He's got it.'
FIRST FELLOW: 'Indeed he has!'
BOTH FELLOWS: (Fading chorus as the funny fellows sidestep off
                 into the wings)
                 'I bought my wife a rabbit,
                 I bought my wife a duck.
                 We put them in the bathroom
                 To see if they would. . . .'
YOU: (Joining in to the Strains of 'Lulu was a Zulu')
                 'Oh Gor blimme
                                        etc.'[1]

You have correctly recalled that whenever mention is made of 'measuring variables' this is merely a convenient and somewhat misleading elision. For measurement is a doubly arbitrary process. In the first place, as the jolly comedians were quick to point out, the *variables themselves* can never be observed. You can only observe certain appearances which you have *chosen as indicators*, as visible representatives of invisible fairy-tale notions. Then a second set of arbitrary decisions is made when *quantitative values are assigned* to those appearances.

Obviously the choice of indicators must be a rather personal business. However, certain guidelines can be suggested.[2]

VI, 1. First *ponder upon your variables* (one at a time!). Feel them out in your mind and consider what they mean to you as second-order constructions of meanings. You may then find it useful to make a quick trip to the LIBRARY to see how other theorists have treated similar ideas.

VI, 2. As you think about your concepts, it may occur to you that many of them are rather complex and involve, not one, but several separable notions. So, *where relevant, break the concepts down into component parts.* For example, Melvin Seeman thought about the concept of *alienation* which has had wide currency in sociological theories since Marx. Seeman decided to treat the notion of *alienation* as consisting in five component parts: *powerlessness, meaninglessness, normlessness, social isolation,* and *self-estrangement.*[3] Another sociologist later decided to attempt to test a theory relating degree of *alienation* to *technology.* When he came to operationalize *alienation* he found Seeman's thoughts useful, but revised Seeman's components slightly because he did not feel that the notion of *alienation* usefully included *normlessness*.[4] You will probably think that *both* of these conceptualizations represent terrible travesties of Marx's own ideas, but this is because the same term appears in three quite different theories and therefore assumes three separate sets of second-order meanings.[5]

VI, 3. Only now does it become sensible for you to *start to think about what sorts of observations might serve as indicators* of your variables. You are looking for sets of appearances which could plausibly be considered as 'epistemic correlates' of your variables.[6]

For example, imagine that you are interested in the *drug-using practices* of people in a certain residential area. You decide that this variable covers three separable kinds of regular activity (the concept has three components), the taking of *medicinal drugs, legal euphoriants,* and *illegal euphoriants*.[7] Now detective ingenuity is called for: what observable variations might be taken as clues to the patterning of these behaviours? Most run-of-the-mill sociologists (but few good detectives!) would think first of all of simply *asking* a sample of the people in question.

But this would be a pretty inadequate indicator, for you would have no way of telling whether or not they were telling the truth$_2$. In the case of consumption of *illegal euphoriants* they would have every reason for lying, and many might even feel inclined to mislead you in regard to their consumption of *legal* ones.

A slightly more ingenious method might be to get them to inform on one another! Again this would involve direct questioning of a sample from the relevant universe; you would have to ask them something like this: '*I want you to think about your closest friend. Do you have any idea how many cigarettes he smokes in an average day? How much alcohol does he drink? etc.*' But this would hardly be very reliable either. And it certainly isn't very good manners!

Well, then, considering *legal euphoriants* alone for a moment, let's see . . . perhaps you could try surveying the customers at local off-licences, public houses, and tobacconists . . . oops! . . . no, snags again! *I* know, what about looking in the dustbins, that way you could get *medicinal drugs* too (from discarded medicine bottles?). Ah but, though you might find booze bottles, cigarette packets might be disposed of by burning; and certainly most users of *illegal euphoriants* are cool enough these days to keep their dustbins clear of all traces of their activities, for the next garbage-snooper might *not* be a friendly bunny RABBIT!

I suppose that one really effective way of getting the information you want would be to infiltrate the group in question, or at least a sample of them, and, seeming to be one of them, to observe what they do. But this method might well seem even more distasteful to you than grubbing around in dustbins and, even if it doesn't, it would certainly be expensive and time-consuming.

Finally, after considering these and other stratagems, you *might* come to the conclusion that *no* plausible indicators can be found at least for one component of your variable, the consumption of *illegal euphoriants*. In that case you would either have to give up completely or take your *ANALYTICAL THEORY* back to the drawing board.

It must be clear to you by now that the selection of indicators is a very tricky business. It is all very well to *say* that operationalization is an arbitrary link between the worlds of FAIRY TALE and reality, established by fiat, but it is only when you come to consider actual examples that it really comes home to you just *how* precarious this link is. The crucial thing to remember is that there is no *logical* relationship between a concept and whatever you decide to treat as its empirical indicator.

Allow me to regale you with another example to illustrate this same point. Take *intelligence*. Suppose that you decide that what you mean by *intelligence* includes *verbal skill*, *numerical skill*, and so on. There is no *obvious* way of measuring any of these components. For *verbal skill* you might decide to listen to people's conversations and categorize them in terms of complexity and/or originality of sentence structure and vocabulary, or you might give people a series of written tests in which they were required to indicate their knowledge of the meanings of words etc. None of these operations would actually amount to measurements of '*verbal skill*', they would simply produce measures of appearances which you were assuming to be empirically related to that abstract property.

As Blalock has said, 'There appears to be an inherent gap between the languages of theory and research which can never be bridged in a completely satisfactory way. One *thinks* in terms of a theoretical language that contains notions such as causes, forces, systems, and properties. But one's *tests* are made in terms of covariations, operations, and pointer readings.' And, of course, this is not a situation which is by any means peculiar to sociology; it is the same for any science. Blalock continues, 'Although a concept such as "mass" may be conceived theoretically or metaphysically as a property, it is only a pious opinion, in Eddington's words, that "mass" as a property is equivalent to "mass" as inferred from pointer readings.'[8]

If even such a straightforward ¿physical? notion as '*mass*' is not amenable to direct measurement, then clearly even those few sociological variables which seem at first thought to be totally non-problematic, as far as operationalization is concerned, cannot be so at all!

Consider the simple demographic variable, *age*, something that you will often want to employ as a standard control in a research programme. Even here the relationship between what you can *measure* and what you really *mean* is not clear-cut. You could work out some scale of age by subtracting dates of birth from the date of the year in which you were doing the research. But would that really be what you meant by *age* when you included the term in your *ANALYTICAL THEORY*? It *might* have been: you *might* have been interested in the deterioration of skin tissues or growth rate of beards, in which case sheer number-of-days-knocking-about-on-earth might have been precisely what you were after; but it is unlikely. It is more likely that you would have been using age as a predictor of knowledge, attitudes (or something like that), in which case you would really be wishing to find an indicator of something slightly different from simple ¿time? – something like experience-of-social-interaction, for instance, which you were assuming to be *empirically related* to chronological age.

All this being so, I suggest that you keep in mind two principles to guide you in the selection of indicators. These principles have been formulated to minimize the uncertainties which inevitably follow from arbitrary acts of measurement.

THE PRINCIPLE OF REPLICABILITY: Choose indicators which are, as far as possible, replicable by other researchers.
THE PRINCIPLE OF TRIANGULATION: Wherever possible choose multiple indicators for each variable. Do this particularly for variables with complex second-order meanings (ones with a number of components) and the key causal variables in your own, or your most damaging rival, hypotheses.

Though the twin principles of REPLICABILITY and TRIANGULATION can never overcome the inherent problems in the whole business of operationalization, they do at least facilitate the governing GOLD-STAR consideration which I have referred to above as COLLECTIVE FALSIFICATIONISM. By REPLICABILITY you ensure that others can at least repeat your rituals if they so desire. (Yet we have seen before,[9] and shall see again,[10] that repeatability, or 'reliability' gives no guarantee of external 'validity'.) By TRIANGULATION you give yourself a means of comparing one indicator with another and thus, clearly, open the possibility that your research will reveal that these different indicators are *not* correlated with one another, thus suggesting that one or more of them are *not* epistemic correlates of the variable in question. For practical reasons – which should become clear later – I suggest that you generally try to pick *at least three* separate indicators for each concept, or, in the case of complex concepts, each component of a concept. (The three here has nothing much to do with the 'tri-' of triangulation, though you might have thought so![11])

VI, 4. Now, *record your initial plans for operationalizing each variable on your 'Inventory of Variables to be Measured'.* Perhaps like Figure 21.

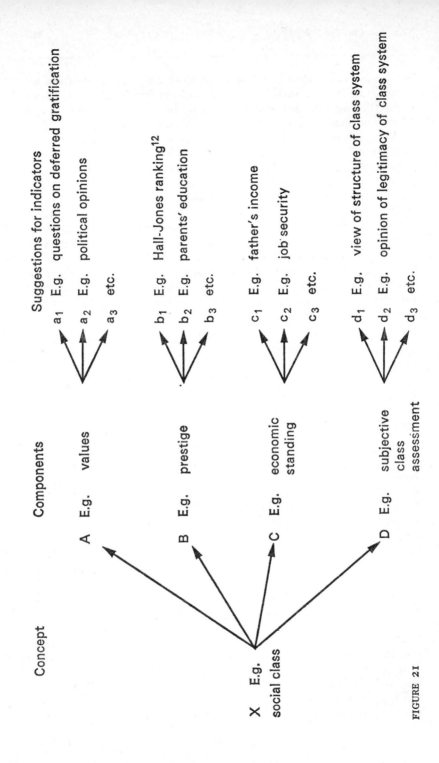

FIGURE 21

Notice that the concept *social class* in the Figure 21 example has been somewhat exploded! What was once a nice vague idea has been shattered into lots of precise fragments. And, though the invisible sum was much greater than this sorry collection of visible parts, these are all you have from which to produce one set of values that you can treat as representative of the variance in the FAIRY-TALE notion *social class*. Somehow you will have to add your separate indicators together again so that, eventually, the processes of operationalization can be represented on your page as in Figure 22.

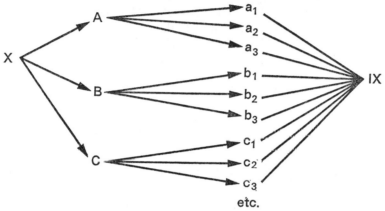

FIGURE 22

Here the various disparate measurements have been reconstituted as one, 'IX', and this *index of X*, though *not X* by any means, will be treated as X's deputy in the real worlds of appearances. This business of putting Humpty Dumpty back together again (or, rather, of making a passable image of him – he himself was broken irreparably when he tried to fall out of the fairy tale!) is called *index construction*. But – hold the king's horses! – you can't do it *yet*!

The actual index construction cannot be done until you have made several other research decisions. You will need to know precisely how you are going to make your measurements (say of *political opinions* in the example above), and how you are going to evaluate them, that is what *scales* you will be employing. But you are not yet even in a position to make *those* decisions. For instance, suppose that you decide that you are going to use direct questioning in order to determine *political opinions*: the form that questioning takes (for example, tick-off postal questionnaires, interviews, or whatever) and the wording of the questions themselves must be suited to the universe to which your tests are going to be applied – and you cannot know about *that* until you have worked out your sampling strategies. For, as we saw in chapter 9, indicators must not only be *objectifiable*, they must also be *subjectifiable*;[13] they must make sense to real people in the real world to which they are supposed to apply. What makes sense to a sample of research scientists would not make the same sense to samples of inmates in mental hospitals, old-age pensioners, or schoolchildren.

But before you can make any further decisions about sampling[14] there is another set of decisions which you will have to make. First you must decide upon your basic *research strategy*: are you going to manipulate your variables – or rather, their representatives, the indicators – *PHYSICALLY, MENTALLY,* or *STATISTICALLY*? Or will you be using some combination of these methods?

As we saw in chapter 6, RABBITS usually believe that the most trusty rituals are those which involve the actual *PHYSICAL* manipulation of variables.

Once upon a time experiments involving small groups of people were quite modish in the sociological warrens. Apart from some rather horrid things they did to guinea pigs kindly held captive by H.M. gaolers,[15] pleasanter experiments were done on kids at holiday camps,[16] paid and unpaid volunteers, and other limited groups of people.[17] Yet it gradually began to dawn on the consciousness of sociologists that, far from being *more* trustworthy, these rituals produced results which could only be considered as bases for generalizations about real lives in real worlds by considerable stretching of the limits of credibility.

This reconsideration of the worthiness of experimentation as a testing ritual is often believed to have begun with an unexpected 'discovery' which occurred during the famous Hawthorne Experiments. Most of these experiments, which were carried out at the Hawthorne Works of the General Electric Company, involved the placing of five girls in a special testroom, the varying of certain INDEPENDENT VARI-ABLES, such as illumination and other physical conditions, hours, rest pauses, modes of supervision and pay incentives, and the observation of the effects of these changes on a DEPENDENT VARIABLE, *productivity*. The observations continued for a period of about two years and are described in boring detail by the researchers under headings like 'The Bank-Wiring Observation Room Study' and 'The Mica-splitting Testroom Study'. During that time, however, the researchers 'discovered'[18] that *whatever* variations were made in the INDEPENDENT factors, *productivity* continued to rise. They attributed this effect to the EXTRANEOUS VARIABLES associated with the *experiment itself*; and this phenomenon has since come to be known as '*The Hawthorne Effect*'.[19] As a result of this work subsequent social science experimenters have been careful to note the possible influence of experimentation itself on the results of testing rituals.

But the Hawthorne Experiments could have been even more instructive than they have been for subsequent researchers. For – apart from a number of boobs resulting from the woolly thinking of the experimenters[20] – they also highlight an *intrinsic* problem of *PHYSICAL* research.

Let me explain. The experimenters found two of the girls in the assembly group uncooperative, so they simply had them removed from the testroom and replaced by two 'more desirous of participating in the test'[21] and chosen by the foreman! Before the change in personnel this group's output had been static or falling, it was *now* that it began to rise. But this would not have been surprising to anyone who, unlike Roethlisberger and Dickson, was using his head! For one of the new girls, a young Italian girl, had a serious economic problem: her mother died shortly before she joined the group and she was responsible for providing the major part of her family's income. Since the group's earnings were related to average output she had every reason for working like stink. Even if it had *not* been for her charismatic personality, and the consequent influence she had upon the other girls, her increased effort alone could have been sufficient to make a substantial impact on the group's output. After all she was 20 per cent of the group – all by herself! This incident reveals another serious problem with experimentation: the number of subjects involved is rarely large enough to enable satisfactory controls to be exercised on the confounding EXTRANEOUS VARIABLES.

So there are at least two important general problems with the use of experiments in social science research. First, the effect of the experiment itself has to be taken into consideration. In order to control this EXTRANEOUS VARIABLE you would need to compare the data from your experimental and control groups with data from a further control group, a group-from-which-no-data-has-been-compiled. This is one of those nearly, but not *quite*, impossible feats: like eating a knickerbocker glory whilst sitting in a lotus.[22] Second, the small samples which are almost inevitable in experimental studies mean that little things (like the motivations of the Italian girl in the assembly group) can confound the results in systematic ways. The assumption that many unconsidered EXTRANEOUS VARIABLES can be ignored because they vary unsystematically simply cannot be made.

Despite these problems with the physical method some of the trendier bunnies have brought out a new-fangled version which rightly enjoys some respect amongst sociologists today. This I shall refer to as the *'ethnomethodological encounter'*. In the ethnomethodological encounter the researcher enters into a real world, either as a stranger – as with our RABBIT parachuting into the land of the Bongy Wongy – or as an already accepted member of that world – as with some of Garfinkel's students in their own families[23] – or in some other guise. But, once in that world, he does not merely try to *observe* what is going on, rather he *intervenes in the situation* and actively alters one or more of the variables which, from a second-order point of view, may be regarded as operating there. Let Garfinkel explain one sort of ethnomethodological encounter, and furnish us with an example.[24]

> Since each of the expectancies that make up the attitude of daily life assigns an expected feature to the actor's environment, it should be possible to breach these expectancies by deliberately modifying scenic events so as to disappoint these attributions. By definition, surprise is possible with respect to each of these expected features. The nastiness of surprise should vary directly with the extent to which the person as a matter of moral necessity complies with their use as a scheme for assigning witnessed appearances their status as events in a perceivedly normal environment. In short, the realistic grasp by a collectivity member of the natural facts of life, and his commitment to a knowledge of them as a condition of self-esteem as a bona-fide and competent collectivity member, is the condition that we require in order to maximise his confusion upon the occasion that the grounds of this grasp are made a source of irreduceable incongruity.
>
> I designed a procedure to breach these expectancies. . . . Twenty-eight premedical students were run individually through a three-hour experimental interview. As part of the solicitation of subjects, as well as the beginning of the interview, the experimenter identified himself as a representative of an Eastern medical school who was attempting to learn why the medical school intake interview was such a stressful situation. . . .
>
> During the first hour of the interview the student furnished to the 'medical school representative' the medical interview facts-of-life by answering (certain *bona fide* questions). . . . With this much completed the student was told that the representative's research interests had been satisfied. The student was then asked if he would care to hear a recording of an actual interview. . . .
>
> The recording was a faked one between a 'medical school interviewer' and an 'applicant'. The applicant was a boor, his language was ungrammatical and filled with colloquialisms, he was evasive, he contradicted the interviewer, he bragged, he ran down other schools and professions, he insisted on knowing how he had done in the interview. Detailed assessments by the student of the recorded applicant were obtained immediately after the recording was finished. . . .
>
> The student was then given information from the applicant's 'official record'. . . . The information was deliberately contrived to

contradict the principal points in the student's assessment. For example, if the student said that the applicant must have come from a lower class family, he was told that the applicant's father was vice president of a firm that manufactured pneumatic doors for trains and buses. . . .

Students wanted very much to know what 'the others' thought of the applicant and had he been admitted? The student was told that the applicant had been admitted and was living up to the promise that the medical school interviewer and the 'six psychiatrists had found and expressed in a strong recommendation of the applicant's characterological fitness which was read to the student'. As for the views of other students, the student was told (for example) that thirty other students had been seen, that twenty-eight were in entire agreement with the medical school interviewer's assessment, and the remaining two had been slightly uncertain but at the first bit of information had seen him just as the others had.

Following this the student was invited to listen to the record a second time, after which he was asked to assess the applicant again.

Results. Twenty-five of the twenty-eight students were taken in.

Notice that though these tactics may be regarded as a *kind of* participant observation they are being employed rather differently than in more usual methods where the assumption is made that the researcher's own behaviour can be ignored or, at best, treated as an EXTRANEOUS VARIABLE. In those cases participant observation is used as a means of compiling data in a research programme in which variables are to be manipulated *STATISTICALLY*. In this case the researcher may be regarded as producing an *experiment*, that is, as manipulating his variables *PHYSICALLY*.

Let us now turn to the second method by which the ritual motions of research can be accomplished, the method of *MENTAL* manipulation of variables. One way in which sociologists have employed this method in the testing of hypotheses makes use of detailed historical case studies. Shall we pop into the LIBRARY for a moment or two to find some examples?

One that comes readily to hand is in the hall marked 'Urban Sociology'. Gideon Sjoberg[25] has recorded the reasoning behind his use of the case-study method to test hypotheses which he drew up in order to assess the relative empirical plausibility of a number of rival explanations of patterns of urban life.

In the first theory *Urbanization* is taken as the key INDEPENDENT VARIABLE: the city itself is seen as a major determinant of the distinctive mode of being-in-a-social-world that characterizes life therein. This

particular causal FAIRY-TALE links *Urbanization* with the DEPEN-
DENT VARIABLE, *urban life*, via a number of intervening fictions
such as *size, density, heterogeneity, lack of isolation, secularization,
secondary group association, segmentation of roles,* and *poorly defined
norms.*[26]

In a rival theory *urbanization* is reduced to the status of an INTER-
VENING VARIABLE which, like other INTERVENING VARI-
ABLES, is subject to the ruling influence of an ANTECEDENT,
Cultural Values.[27] And in still other theories *Technology* and *Social
Power* are treated as ANTECEDENT to both *Urbanization* and *Cultural
Values.*[28]

Sjoberg has an *IMPLICIT THEORY* of his own which, if drawn up
as an *ANALYTICAL THEORY*, might look something like Figure 23.

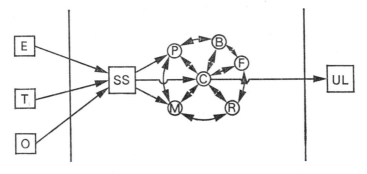

FIGURE 23

Here Sjoberg takes the *Ecological Base, Technology,* and *Social
Organization* of a society as INDEPENDENT FACTORS. In the
diagram I have labelled these 'E', 'T' and 'O' respectively. He treats
these rather as *attributes* than as variables, however, as he is satisfied
simply to dichotomize their values: he argues that certain values of these
factors ('favourable' E, 'advanced' T and 'complex' O) are prerequisites
for the development of city life. Thus he is interested in the mere
presence or absence of these values rather than the whole *range of variation*
which might be exhibited by the factors in question. Linking these
three causal factors with his DEPENDENT VARIABLE, *urban life*
(call it 'UL'), are a number of INTERVENING VARIABLES: *social
stratification* ('S'), *political structure* ('P'), *economic structure* ('M'),
religion ('R'), *bureaucracy* ('B'), *family life* ('F') and *communications* ('C').
(Anyone who has read *The Preindustrial City* may think that I have been
rather free with Sjoberg. But Sjoberg's *IMPLICIT THEORY* is
difficult to schematize as an *ANALYTICAL* one, both because he is con-

cerned with explaining a *being* rather than a *becoming*,[29] and because he is, by his own admission, adopting a functionalist approach here and, as we have seen, functionalists are rather reticent about admitting their causal assumptions.[30])

Though a number of crucial hypotheses could have been drawn from the above theory, Sjoberg was particularly interested in one: 'in their structure or form, preindustrial cities . . . whether in medieval Europe, traditional China, or elsewhere . . . resemble one another closely and in turn differ markedly from modern industrial urban centres.' In other words Sjoberg was hypothesizing that, whatever else is also going on,

$$T \to UL$$

and, given this guiding hypothesis, his research strategy was disarmingly simple: select some historical cases for comparison in such a manner that T is held constant and examine the relationships between the INTERVENING FACTORS and UL. So, instead of arguing from detailed descriptions of the city in modern America, as Wirth and the others had done, Sjoberg proposed to examine the preindustrial city.

His research design had another interesting feature which may also be instructive to us. In addition to controlling T by the manner in which he selected his cases, he also wished to control an INTERVENING VARIABLE, S. He considered that *social stratification* could be viewed as an uncontrolled CONFOUNDING factor in much of the earlier work. So he attempted to hold this variable constant by seeking to compile data from the 'mass' of the population and the outcaste minorities, as well as from the ruling élite whose antics had been subject to the most scrutiny from students of urban history.

It took Sjoberg ten years to complete his detailed analyses of preindustrial cities and as a result of this monumental effort he donated to the library three hundred and fifty pages of fascinating reading, as well as a number of methodological notes. For example, he drew the attention of visitors to the LIBRARY (like ourselves) to the problems arising from sloppy thinking in the use of the method of *MENTAL* experiment. Redfield, for instance, had been making meaningless and illegitimate comparisons between parts (modern cities) and wholes (folk societies).[31] Sjoberg also noted the problems which are presented by the unfortunate necessity for sociologists testing their hypotheses in historical settings to rely upon data compiled by scholars outside their field, data which are bound to be tempered by different 'domain assumptions',[32] or meta-theories.

These are not the only problems with this kind of research, but, on the other hand, it is foolish to denigrate the use of historical case studies to the degree that Santayana did when he said that 'Inferred past facts are more deceptive than facts prophesied, because while the risk of error in the inference is the same, there is no possibility of discovering that error; and the historian, while really as speculative as the prophet, can never be found out.'[33] No: we have already seen that prophecy and prediction are not the same thing.[34] Prediction *backwards* ('retrodiction' as Ryle called it)[35] is not logically distinct from *synchronic* prediction such as that used by scientists preferring the method of manipulating variables *STATISTICALLY* via indicators measured at a frozen moment in present ¿time?. Both *can* be equally risky. On the other hand both *may* involve unscientific legerdemain where risk-taking is avoided. Not the historian, then, but only the *prophet* is *necessarily* false$_2$. He is never recognized in his own land for the simple reason that he takes no risks with his predictions; he is certain that no one can know – yet – whether he has truth$_4$ on his side. But genuine predictions *may* be made about the past as well as the present and this gives a special sense to the cliché that history is for ever in the making!

Of course, the case-study method is not limited in applicability to historical data. This method has been employed to test hypotheses drawn from theories devised to explain variations in second-order happenings such as formal organizations, families, and individual biographies, as well as whole societies and smaller communities, both past and present.[36]

But, like the method of *PHYSICAL* experimentation, the case-study method raises serious methodological problems for RABBITS seeking to make reliable judgments about the truth$_4$ of their theories. Avid proponents of this approach frequently make a very naughty assumption: they often 'assume that we must accept their hypotheses as true (i.e. true$_4$) until such ¿time? as a case may be discovered which will falsify them'.[37] This is a sort of upside-down falsificationism which is, of course, only a particularly dodgy kind of *verificationism*.

As several scholars have pointed out, a major difficulty arises from the *MENTAL* experimenter's inability to specify the precise circumstances under which his theory is believed to obtain.[38] Suppose, for example, that you wish to test a lousy theory relating an INDEPENDENT VARIABLE, *Family breakdown* to a DEPENDENT VARIABLE, *Juvenile delinquency*, via a number of INTERVENING fictions such as *anomia, inadequate socialization*, and so on. You choose a number of families for which case histories are available and in which a junior member has been categorized as *delinquent*. Then you scan the case histories for material relevant to the estimation of values for the variables *Family breakdown, anomia*, etc. Now suppose that you find that, in the vast majority of cases studied, these variables can be interpreted as behaving in ways which do not contradict your hypotheses. What does this enable you to say about the truth$_4$ of your theory?

Of course all that you can legitimately claim is that you have failed to falsify your theory when you applied it to a certain group of families with '*juvenile delinquent*' members. You have no idea whether or not '*family breakdown*' is as common in totally law-abiding families. And, even if you could get hold of some case histories of some such families for purposes of comparison, you would still have no way of ruling out the highly plausible rival suggestion that families for which case histories are available differ in significant respects from those for which there are no such records.

Think back to Sjoberg's study of preindustrial cities for a moment. Was he really testing generalizations about '*the*' preindustrial city in a way which enables other scholars to assess their applicability to the whole universe of residential set-ups falling within that definitional boundary? No. Of course he was not: he has tested his theory only within a limited working universe. So he has only permitted us to make judgments about its plausibility with respect to that limited universe, a-group-of-preindustrial-cities-for-which-Sjoberg-managed-to-get-data. Can his generalizations be applied to the Aztec cities, for example, or Ancient Atlantis? We simply do not know.

Sjoberg himself has put this problem another way. He says, 'we cannot avoid the question: Are the cases we are studying normal, typical, or extreme?'[39]

This amounts to a *sampling problem* and should serve to remind us that in the *MENTAL* method of manipulating variables, no less than in the *PHYSICAL* and *STATISTICAL* methods, the selection of segments of empirical reality to serve as test grounds for hypotheses is of paramount importance. For, in order to examine the relationships between particular variables it is always necessary to attempt to restrain the influence of certain other relevant factors which could be operating to confound the test situation.

One way of holding major variables constant is to select instances of the phenomena in question which can be taken as '*normal*' or '*typical*'. But this presents a conundrum: how can you know what is typical unless you know what is typical! How can you be sure that your sample is representative of some larger universe when the only data you have on that larger universe is drawn from that same sample?

In order to avoid this riddle, some proponents of the case-study method prefer to select '*extreme*' rather than '*typical*' instances. They choose cases thought to be representative of the conceptual poles of their variable scales, rather than the great mass of cases which they believe to fall within those poles. And another strategy relies upon the selection of '*deviant*' cases, those which are believed (on the basis of previous research or mere hunch) to lie outside the sphere of competence of some theory. But while the analysis of extreme and/or deviant cases could form a useful part of a falsificationist research programme, it rarely does so. More often it is used in the initial construction of theoretical ideas from descriptive material,[40] or, at least, it serves as a basis for the revision of a theory which has already been found to be empirically inadequate.[41] Indeed, I think that it is fairly safe[42] to say that, whether he relies on analysis of typical, or extreme, or deviant cases, the typical *MENTAL* experimenter conceives of his case analysis as an inductive rather than a theory-testing ritual.[43] And, in the course of our adventures in the MAGICAL MOUNTAIN of science, we have oft been reminded that the DIRTY LINEN of theory construction ought not to be considered appropriate costume for the DERVISH DANCE which celebrates truth$_4$. Let Sjoberg have the last word on the method of manipulating variables *MENTALLY*, before we rush out of the LIBRARY to soothe our headaches with more tea.[44]

> To generalise about a complex society from one or a few cases – be they individuals, communities, or organisations – is admittedly hazardous. . . . For this reason many sociologists question the case-study approach as a valid sociological tool for testing hypotheses.

I always feel a little confused when I emerge after a spell in the LIBRARY, don't you? It's so hard to remember where one had intended to go next. If you didn't have the presence of mind to bring along one of those handy balls of string with which boy scouts can always find their way back to the beginning, I'll let you have another look at the plan in my pocket. (See Figure 24, The Dervish Dance of the Rabbits.)

Oh dear! Nothing ever seems to stay the same for long around here. I thought this was supposed to be a plan of the LIGHTS on the roof of the hall. It looked like that a moment ago. But now I can't seem to make it out at all. Ah! I see: it is the choreographical score for 'The Dervish Dance of the Rabbits'. Oh yes, there is a legend on the back. It explains that each movement in the DANCE is numbered with Roman numerals in order, and that the steps involved in each movement are shown by loops represented by Arabic numerals.

You have already taken a few spiralling steps of the DERVISH DANCE. First you got your golden key, the token for admission to the dance, (step I, 1). Then you went through some formal routines involving four steps, at the end of which you found that you had turned your *IMPLICIT THEORY* into an *ANALYTICAL* one (steps II, 1–4). Then you *may* have embarked upon the optional third movement (III, shown on the diagram by broken lines). *If* so, you will have undertaken some advanced high-stepping motions in order to turn your theory into a proper deductive nomological explanation, or *EXPLANATORY THEORY*. However, it is very probable that, even if you had succeeded in so doing, you would still have to translate your theory back into the form of an *ANALYTICAL* one for the practical reasons of mnemonic simplicity and ease of communication.

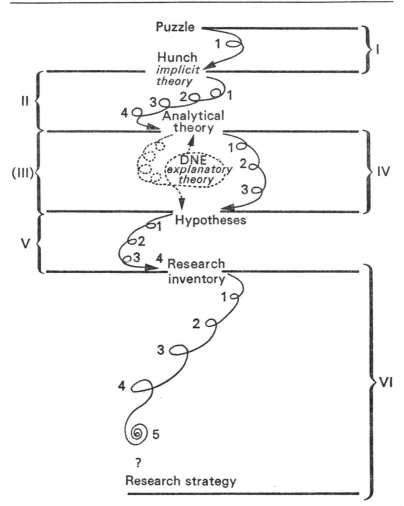

FIGURE 24 *The Dervish Dance of the Rabbits*

Next you whorled through the three steps of the fourth movement of the DANCE (IV, 1–3), thus effecting a complete listing of the *HYPO-THESES* to be tested in the course of the research programme. Then, gathering up all these multicoloured tapes at once, and whizzing around an imaginary maypole, you advanced a further four steps (V, 1–4); whereupon dazed and dizzy from these exertions you fell back on the bank by the BRIDGE. As you lay there, panting and contemplating the horrors of making the crossing, you realized with great relief that you had not come this far empty-handed. Clutched tightly in your left paw was your little tin of bacon sandwiches. And – lo and behold! – in your right paw there was a scruffy shopping list of variables to be measured, that is your *RESEARCH INVENTORY*.

Thus assured, you began the tricky steps of the sixth movement. After four steps (VI, 1–4) you found that you had advanced across the BRIDGE to within a hair's breadth of the opposite bank: you had made some crucial operational decisions (VI, 1–4) and thus all-but selected a chorus of little indicators to mimic your spiralling motions. But then – as you lifted your right leg for the fifth step – you encountered a problem. There you were in mid-air and there were three quite different scores you could have followed from there: *PHYSICAL, MENTAL,* and *STATISTICAL.*

Since you weren't quite sure which way to choose, you allowed me to con you into making another trip back to the LIBRARY to find out what previous dancers had done. All this did for you – apart from giving you a headache – was to confirm you in what you thought you knew already. You have come out of the LIBRARY with some firm convictions about research methodology. You reckon that, in both the methods of *PHY-SICAL* and of *MENTAL* manipulation of variables, serious problems arise from the difficulties of achieving adequate control over the behaviour of the snivelling little understudies, called 'indicators', which are standing in for variables – because the latter cannot get into the DANCE. You know that sophisticated sampling procedures are available to anyone who wishes to use the *STATISTICAL* method instead, and that these are generally believed to permit the choreographer greater control over the dancers. But you have a sneaking suspicion that, if you opt for this variation, you will find yourself having to get into some very tricky postures later on!

I don't think it will be necessary to make *another* weary journey back into the LIBRARY to find an excuse for confirming this suspicion as a conviction, do you? I assure you that the details of the *STATISTICAL METHOD* will become uncomfortably clear later in the DANCE. And you have already grasped the fundamentals: you know that the design of a *STATISTICAL* survey to test hypotheses relies, like any other method of testing, upon effective control of the variables, and that this can be simulated by direct selection and/or randomization, as well as by actual measurement.

Which of the three variations you choose will, naturally, depend upon what you are choosing them for. This is a matter for you and your *ANALYTICAL THEORY* to sort out between you. Your *ANALY-TICAL THEORY* has dictated which variables are to be manipulated, and the method by which you attempt that manipulation must depend both on the indicators you choose and on your research resources. For you do not need me to tell you that ¿time? and money are scarce and that some data are easily (and ¿ethically?) come by while some are not. Research strategy, like most other things in real worlds of everyday life, is bound to be a compromise: you have to consider not only what your theory and your methodological convictions seem to demand, but also what restraints are imposed by your limited financial and other resources and the differential accessibility of data.

But wait a minute. Before you decide, allow me to make another suggestion.

When we were overcome by the uncertainties, which the arbitrary selection of operational indicators of fictional notions necessarily involves, we hit upon a useful principle which to some extent permits the greedy bunny to have his knickerbocker glory and eat it too. Sharing Ambrose Bierce's attitude to *quantity* – 'A good substitute for quality, when you are hungry'[45] – we hit upon THE PRINCIPLE OF TRIANGULATION as a cunning way of missing one bird with several stones.

Now let me show you how you can trump that display of rabbity exhibitionism. Allow me to introduce you to the wonders of THE PRINCIPLE OF PHEWANGULATION.

The word 'phew', as all enterprising lexicographers already know, comes from the ancient Arachnoid term 'phewww!' Far from being 'int. expr. impatience or disgust', as the compilers of *The Concise Oxford Dictionary* would have us believe, this is actually an expression of tentative relief.[46] PHEWANGULATION, then, is the sort of angulation that leads you to say 'phew' if you ever manage to do it!

The principle may be expressed thus,

THE PRINCIPLE OF PHEWANGULATION: Wherever possible employ more than one research strategy to manipulate your variables.

Like Triangulation, PHEWANGULATION has a paradoxical effect on RABBITS. It enables them to feel more comfortable about their research decisions, whilst actually maximizing the risks they take in their testing rituals. For there is the clear possibility that, where PHEWANGULATION is effected, different methods of manipulating variables will produce different results. So, as well as ensuring a closer approximation to the primary research principle of COLLECTIVE FALSIFICATIONISM, this trick also enables useful analyses of the possible sources of any divergence in the results. Which variables are controlled in one method and uncontrolled in another? How might these be interacting with the INDEPENDENT, INTERVENING and DEPENDENT variables in the theory? These are the sorts of questions which are raised by PHEWANGULATION.

Let us explore an imaginary example.

Imagine that you wish to test a theory which proposes that the activities of the anti-pornography lobby are a major cause of increasing sexual activity in 'The Permissive Society'. You undertake a statistical survey in which you measure a number of indicators of the INTER-VENING VARIABLES: *exposure* (to the views of the anti-pornography lobby), *sexual attitudes* and *erotic opportunities*, and of the DEPEN-DENT VARIABLE *sexual activity*. As a result of your analysis you find that, amongst other things, you are unable to falsify the hypotheses that *exposure* and *sexual attitudes* and that *sexual attitudes* and *sexual activity* are correlated. However, being an ardent phewangulator, you have the foresight to realize before undertaking your research that results like this could equally be explained by a rival theory which suggested that it is increasing *sexual activity* which is a cause of the rising *agitation* of the anti-pornography lobby, rather than the other way around.

In order to sort out the relative plausibility of these two opposing theories you would need to control '¿*time?*'. For in this, as in most statistical research, ¿time? may be regarded as an EXTRANEOUS, and quite probably confounding, variable which is not subject to the re-searcher's control. We normally assume that causes precede effects in ¿time?, but the method of *STATISTICAL* manipulation of variables rarely enables us to analyse the correlates of this factor since the measure-ments present only a sort of statistical snapshot taken at a particular moment when everyone was supposed to be saying 'Cheese is yellow too!'

So you, very sensibly, decide to devise an experiment with which to supplement your *STATISTICAL* analysis. In this experiment you take a number of male volunteers and divide them randomly into an experimental group and two control groups. The experimental group is exposed to a film in which Mrs Mary Whitehouse and Lord Longford are seen discussing pornography in a BBC studio. The two control groups are positioned in identical seats in front of an identical screen and shown two other films of the same length, one a rude movie and the other a short documentary on the yachting prowess of Mr Edward Heath. For reasons of good taste you do not actually select direct indicators of the DEPENDENT VARIABLE in the experimental situation, instead you measure an INTERVENING VARIABLE, *sexual arousal* using a cunning device known as a penisometer. This gives a clear reading for *sexual arousal* using Archimedes' theorem about displacement of water.

The use of this method does enable you to take control of ¿time?: the penisometer readings are taken before and after exposure to the films. However, a number of other problems arise from your experiment. Most of these centre around the perversities of your sample; the facts that they are males and volunteers may both be systematically related to the variables in which you are interested. Also the unique nature of the experiment itself may throw out interesting hypotheses which you had not considered before undertaking the research and which would never have occurred to you at all if you had restricted yourself to the *STATIS-TICAL* method. Suppose, for example, that the experimental group do show increases in penisometer readings after seeing the film, and that these increases are much greater than any recorded in the two control groups, might this be something to do with the physical appearances of Mrs Whitehouse and Lord Longford, or their gestures? And might not these two characters be personally responsible for the outbreaks of sexual excess and indecency which, on their own admission, are ravaging the country?

In order to effect control of such EXTRANEOUS VARIABLES as *Mrs Whitehouse's limb control* and *Lord Longford's trousers* you might wish to go in for some top-flight phewangulation and supplement both *STATISTICAL* and *PHYSICAL* methods with case-study analysis, say of documents compiled on sexual offenders entertained at Her Majesty's pleasure. And discrepancies between the results of these three different strategies for manipulating variables might lead you to some interesting speculations based on analysis of the differential control over EXTRANEOUS VARIABLES afforded by these three methods. Such speculations might well lead to further hypothesizing, and eventually to further tests. But I will leave the rest to *your* imagination.

'Golly Gee!' (as a famous sociologist once remarked[47]) I'll bet you're glad you brought your imagination along. Standing there with only one foot on the ground, you know that, as the next note of that infernal music sounds, you must trace several separate, but interwoven, patterns with the other foot, eventually making an elegant landing on the solid reality which you believe so firmly to lie across that accursed BRIDGE!

If you have managed to do it then, as you know, it is obligatory to say 'phew!'

And there is something else that it is obligatory for you to do before proceeding with the dance. You must make a clear record for your research notebook of the postures involved in that latest crucial step.

VI, 5. Decide upon your research strategies. (Do this by first looking back at your *ANALYTICAL THEORY* (see pp. 224–33), and at the reasoning which culminated in your Research Inventory (IV, 4, see pp. 235–40), and then at your plans for selecting indicators. You may also find it helpful to refer back to chapter 6 above.)

Some of you may find that you are dancing on ahead, whirling elegantly in the old style and creating startling new variations, as the sounds of the distant GOLD-STAR piper light upon your ears. But for those of you who, like me, have tin ears and eight left feet, a little guidance may be welcome.

In the next two chapters I shall discuss some recipes for concocting samples (or sampling concoctions as the RABBITS prefer to put it!).

But after all that energetic dancing I'm sure you will need a nice cup of tea before you do anything else.

the King called out,
'Ten minutes allowed for refreshments!'

Chapter 14

A Most Unlikely Story

'Hurry up now! No more time for dallying over tea, we have to get on. Are you sure that you remember your theory? You are going to need that where you're going next. Better check now!'

'Stand up and repeat "*'Tis the voice of the sluggard*",' said the GRYPHON.

'How the creatures order one another about and make one repeat lessons!' thought Alice. 'I might as well be at school at once.' However, she got up and began to repeat it, but her head was so full of the Rabbits' Dervish Dance, that she hardly knew what she was saying; and the words came *very* queer indeed:

> ' 'Tis the voice of the Rabbit: I heard him declare
> "You have baked me too brown, I must sugar my hair."
> As a duck in a dance so the Rabbit instead
> Put his bowl in his spoon as he stood on his head.
> When all facts are in view, he is gay as a lark,
> And will talk in contemptuous tones of the SNARK:
> But when nasty tangles and SPIDERS come round
> His voice has a timid and tremulous sound.'

'That's different from what *I* used to say when I was a child,' said the GRYPHON.

'Well, *I* never heard it before,' said the MOCK TURTLE; 'but it sounds uncommon nonsense.'

Alice said nothing: she had sat down with her face in her hands, wondering if anything would *ever* happen in a natural way again.

'I should like to have it explained,' said the MOCK TURTLE.

And so should *I!*

We could go into the LIBRARY to find some textbooks on Sampling and Sampling Statistics for Sociologists, but *I* don't advise that at the moment. We have spent far too long in there already, and anyway, I don't know about you, but *I* find that the smell of sums mingled with SPIDERS had a soporific, if not indeed nightmarish, effect!

'No, no! The adventures first,' said the GRYPHON in an impatient tone: 'textbook explanations take such a dreadful time.'

All right then? Let's get on with the adventures. In the course of these we are about to meet up with the GRYPHON, the MOCK TURTLE, some very surprising SOOOOUP made thereof, some rabbits who put their bowls in their spoons and stood on their heads for centuries, some very silly frogs, some old friends, a red herring, and, of course, oodles and oodles of SPIDERS!

'What fun!' said the GRYPHON, half to itself, half to Alice.

Let us first be sure that we are quite clear about the object of sampling.

When he draws a sample the researcher is choosing some chunks of reality to serve as testing-grounds for his hypotheses. For the universe to which his theory is alleged to apply is, of course, only a FAIRY-TALE place where explanatory sagas are enacted by the shadowy phantoms called variables rather than by concrete observables. Yet measurement rituals are applied, not to the variables themselves, but to indicators. And these indicators must be chosen from observable features of real worlds taken for granted. Just as indicators are mere stand-ins for variables, so samples are mere stand-ins for theoretically defined universes.

Clearly the dearest hope of the RABBIT is that he can gaily assume isomorphism between his sample and his theoretical universe. He would be blissfully happy if only he could truly$_2$ say, 'As the sample so the universe.' For in those Utopian circumstances, the RABBIT could be sure that the results of various testing rituals performed on indicators measured within his sample could be generalized to his theoretical universe.

Suppose, for instance, that a RABBIT has decided to test some absurd theory from which, amongst others, he has derived the hypothesis that changing tastes in lingerie are a causative factor in the sadly declining state of the gardening industry in England and Wales. From where in the tangle of real Englands and Wales would he draw his measurements of lingerie tastes and of consumption of gardening equipment and materials? If he decided to draw a sample of men and women of gardening age from certain residential areas (with large gardens) in Glossop, could he be sure that these Glossoponians were *representative* of Glossoponians in general, and that Glossoponians were *representative* of all those English and Welsh people of gardening age to whom he might wish to apply his theory? Might he be better advised to employ different tactics, such as placing observers in underwear and gardening departments of large stores in a number of English and Welsh cities? And if he did so, could he assume that sales in those stores were *representative* of sales in general, and that these particular large stores were *representative* of large stores throughout the countries in question?

All sampling questions are questions about *representativeness*. So discussions of sampling methodology, both in texts and handbooks on the subject and in reports and criticisms of actual pieces of research, are, as Willer has said, 'almost obsessed with the need for representative samples'.[1] And anyone who ever sat through an undergraduate course of statistics will remember *that* at least. *I* remember a small bespectacled gentleman who told us, once a week for forty-five terrible minutes, 'You've got to have a representative sample.' Unfortunately he found that by the end of the year his sample of second-year sociologists was not only thoroughly unrepresentative but also so small that he could never do a chi-squared on it! Once (before I joined the ranks of the truants) I made so bold as to stick up my hand and ask, 'What *is* a representative sample?' He didn't reply but looked at me pityingly and returned to the sums on the blackboard.

It is not at all unlikely that you have had similar experiences. But don't be daunted, you are free to ask the question again if you wish: *What is a representative sample? I* suggest the following contrary definition:

> A representative sample is any sample alleged to be selected from a given universe, which is *not unrepresentative* of that universe.

If you have not fallen asleep already you will no doubt be wondering if there is any point at all in posing the further question: *What is an unrepresentative sample?* There is, indeed a great deal of point in asking *that* question for, unlike the first question this one can be answered very easily:

> An unrepresentative (or biased) sample is one which differs in relevant respects from the universe from which it is supposed to be drawn.

And of course there is no need to ask what respects may be regarded as *relevant* respects, for you will know by now that *that* depends upon the theory being tested and any rival theories which can be brought to bear upon it.

The point of sampling strategy is, then, to select real locations for measurement operations in such a way that efficient control of the EXPERIMENTAL (that is INDEPENDENT, INTERVENING or DEPENDENT) and/or EXTRANEOUS variables is facilitated. Now we have already seen, in chapters 6 and 13, that one simple method of controlling a variable by sampling strategy is to make selections on the basis of that factor. You may remember the boring example which I gave of a test of a hypothesis relating an INDEPENDENT VARIABLE, Eating habits, to a DEPENDENT one, 'fatness'. I pointed out that any relationship between those two EXPERIMENTAL VARIABLES might be an artefact of an EXTRANEOUS factor, *exercise*. I went on to suggest that one way to keep this nuisance factor under control was to select on the basis of it, and one way of doing that is to select a sample that can be regarded as homogeneous in that respect (say all avid exercisers or, on the other hand, all lazy sedentary types).

So the most straightforward form of sampling strategy involves *the deliberate selection of chunks of reality according to certain required values on particular variables*. This may be termed PURPOSIVE SAMPLING.

Of course PURPOSIVE SAMPLING is not restricted to the selection of units which exhibit *homogeneous* values with respect to specific variables, as in the example just cited. One may obviously go about it the other way around and select units deliberately to display a pre-defined range of *heterogeneity*, so that comparisons may be made between groups assigned different values on the variables in question. An example would be where the researcher, wishing to test the above hypothesis about gluttony, decided to select, say, three groups with high, medium and low scores on the EXTRANEOUS factor, exercise, so that he could make comparisons between them with regard to the two EXPERIMENTAL VARIABLES being measured (Eating habits and fatness) and their interrelationships.

There is a variation of sampling by *heterogeneous* selection which has enjoyed some favour among sociologists, particularly those employing the strategy of *MENTAL MANIPULATION* of variables, and most especially where that strategy has been applied to the study of cultural variations between social worlds located at different points in ¿time? and ¿space? (that is, in research employing 'historical' and/or 'anthropological' data). I shall call this sort of heterogeneous sampling, *typological sampling*. The method of typological sampling is as follows:

(1) Decide upon the variables in terms of which you wish to make your selection. (These variables may, of course, be either EXPERIMENTAL or EXTRANEOUS variables or a combination of the two; which they are and how many variables you wish to control in this way will, of course, depend upon the decisions about your basic research strategy which you have already made.)

(2) Now 'break' these dimensions arbitrarily into a number of values.

(For reasons which will become clear later, it is rarely practical to do much more than dichotomize or trichotomize.)

(3) 'develop a typology that includes the various combinations of values on these dimensions. . .

(4) [Then] use this typology as a sampling frame for selecting a small number of cases from the universe, typically drawing one case from each cell of the typology.'[2]

Imagine, for example, that you wish to sample slave societies according to three variables: relegation of the slave to property status, ascription of slave status along caste lines, intervention of doctrines of organized religion. You might simply dichotomize all three variables to produce the following typology.

	slave defined as property		slave defined as person	
	caste	non-caste	caste	non-caste
no code of slave rights	1	2	3	4
code of rights defined from religious standpoint	5	6	7	8

You would then hope to select one or more cases to cover each type, perhaps with the exception of certain combinations which seemed to be theoretically impossible (say, for instance, types 5 and 6 in the above sampling frame). So you might choose the case of the ante-bellum south of the United States to represent type 1, and so on.[3]

Still another way to control variables by selection, or by PURPOSIVE SAMPLING, involves the straightforward simulation of experimentation by using *matching* groups. This is a sort of combination of homogeneous and heterogeneous selection. The rationale is exactly the same as that employed in the simplest of experiments where an experimental or 'test' case is compared with a control case, the latter being contrived to match the former in respect of all variables considered to be relevant bar only the 'test factors' under scrutiny. This technique was very popular amongst sociologists at one ¿time?, especially in research based upon the case-study method, but for practical reasons it was generally restricted to studies of case histories of individual persons or families,[4] rather than larger and more 'complex' social units like slave societies, cities, etc. *Matching* simply involves the grouping of cases into pairs in such a way that each pair is homogeneous in respect of all the variables defining the sampling frame except one, the 'test factor'. Where matching is satisfactorily achieved, differences between paired partners in respect of any other variables are assumed not to be attributable to the matching variables and therefore – by elimination – are regarded as effects of the variation in the 'test factor'.

In addition to controlling variables by *homogeneous* and *heterogeneous* selection and the combination of these two tactics in *matching*, there is a more complicated form of PURPOSIVE SAMPLING which we may call *structural sampling*. In a structural sample units are deliberately selected to display specific values on particular variables in order to mimic the composition of values on those same variables which the researcher believes to obtain in the universe to which he wishes his theory to be applied. This tactic can perhaps be best explained by reference to a variation of *structural sampling* which can be found in most texts and is usually described as *Quota Sampling*.

Suppose that you wish to draw a sample of schoolgirls from a certain large school, which we will call the Dame Alice Harpur School for Young Gentlewomen. You have, at the start, certain information about those girls which you may have gleaned from the registers, the headmistress, the school secretary and, say, John Cringle's previous research on the school.

According to this information:

There are 1,000 girls in the school

		%
Of these	154 are in the first year	(15·4)
	151 are in the second year	(15·1)
	148 are in the third year	(14·8)
	147 are in the fourth year	(14·7)
	150 are in the fifth year	(15·0)
	139 are in the sixth year	(13·9)
	81 are in the upper sixth	(8·1)
	and 30 are in the further sixth	(3·0)
	——	——
	1,000	100

At the same time,

324 girls are known to wear the regulation navy-blue knickers	(32·4)
610 girls are known to wear non-regulation knickers	(61·0)
and 66 girls are known to wear no knickers at all	(6·6)
——	——
1,000	100

Now suppose that you wish to draw a 10 per cent quota sample of these girls. You would simply pick your sample in such a way that,

%
15·4 were in the first year   (15 girls)
15·1 were in the second year   (15 girls)
14·8 were in the third year   (15 girls)
14·7 were in the fourth year   (15 girls)
15·0 were in the fifth year   (15 girls)
13·9 were in the sixth year   (14 girls)
 8·1 were in the upper sixth   (8 girls)
and   3 were in the further sixth (3 girls)

and that

%
32·4 were navy-blue knicker wearers   (32 girls)
61·0 were non-regulation knicker wearers (61 girls)
 6·6 were non-knicker wearers   (7 girls)

In quota sampling, then, a deliberate attempt is made to draw a sample which is quantitatively isomorphic with the assumed composition of the universe from which it is alleged to have been drawn. But quota sampling is only one sort of structural sampling and not all structural sampling aims at *numerical* isomorphism, much (such as the 'reputational' and 'snowball' techniques which will be introduced in the following chapter) involves a different sort of isomorphism.

Now, whether it is achieved by numerical rituals or by some other selection techniques, which we will be considering later on, PUR-POSIVE SAMPLING has two serious limitations which are widely thought to render it inappropriate for many sorts of sociological research. These may be termed the problems of *attrition* and of *relevant bias*.[5]

The problem of attrition is quite simply a question of wastage: 'the loss of cases on which data have already been collected'[6] in the process of selecting the sample. Think for a moment about the business of *matching*, for example. Any researcher who uses this mode of PURPOSIVE SAMPLING will have to face the fact that in the process of selecting pairs or groups which are matched on particular variables, he will end up chucking a lot of information in the wastepaper basket. One poor RABBIT's experiences may serve as a warning:[7]

'A classic example of attrition is Christiansen's matched sample of high school graduates and high school dropouts. Some 96 per cent of his completed interviews were discarded in achieving a final matched sample of forty-six cases.'

If you now look back at the strange case of the girls from Dame Alice you will see that this business of attrition constitutes a variable nuisance. It does not arise when there is ready-made information available to guide you in the selection process. The school secretary could tell you how many girls there are in each year group and you could identify the girls from the different forms with the aid of the teachers with very little effort indeed. But consider the matter of the knickers! Even if John Cringle's previous research in the school has provided you with a breakdown of the girls' knicker-wearing habits he will certainly not have identified the girls with varying values on this variable by name. So you would need to make some measurements in advance of selecting your quotas on this variable. Whether you did this by questioning the girls, or by making them all line up and walk in single file over an air vent, or by some other operational trick, you would certainly end up looking very silly indeed. For, as we saw above,[8] if you are going to have to measure something anyway then you might just as well retain your data and make your controls statistically, rather than squandering effort and imagination in this way!

It is probably obvious to you that the nuisance value of *attrition*, whether in homogeneous, heterogeneous, matched, or structural sampling, is related to the number of variables defining the sampling frame.[9] The more variables you wish to control at once, the more information you will have to throw away. It is often hard enough to achieve adequate selection according to one or two variables so the wastage involved in trying to control more than three or four variables in this manner is likely to be so great as to render such sampling futile.

The problem of attrition relates also to the second major limitation of PURPOSIVE SAMPLING. This is the question of *relevant bias*. Relevant bias is the sample distortion produced by the selection itself. A biased sample is, as we have already seen, one that is in relevant respects unrepresentative of the universe which it is supposed to represent. Another way of putting that is to say that the sample and the universe from which it is supposed to have been drawn differ from one another in respect of certain variables which, from the point of view of either the theory being tested, or some rival theory, might arguably be interacting with the variables under scrutiny.

For, in PURPOSIVE SAMPLING, only those variables specifically defining the sampling frame can be safely assumed to be under the researcher's control. But there may always be other variables which could be claimed to be interacting with *both* these sampling frame variables *and* with the variables whose indicators are to be measured within the sample. Usually these other, nuisance, variables will be what we have been calling EXTRANEOUS ones, that is ones which could be posed from the point of view of some rival theory. But if the rabbit is careless enough, and some rabbits are, they may even jump out of his *own* theory to jeer at him.

The problems of *attrition* and *relevant bias* are related. Bias must increase with attrition because as the proportion of information in your wastepaper baskets begins to outweigh that in your filing cabinet, the likelihood of relevant differences between the cases represented in each of these paper receptacles is bound to increase. At least, so the statisticians would have us believe. They do not doubt that the smaller the proportion of the universe represented in the sample the greater the probability that the sample is biased.

But it is not the whole point of PURPOSIVE SAMPLING to get a determined grip on as many variables (or at least their representatives, the indicators) as possible, and to force them to stop their infernal jigging about and to keep still for a moment so that we can perform our test rituals without their interference? Presumably then, the purposive sampler will find – as he ponders upon his own ANALYTICAL THEORY, realistically anticipates criticisms from rival points of view, and considers the practicalities of measuring his variables – that he will need to cope with allegations of bias in his sampling by *increasing* rather than decreasing the number of variables in terms of which he makes his selection. But as he increases his sampling frame variables as a defence against allegations of *bias* so *attrition* must increase, and with it, *bias*! This is just another of those Catch 22 situations with which we seasoned adventurers in the mountain of madmen have become all too familiar!

So PURPOSIVE SAMPLING has a serious limitation. It does enable the RABBIT to get a grip upon those EXTRANEOUS VARIABLES which he has actually *anticipated*, and in terms of which he has constructed his sampling frame. But it leaves him speechless in the face of the possible accusation that his sampling frame variables might be systematically related with *other* variables which could be invoked in conflicting theories to explain the same events. Unimagined EXTRANEOUS VARIABLES can never be controlled through PURPOSIVE SAMPLING precisely *because* they are unimagined. What then is a poor RABBIT to do?

Let us take up the story at the point where a certain Mr Fisher entered the lily pond. His idea was to go about the whole business of casting for samples the other way around. If you can select imaginary variables to render them systematic, then, he reasoned, perhaps you can *un*select the *un*imaginary ones to render them *un*systematic. If you can be reasonably sure that their variation is indeed unsystematic from the point of view of your theory, then you can assume that any biases in your sample are also unsystematic, so these biases can be regarded as *irrelevant* from all conceivable points of view and thus can be ignored. Fisher therefore suggested the application of a series of scrambling rituals to sampling design in order to neutralize the effects of uncontrolled EXTRANEOUS VARIABLES.[10] These rituals and the statistical calculations which assume them are the procedures and techniques of PROBABILITY SAMPLING.

PROBABILITY SAMPLING is the opposite of PURPOSIVE SAMPLING in that, though both are used in attempts to increase the representativeness of a sample by decreasing relevant biases in sampling, the former seeks to render all uncontrolled bias as *un*systematic rather than as systematic: the assumption behind PROBABILITY SAMP-LING is that *randomization removes the systematic influences of uncontrolled EXTRANEOUS VARIABLES*. In short, if a sample is picked 'at random' then, since there are no good reasons for assuming that there are *relevant* differences between that sample and the universe which it is chosen to represent, it is reasonable to assume that any differences between the sample and the universe are *irrelevant*.[11]

> Once or twice something moved about with a rustle and a splash amongst the rushes at the side of the pond. 'I trust that is not a rat,' said Mr. Jeremy Fisher.

Well, it certainly smelt a bit ratty to me! Perhaps we had better examine the idea of randomization at closer quarters. What does the probability sampler mean when he says that he has selected his sample 'at random'? Suppose, for example, that he wants a random sample of the people present at a certain football match on a particular Saturday afternoon. Selecting his spectators 'at random' obviously does *not* mean selecting the first few spectators that he happens to encounter; for any dozen samples collected in this way might well differ considerably from one another (one sample gathered near the gate might include a disproportionate number of latecomers, one gathered in the Directors' Box an unusually high number of cigar smokers, one at the Shed end might be almost totally composed of Chelsea supporters, and so on). So sampling randomly is clearly not sampling any-old-how. The word 'random' in this context clearly does *not* mean 'haphazard'. Then what *does* it mean?

Any textbook (unselected haphazardly) will give you more or less the same answer:[12]

> A selection process is random if it favours no member of the population over any other member; that is, if every member of the population has the same chance of being selected. We may define *random selection as any process that gives each member of the population an equal chance of falling in the sample*.

That seems clear enough doesn't it? All you have to do to unselect EXTRANEOUS VARIABLES by random sampling is to ensure that every member of the real population, that you are taking to stand for your theoretical universe, has an equal ¿chance? of landing up in your sample. So if you want a random sample of the spectators at a certain football match, all you have to do is to give each spectator at the match a number, write down each number on a piece of paper, fold all the pieces of paper carefully making certain that none get blown away, then put them all into a giant hat and invite Diana Dors to dip her hand into the hat and draw out the required proportion from the hatful. If that sounds a little impractical, you can always write down every name in a long list, get someone to blindfold you and spin you around a few times, then pick a certain number of names with a pin. And if that doesn't take your fancy you can try using a table of random numbers:[13]

> A table of random numbers may be made in a number of ways, one of which is to program a computer to produce a table in which any number between o and 9 has the same probability of appearing at every place. In a table of random numbers, there is no connection whatsoever between a number that appears in one place and any number that appears in any other place in the table.

Now, according to the RABBIT who coined the term 'PROBABILITY SAMPLING', such sampling has a special feature which should make it overwhelmingly attractive for RABBITS who are tired of standing dumb-founded in the face of the Unknown.[14]

> The special feature of Probability Sampling is that it permits the use of the theory of probability for the computation, from the sample itself, of probability limits of sampling variation.

In other words, if you can be sure that every member of the real universe which comprises your population has an equal ¿chance? of landing up in your sample, then you can use all kinds of clever mathematical formulae for calculating the ¿probability? that your sample differs from the universe from which it was drawn and thus, by elimination, for calculating the ¿likelihood? that your sample is biased in some relevant respect. (Have *you* tracked down that rat yet?)

So random selection was conceived by its proponents as a sort of stirring ritual. Rather than trying to fish out from a real universe a number of units chosen in such a way as to represent his idea of the universe in relevant respects, the random sampler indulged in an opposite kind of activity. Instead of attempting to render the un-imagined EXTRANEOUS VARIABLES as *systematic* he tried to take advantage of the very fact that, from his point of view, their variation could be regarded as *unsystematic*. Faced with the unsystematic, with that which cannot be predicted by deduction from any known laws, the RABBITS fell back upon a strange medieval theory of the Unknown. Let Mr Byrne describe how that theory came to acquire the impressive freight which it carries today.[15]

In the course of time, Cardano and then Pascal and Fermat came to recognise that gamblers' rules already in existence might provide a more effective instrument to deal with the [unsystematic]. These gamblers' rules they and then others developed and systematised.

That this more or less systematic instrument of the non-systematic came to be known as a *calculus* is due not only to its character as a mathematical instrument but to imitation and adulation of the great new instrument of the systematic, the calculus of Leibniz and Newton. . . .

That this *calculus* of the non-systematic came to be called a calculus of *probability* is due to ingredients of the intellectual milieu which go back deep into the Middle Ages. . . .

As for the calculus itself, the new instrument thus inaugurated was eventually systematized by Laplace according to standards of his day and by Kolmogorov and others according to standards of our day. But it is important to bear in mind that what is now a demonstrative system in its own right began as *an instrument to deal with the non-systematic on the basis of a new theory about how to express the non-systematic.*

And a very odd kind of theory it was too, at least so far as the rabbity imagination is concerned! For the theory behind the impressive Calculus of Probability is one which is quite different from those normally entertained by scientists. Indeed I will go so far as to say that it is one which cannot even be *understood* within a scientific frame of reference. For it is not so much a theory as an *un*theory. It does not posit a cause or causes to account for puzzling particulars, but rather invokes an unimaginary monster, called *Chance* to be the *un*cause of the otherwise unaccountable.

Such an untheory is, of course, the sort of story at which the GOLD-STAR RABBIT sniffs in the utmost contempt. It cannot possibly be scientific – in the sense in which GOLD-STAR RABBITS use that term – because it can never be put to the test. For, though the theory behind the Calculus of Probability is exclusively concerned with the business of risk-taking, it takes none itself: there is nothing which it forbids to happen, for its pivoting premise is the tantalizing proposition that 'Anything can happen!'[16] One of our favourite connoisseurs of the GOLD-STAR standard, Professor Popper, has described this peculiar untheory of *Chance* as a sort of conspiracy theory of errors: a great big untestable pseudo-theory which can always be defended by conventionalist stratagems. For Popper it is at least problematical whether probability statements have any place in the GOLD-STAR RABBIT's vocabulary, because taken by themselves, they are 'non-falsifiable' and therefore without empirical significance.[17]

But long before Popper's day the whiskers were twitching in the warrens. Some of the RABBITS had already sensed the bizarre danger. For, even in those days, no RABBIT liked to be caught with his GOLD-STAR BADGE off and his feet up, casting the *I Ching*. Nor contemplating Pope's unscientific views on the unpuzzle in question,

> All nature is but art, unknown to thee;
> All chance, direction which thou canst not see;
> All discord, harmony not understood;
>
> > *(An Essay on Man)*

So the RABBITS tried frantically to provide themselves with alibis. They claimed that the revered calculus could make perfect (mathematical) sense by itself, without any reference to nasty metaphysical monsters like *Chance*, and its outriders, *Accident* and *Coincidence*. So, towards the close of the nineteenth century, when the rabbity empire was spreading its intellectual bounds 'wider still and wider', John Venn, amongst others, claimed that[18]

> When Probability . . . is divorced from direct reference to objects, as it substantially is by not being founded upon experience, it simply resolves itself into the common algebraical or arithmetical doctrine of Permutations and Combinations.

But the monster did not remain at bay for long. Poincaré found himself forced to admit that he could not provide a satisfactory definition of the key term '*probability*' without stepping outside of the formal system of mathematics.[19] To define 'probability' by reference to the beast itself would clearly be metaphysical. Not to define it at all, on the other hand, would be giving the beast the last laugh. Some more, rather elegant, retreats were accomplished and indeed the efforts of Servien and Russell could be regarded as highly successful in that most RABBITS were eventually lulled into thinking that the monster had been definitively banished from the warrens. As far as they were concerned the Calculus of Probability stood on its own as a formal mathematical mechanism, all of which could be built up on the basis of elementary set theory without any reference at all to the extramathematical ideas which had directed the thoughts of those bygone RABBITS who first began to erect it.

Yet, though the courageous efforts of those who maintained a distinction between the formal Calculus of Probability and any interpretation given to that mechanism did produce in the burrows a sense of confidence and a diminished fear of the Unknown, the beast was still lurking amongst the cobwebs. And still today his mischievous forays into the testing-grounds are explicitly recognized in the reports from the researchers. When drawing up their data these run-of-the-mill RABBITS frequently apply themselves to the task of estimating the '*probability*' that such and such a variation is *not* due to the extrascientific intruder *Chance* and that, *ergo*, there is some empirical support for a particular hypothesis. They do this in the true$_2$ belief that, because they have selected PROBABILITY SAMPLES, they have performed the stirring ritual of randomization and thus neutralized the effects of all those mysterious uncontrolled EXTRANEOUS VARIABLES which might otherwise be systematically sabotaging their research rituals. If you do your stirring properly, they claim, you may safely assume that all plausibly relevant variations between your sample and the universe from which it is supposed to have been drawn have been so confused with one another that they may be regarded as irrelevant. So the run-of-the-mill RABBITS have got into the habit of performing a special trick to mix up all the uncontrolled EXTRANEOUS VARIABLES and fashion them into one abomination called *Chance*. Then, faced with that unimaginable idea, they resort to gamblers' superstitions as they make random lunges against the beast.

But while the run-of-the-mill bunnies are getting on with their target practice, the GOLD-STAR RABBITS are still scratching their furry heads. In their understandable eagerness to rid themselves of the medieval connotations of the idea of *Chance*, they naturally have very great difficulty in conceiving of the notion at all. On their own definition it is, after all, unimaginable. It can only be imagined by transcending the scientific point of view and reverting to the metaphysics which they are so desperately striving to escape. If they remain steadfast in maintaining that the Calculus of Probability must be regarded as a set of (mathematical) propositions which has no necessary connection with metaphysical notions on the one hand, or with empirical judgments on the other, then they must admit that they are left with a key term which is undefinable. For, no matter how much they attempt to abolish the term *Chance* from their judgments, they are left with attendant notions like 'randomization' and '*probability*' itself, which cannot be defined except by reference to such a concept. On the strictly 'logical theory' of probability, then, the terms '*chance*' and '*probability*' can always be replaced by any other words anyone might choose without in any way affecting the structure of the formal system.[20]

In other words, the run-of-the-mill bunnies in the warrens today might just as well be muttering, 'Now I think I can say with a confidence level of 0·001 that these variations are *not* due to *a patent elastic summer-house, capable of being compressed into the waistcoat pocket*, it therefore seems reasonable to assume that they are due to something else'; or, 'No, my dear fellow, that result could not have been expected on the basis of *special herbal toothpaste (with bio-flavoids)*. I think we are on to something interesting!; or, 'That relationship is no greater than that which might be expected on the basis of mere GRYPHON'.

' "*Mere*" indeed!' sniggered the GRYPHON as he tickled the rat amongst the rushes. The tickling stirred up such a commotion on the surface that Mr. Jeremy Fisher and his butterfly sandwich fell right off their lily leaf. Plop!

Down, down, down goes that unfortunate angler: he is well and truly in the SOUP. For, over the years, the run-of-the-mill RABBITS have been cooking up a most extraordinary potion. They have thrown together all their niggling doubts – all the uncontrolled, extraneous, and confounding variables which they feel to be outside of their control, if not, indeed, of their very understanding. Then they have – or so they believe – thoroughly stirred all the uningredients by the reliable trick of randomization. And, lo and behold! They have before them a most surprising SOUP!

It is the RABBITS' superstition that, if the SOUP is properly made up by the correct unarrangement of the uningredients and the right sprinkling of ¿time? for flavour, the result is a most powerful antidote to the GRYPHON. For, to prevent that beast from interfering in mischievously systematic ways with the activities of the variables involved in the tests, all you have to do is to surround it with the curious MOCK TURTLE SOUP. Once you have done this, the RABBITS will tell you, you have not only stopped the creature from messing up your research, but you have actually forced it into the indignity of acting as an unpaid research assistant in your testing rituals! Indeed, provided that your samples are selected 'at random' from the SOUP, you can be sure that the GRYPHON's ineffectual flailings will be doing the thoroughly useful job of keeping the SOUP nicely stirred, so that there are no good reasons why any one randomly selected ladleful of SOUP should be relevantly different from any other. Any RABBIT worth his salt will assure you that, under such circumstances, the respective probabilities of bringing up a ladleful of gargling Chelsea supporters, knickerless schoolgirls, or Glossoponians with damp cigars, can be clearly specified. For, if the GRYPHON is forced to keep on stirring, or, as the RABBITS put it, 'if chance is free to vary', then every drop or particle of SOUP has an equal chance of landing up in the ladle each time that ladle is dipped randomly into the SOUP. So the impressive Calculus of Probability can then be employed in estimating the probability that any particular ladleful differs from the rest of the SOUP in relevant ways, that is, *the probability that any sample is unrepresentative of the universe from which it is supposed to have been drawn.*

Ugh! What a thoroughly horrible idea, this MOCK TURTLE SOUP! It has been defined to include anything you care – or even don't care – to think about, not to mention the rat whose presence we have already smelt, several SPIDERS and a RED HERRING who will be swimming into the picture a little later on, *and* J.F. and the now-soggy butterfly sandwich.

And yet at the same ¿time? this abominable SOUP has not been defined
at all. Only one ¿true? proposition can be made about it: it is surprising.
You can say nothing else at all about it. You can't say how deep it is,
how wide it is, how thick it is, how hot it is, or, indeed, *how* it is; for if
you tried to say any of those things you would be accused, justly, of
metaphysics. You can rely on that SOUP *only* to surprise you.

So, believing the GRYPHON to be effectively reduced to the status of a
'*mere*' SOUP-stirrer, the RABBITS have come to forget their obsessive fear
of the creature itself and, instead, are somewhat overinvolved with the
SOUP. When they grow tired of casting for samples in it, they sometimes
praise it in song, like this,

> 'Beau--ootiful Soo--oop!
> Beau--ootiful Soo--oop!
> So--oop of the e-e-evening
> Beautiful, beauti--FUL SOUP!'

'Chorus again!' cried the GRYPHON, and the Mock Turtle had just
begun to repeat it, when a cry of 'The trial's beginning!' was heard in
the distance.

We have already had the pleasure of meeting the monk and most of the
cricket UMPIRES who made up the panel of judges presiding over the
trial. In the dock were most of the run-of-the-mill RABBITS from the
warrens of social science, some from other parts of the MOUNTAIN, and
a number of rather weightier figures one of whom, a certain Galileo
Galilei, was conspicuous for his arrogant manner and flamboyant dress.

Counsel for the Prosecution could not resist a twitch of his long ears
and a slow, sad shaking of his head as, replacing his large gold watch in
his waistcoat pocket, he stated the case against the accused. The charge
was one of abusing the MOCK TURTLE with intent to insult the GRYPHON.
Allegedly the RABBITS had been too greedy with the SOUP. So eager had
they been to sample it, that they had been trying to put their bowls in
their spoons, turning silly somersaults in the process, and landing up
in the SOUP. Plop! Plop!

'Call the first witness,' said the King; and the White Rabbit blew
three blasts on the trumpet, and called out 'First witness!'

The first witness was the Hatter. He came in with a teacup in one
hand and a butterfly sandwich in the other. 'I beg pardon, your
Majesty,' he began, 'for bringing these in; but I hadn't quite finished
my tea when I was sent for.'

SPIDERS do have horrible habits, even when they make hats for a
living, but *that* was inadmissible evidence. Counsel for the Prosecution
began to examine the SPIDER.

'Let us confine ourselves for the moment to the matter of social science,' he began, 'to the everyday, common or garden, run-of-the-mill research rituals of the psychologists, sociologists, and fellow travellers in the dock.' The Hatter said nothing at this point but made several rude gestures with some of his hairy legs.

'Why would you consider that the ordinary social scientist normally tries to perform PROBABILITY SAMPLING?' the RABBIT continued.

'I have heard it said,' replied the Hatter, 'that "It is through probability sampling that scientists attempt to achieve representativeness".'[21]

'That is hearsay!' said the MOCK TURTLE, quite out of turn, 'and anyway, I don't understand it. I would like to have it explained.'

'Well, I don't understand it either,' declared the witness, but I have also heard it said that:[22]

Random selection produces a representative sample by the continued operation of probabilities. Suppose that men with beards make up $1/20$ of our population. Random sampling in which each member of the sample has the same chance of selection gives bearded men, as a group, one chance in twenty of having their members selected. If we repeat the selection over and over again – take a large enough sample – then $1/20$ of our sample, just the same proportion as the proportion in the population, will be bearded. The same will hold true for every other characteristic. We can be sure that if we only take a large enough sample, the proportion in our sample of individuals with any given characteristic will be virtually identical to the proportion in the population.

At this point there was such a chuckling in the court that Counsel could barely be heard as he surmised that if one knew enough about a population to ensure that each member of it had an equal chance of being selected for a sample, one would hardly need to resort to PROBABILITY SAMPLING. But it was not necessary for him to say anything, for the SPIDER was eager to continue.[23]

'They say too that,

It can be demonstrated mathematically that where there are only two alternative outcomes to an event, e.g. heads or tails with a spun coin, and the coin is tossed so that chance alone determines which way it falls, then if the experiment is repeated a very large number of times, the distribution of results can be predicted. Take, for example, the experiment of tossing ten coins simultaneously and noting the number of heads. In the early stages one head might follow six heads and then three heads; no particular order would be apparent. But as the number of tosses grew, so the distribution of frequencies of particular numbers of heads would take on a definite pattern. Such a frequency distribution could be represented graphically with the values 0–10 heads marked off along the base and the corresponding proportionate frequencies marked off along the vertical axis.'

'Apparently,' witness went on, ignoring the rising mirth in the chambers, 'if the coin-tossing were repeated lots and lots and *lots* of times the resulting distribution would form a normal curve.' And he proceeded to draw a rather boring picture in the dust on the edge of the witness-box (Fig. 25).

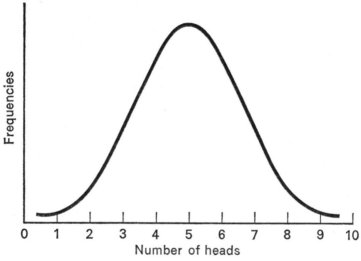

FIGURE 25

'Wash it away! Wash it away! Fetch the BATHWATER and wash it away!' went up the cry. For everyone present had seen through the SPIDER's story. The trouble was, of course, that the ladling of MOCK TURTLE SOUP cannot legitimately be compared with the tossing of coins.

The fact that a coin has only two faces, one called 'heads' and one called 'tails', has nothing at all to do with the GRYPHON. It is not by 'accident' that the coins which probability theorists keep in their pockets for the purposes of demonstrating their arguments have two sides, and that neither heads nor tails are favoured by their tossing technique. Nor is it 'coincidence' that dice have six sides, all equally capable of landing face upwards after a throw, or indeed that 478 raffle tickets in a hat each have an equal ($1/478$) chance of being picked out by the celebrity.[24] These games of chance have all been *set up* to yield a deliberate, finite, and well-defined set of possibilities. But the games of chance situations with which probability theory was designed to cope rarely resemble the circumstances of sample selection.

For the MOCK TURTLE SOUP was never set up according to the same kinds of rules, if, indeed, its uninvention could be said to be attributable to any rules at all. This undefined concoction is the very antithesis of the die, roulette wheel, Tarot deck, or pinball machine. For the latter machines of chance are defined in terms of all game-related parameters, that is to say that *everything relevant is known about them*. The MOCK TURTLE SOUP, on the other hand, is distinguished by the very fact that *nothing relevant is known about it*, or, contrariwise, the only thing that is known about it is that it is irrelevant, unsystematic and SURPRISING.

Of course the most important thing that the run-of-the-mill RABBITS (particularly the sociologists, psychologists, and fellow travellers) *didn't* know about the SOUP was where it began and where it ended, so it is hardly surprising that so many of them had been caught with soupy whiskers. If there had been some sort of giant tureen to contain the SOUP it would have been simple, they could have sat safely on the edge and dangled their bowls into the murky depths. But since they had forgotten to invent the tureen they were feeling very foolish, as they stood there in the dock.

The more meticulous RABBITS had tired themselves out issuing two clear warnings:

(1) A random sample can only be drawn from a clearly defined population by methods which guarantee every well-defined unit in that population an equal probability of selection.
(2) Statistical calculations of probabilities cannot be employed to assess data from samples which are not random.

And one of the judges[25] now repeated the salient point for the benefit of the jury: 'it is only from a finite collection that a random sample can be drawn'. At this point the SPIDER thrashed about hysterically in the BATHWATER splashing all and sundry, particularly sundry.

However had it happened that so many RABBITS had forgotten to invent their tureens? Was it perhaps because they were so hopeful of ¿discovering? *universal* laws that they had intended to give the impression that their generalizations were unlimited. Or was it that some of them really believed that history and geography had conveniently conspired to draw boundaries for them, as did the RABBIT who testified that:[26]

books on logic and the scientific method often take baskets of apples or jars of coloured beads for their examples. Boundaries must be established when sampling any finite collection. A time period and the geographical boundaries of the country provide the sampling frame for a nationwide population sample, while a basket suffices for the boundary when sampling the apples.

But that testimony only seemed to lend weight to the Prosecution's case! The GOLD-STARRED and bewigged legal gentleman submitted to the court that the somersaulting had scrambled the brains of the run-of-the-mill bunnies. For, without realizing it, they had tried to perform an absurd epistemological leap from their own familiar FAIRY-TALE MOUNTAIN into the real worlds outside, by way of Brighton pier and the MOCK TURTLE SOUP.

For, whatever else may be said – or left unsaid – about that horrible SOUP, one thing is clear from our viewpoint: it cannot be a *real* soup. Like the unimagined variables from which it is supposed to have been concocted its proper existence is in the FAIRY-TALE realm of imagination. It is a conglomeration, not of un*events*, but of un*judgments*. But, in their ordinary everyday practice, the bunnies, understandably keen to banish *idealist* metaphysics from their minds, had had recourse to another, and no less metaphysical, way of imagining the SOUP. Into the use of probability sampling and probability calculations had crept a bundle of *positivistic* notions. For them the GRYPHON, *Chance*, was not seen as a name for incomplete *knowledge*, but as a *real* force, really operative in real worlds: a source of the sort of unsystematic variation in events themselves which could be described by the unashamedly systematic devices of probability statistics.

Some say that the psychologists and sociologists were most guilty in this respect. The vast majority of them had simply taken the presence of the SOUP for granted. For them it was somehow 'there' lapping at the doors and windows of their dingy research rooms. Quite where it began or where it ended they did not care to think, but it was bubbling away out there all the same, and when they wanted a sample they felt that they had only to dip in their bowls. And they firmly believed that the larger the bowl used in sampling, or indeed the more times a smaller bowl was dipped, the greater the probability that the sampled SOUP would be representative of the SOUP left unsampled. This was, of course, a thoroughly reasonable assumption *if and only if* the SOUP could be regarded as a finite collection of units, like a basket of apples or a jar of coloured beads. So, naturally, a positivistic world view, on which vision *reality itself was finite but unbounded*, provided a comforting faith for those RABBITS who were too lazy to invent their own tureens.[27]

But, before the sentence was to be passed, there were more ill-doings to be discovered. It seems that, in their habitual performances of the ritual methods of sampling and estimating probabilities, the RABBITS had not only fallen prey to the rats and spiders who breed positivism in the burrows, but had also been consorting with the carriers of that other dreaded plague, *inductivism*. Just as they had fallen into the way of taking it for granted that variable probability is a characteristic, not merely of *judgments*, but of *events themselves* (so that the GRYPHON *Chance* became an actual feature of reality, rather than a convenient myth) so also had the silly bunnies fallen into regarding calculations of probability as valid *sources of theory*. Thus, over the years, these common or garden bunnies had come to believe that *probabilistic laws* could be induced from observations of the frequency distributions of specified happenings.

Indeed the use of the Calculus of Probability for the purposes of statistical induction of theory has become very widespread indeed. And, particularly since the development of quantum theory in physics, this is as much the case in the warrens of physical science as it is in the domain of the social sciences.

The *positivistic-inductivistic* recipe for MOCK TURTLE SOUP goes like this.

1. First make a number of quantitative observations in respect of units assumed to be randomly selected from a (rarely well-defined) universe.

2. Now plot these observations in terms of the frequency distributions of certain ¿interesting? features.

3. Where these frequency distributions deviate from the normal distribution (the one which one would expect on the basis of 'mere chance') seek correlative or associated variations in other groups of observations from the same universe.

4. Employ descriptive statistical techniques (such as graphs, means, and standard deviations) to collate this information.

5. 'Test' 'hypotheses' 'suggested by' this data by means of statistical 'tests of significance', or other devices derived from the Calculus of Probability.

6. Progressively subsume each level of statistical description under a more general judgment of probability.

The probability generalizations, or probabilistic laws, produced by this method are forms of judgment which might well be translated into words as laws of the form 'Men usually wear trousers', 'Leaves practically always fall off trees in autumn', and so on. These are built together in levels of increasing generality to form stories rather similar to deductive nomological explanations. But there is a crucial difference between *deductive nomological explanations* and *inductive statistical generalizations*: 'the former effect a deductive subsumption under laws of universal form, the latter an inductive subsumption under laws of probabilistic form.'[28] That is to say that, while the former are *categorically* causal, the latter, if they are explicitly causal at all, are merely *casually* so.

Now there are many rabbits who believe that such methods *can* yield valid *explanations* of the epidemiology of happenings, though many admit that these stories are 'of a less stringent kind'[29] than deductive nomological FAIRY TALES.

These fellows will admit that, while the *explanandum* of a true deductive nomological explanation, or proper *EXPLANATORY THEORY*, is necessarily true$_4$ (provided that the judgments in the *explanans* are believed to be true$_4$), the *explanandum* of an inductive probabilistic explanation is only '*probably true$_4$*'. But they claim that, where the focus of interest is *classes of events* rather than single events, probability generalizations will provide accurate and reliable approximations to truth$_4$. For instance, if you are interested in the social distribution of the venereal affliction currently known as Non-Specific Urethritis (NSU) then, for example, the following series of generalizations might form a useful basis for prediction and action:

EXPLANANS   Persons in 'relevant' contact with NSU cases prac-
             tically always get a dose.
             The more 'urban' the environment the more likely it
             is that social contacts will involve NSU cases.
             The more 'friendly' the community the greater the
             likelihood of social contact between individuals.
             The more 'deviant' the community the more likely it
             is that social contact will involve 'relevant' contact.

EXPLANANDUM   'Friendly urban deviants' stand a good chance of
               getting a dose.

Now, of course, the use of percentages and statistics instead of statements like 'practically always', 'more likely', and 'a very good chance', ought not to obscure the fact that inductive probabilistic 'explanations' such as the above, do not have the same logical status as proper *EXPLANATORY THEORIES*.

In truth$_2$ I, personally, find it hard to see how statements of the kind 'things like that usually do behave like that' can inspire causal thinking. But it is no part of my argument to deny that some theorists may find the Calculus of Probability (perhaps supplemented by axiomatic set theory) to be a useful tool for theory construction. The point to be made is simply that: *the methods by which a theory is constructed in the first place give no guarantee of the truth$_4$ of that theory, nor even of its 'probable truth$_4$'*. 'Probable truth$_4$', like 'necessary truth$_4$', can only be established through testing rituals, and the business of testing has, as we have seen, nothing at all to do with the essentially private and personal preferences which theorists may have about the various ways in which inspiration may be acquired.

The danger with the use of the Calculus of Probability at the stage of theory construction is, of course, that numbers may create even more awesome magic than words: there is a spurious authority about sums.[30] Those RABBITS who happen to be good at their sums often get a sort of quantomania which, like that other rabbity ailment, myxomatosis,[31] causes their heads to swell. As a result, they tend to show off their (statistical) theory construction procedures in public and thus often trick innocent passers-by into mistaking these mathematical UNDER-GARMENTS for the respectable garb of truth$_4$. This is how it comes about that what should properly be regarded as a prologue for, or propaedeutic to, the scientific business of testing hypotheses is mistaken for science itself. What Byrne has said of the physical sciences goes equally for the social sciences:[32]

> In briefest terms, what is of the utmost importance about the present role of the calculus of probability is precisely the fact that it is no longer viewed as a preparation for or auxiliary to *scientia*. On the one hand the *scientia* that was the Newtonian celestial mechanics has given way to Einstein's theory of relativity, and in the process man has lost confidence in the absolutivity of *scientia*. On the other hand, and almost simultaneously, that which had been viewed as the propaedeutic to *scientia* has suddenly found itself as the systematic representation of a large and important sector of *scientia* itself.

How have these positivistic and inductivistic SPIDERS crept into the background of assumptions which so many common or garden bunnies take for granted when they pick up the tools of probability statistics?

In my view the trouble has derived from the willingness of so many of us common or garden bunnies to make do with hearsay, rather than finding out for ourselves. Anyone who has delved far enough into the archival records available in the LIBRARY, could see for himself that the Calculus of Probability was originally conceived as a replacement for medieval methods of disputation. And such disputation was considered appropriate only in the realm of non-scientific discourse, that is of the sort of proto-scientific *speculation* which, once upon a time, St Thomas Aquinas called '*opinio*' in contradistinction to *testable* knowledge or '*scientia*'.

Now two of the most astute judges at the trial which we are at present attending, Professors Popper and Carnap, have distinctly ruled that speculation and science must be kept apart. Though the former may be an essential source of the latter, the two must not be confused. Our theories may have their origins in *opinion*, but only through *scientia* can we arbitrate their truth$_4$ within the indubitable limits of reason. Thus these venerable judges reiterate the GOLD-STAR principle of separation between the *sources* of theorizing or modes of theory construction, and the assessment of truths$_4$.

And, of course, a theory can no more be *proved* to be 'probably true$_4$' than it can be proved to be true$_4$. For however closely a probability statement seems to approach unity, it can never attain that value. For a statement of certain truth$_4$ (one where P = 1) is merely introduced into probability theory as a fictional criterion against which judgments of probabilities 0–1 (exclusive) can be compared. Of course, where there is a clearly defined universe, the progressive sampling of more and more subsets from that set will result in statements with increasing probability values. The probability (P) of each sample (S) representing an unbiased reflection of the universe will continue to increase *towards* '1' as the sample itself increases *towards* the universe. *But*

> 'Many a slip
> Twixt S 00000000000 P
> And S 1 P'

Thus sniggered the rat, as he pulled the feather from the grand hat of one Galileo Galilei. 'Indeed, indeed', murmured the whole company of judges before lending their ears to the quiet-voiced monk, who merely repeated the words he had spoken in the Observatory: 'unde hoc non est demonstratum, sed suppositio quaedam.'

No wonder the gaudy Galileo is in the dock with the rest of the accused! He has again taken up the loud mantle of an arch-villain in our FAIRY TALE. For much of the subsequent confusion within the scientific kitchens, and the resultant spoilt broth, can be seen as a curious admixture of speculative and demonstrative methodologies. It may be argued that it was not until the so-called Galilean Revolution that the horrible metaphysic of the MOCK TURTLE SOUP was considered thick enough to fill the gap which Nature already abhorred! But that is another story and, as you will *probably* be getting a little anxious about tea, I will save it for another day.

But let us dally in the courtroom a little longer. You may find it ¿interesting? to hear the case against a certain M. Laplace who has been singled out for separate examination because of his alleged role as a ringleader. It is said that he has had a very strong influence on subsequent users of the Calculus of Probability.

Laplace's contribution to Probability Theory is sometimes called the *Principle of Insufficient Reason*. According to this principle, where a RABBIT is faced with insufficient reasons for expecting one happening over another, then he should assume that all happenings are equally likely to occur, that is,[33]

The theory of chance consists in reducing all the events of the same kind to a certain number of cases equally possible, that is to say, to

such as we may be equally undecided about in regard to their existence, and in determining the number of cases favorable to the event
whose probability is sought. The ratio of this number to that of all the
cases possible is the measure of probability, which is thus simply a
fraction whose numerator is the number of favorable cases and whose
denominator is the number of all the cases possible.

The distinguished Frenchman is more than a little embarrassed at the
totally uncalled-for laughter in the court. He protests that it is not he
who is guilty of letting the SPIDERS into the SOUP. As he says, he made it
quite clear that the use of the calculus should be regarded as a mark of
imperfect knowledge, that probability statements are non-demonstrative
statements, and that probability theory is an instrument of the unsystematic. Thus, clearly defining probability theory as a mode of *opinio*, of
proto-scientific speculation, he had formulated his theory in terms of
the following three pivoting assumptions.
   1. What never happens has a probability of 0.
   2. What always happens has a probability of 1.
   3. By making properly guided observations of the frequency of
events, we can make generalizations which will go on increasing in
probability value until they attain certainty, 1.
   So stated, Laplace's statistical methods were quite definitely to be
regarded as routines for inducing theoretical generalizations from rather
large numbers of observations, made with respect to clearly specified
universes. 'Eef zere are people who want to confuse my method wiz ze
techniques of testing hypozeses, zen zat ees zeir own business,' protests
Monsieur Laplace, twitching his nose miserably in the dock.
   But, at the judges' bench, Professor Carnap is not at all impressed
with this defence. His summing up of the situation leaves very little
doubt that in his written works Laplace had slipped in a second referent
for the term 'probability'. As well as using this word to denote *the degree
of certainty with which a judgment was held*, he also employed it to mean
something rather like '*the true₄ frequency of events*'. Thus, in addition to
a concept of 'probability' as an aid to theory construction, the distinguished French mathematician had used the same word to mean
something quite different.
   So it is that Laplace stands in the dock, accused with the others of
contributing to the growing *confusion of probable propositions about
events with propositions about probable events*. And this is a confusion
without which, as the judges are eager to point out, that school of
statisticians represented by the other frog, Mr Jeremy Fisher, could
never have developed at all! For the methods of these positivistic and
residually inductivistic statisticians involve a conception of 'probability',
and thus of the beast *Chance*, which has its locus in a real world of real

events. And it is in this sense, rather than in the sense of a machine for the arbitration of *judgments* that most common or garden bunnies take the calculus of probability for granted.[34]

'That's very important,' the King said, turning to the jury. They were just beginning to write this down on their slates, when the White Rabbit interrupted: '*Un*important, your Majesty means of course,' he said, in a very respectful tone, but frowning and making faces at him as he spoke.

'*Un*important, of course, I meant,' the King hastily said, and went on to himself in an undertone, 'important – unimportant – unimportant – important – ' as if he were trying which word sounded best.

Some of the jury wrote it down 'important,' and some 'unimportant.'

Perhaps, at any rate, it would be a good deal less important if the spidery incubi of positivism and inductivism had confined their whisperings to the floppy ears of the *common or garden* bunnies. But some of the weightiest figures in the contemporary warrens have been caught by *Chance* with their GOLD-STAR BADGES off.

Professor Hempel, for example, is generally the strictest of deductivists, but his covert positivism leads him to a residually inductivist position with regard to the issue of 'probability'. Recognizing the double meaning of the term, Hempel has adopted the logico-positivist stratagem of distinguishing '*logical probability*' as a 'quantitative logical relation between definite *statements*', from '*statistical probability*' which he characterizes as a 'quantitative relation between repeatable kinds of *events*'. And, as any of our judges could point out, this characterization of the 'statistical' notion of 'probability' reveals Hempel to be as guilty of abusing the MOCK TURTLE SOUP as are any of the common or garden bunnies whom no one expects to know any better.

Consider the following statement upon which the 'statistical' interpretation of the calculus of probability is pivoted.

$p(O,R) = r$

This statement, as Hempel says, 'means that in a long series of performances of a random experiment R, the proportion of cases with outcome O is almost certain to be close to r'.[35] But what kind of a statement is that? If this, as Hempel has claimed, is a judgment about events, rather than merely about other judgments, then it must be a metaphysical statement: it must be a statement of belief about the consequences of evoking the real GRYPHON in a real world through the real trick of randomization.

The King turned pale, and shut his notebook hastily. 'Consider your verdict,' he said to the jury, in a low trembling voice.

'There's more evidence to come yet, please your Majesty,' said the White Rabbit jumping up in a great hurry: 'this paper has just been picked up.'

The paper in question is a very famous article which first appeared in the *American Sociological Review* in 1957.[36] In this paper Hanan Selvin carefully described the method of randomization developed by the hard-done-by Mr Fisher.[37] And he summed up the use of probability methods of sampling and estimation in sociology by explaining that, by such methods, sociologists first assume that random sampling has introduced random differences between units grouped together on the basis of some variable(s), then they calculate the 'probability' that any differences which they observe between such groups 'can be attributed to chance'. Another way of putting that is to say that they calculate the likelihood that the samples have been drawn from the same homogeneous population (or, if you like, are included in the same set). The article then makes the point that such methods involve the illegitimate assumption that randomization has necessarily neutralized the impact of all the UNCONTROLLED EXTRANEOUS and CONFOUNDING VARIABLES which might be operating in systematic ways to mess up the results of the testing operations. And, assuming for some reason that this is a situation peculiar to the social science, Selvin continues.[38]

> In design and interpretation, in principle and in practice, tests of statistical significance are inapplicable in non-experimental research. Sociologists would do better to reexamine their purposes in using the tests, and try to devise better methods of achieving these purposes than resort to techniques that are at best misleading for the kinds of empirical research in which they are engaged.

But this important paper is turning into a RED HERRING before the very eyes of the jury! For, though Selvin was right to urge caution in the use of probability statistics, particularly the so-called 'tests of significance' which we will be examining in greater detail below, the perils he has stated so carefully are not confined to social science. For, *wherever in science there is a taken-for-granted metaphysic of positivism, then inductivistic methodology is bound to flourish amongst the common or garden bunnies.* For, as they find themselves busily assuming that reality itself is like the dreadful MOCK TURTLE SOUP, finite but unbounded, so they inevitably come to use the mathematical instruments of probability theory as means of inducing statistical regularities from data.

It is this sort of common or garden positivistic inductivism, or *verificationism*, which leads so many empiricists to slip into the error of confusing *statistical* with *substantive* significance. What happens is that they translate all the values of all the units under consideration into numbers, use their counter-sorters and computers to sort these numbers into comparative tables, and then calculate the extent to which these distributions deviate from the patterning which might have been expected on the basis of no theory at all, in other words by the bare metaphysical assumption of *Chance*. They then state these results in terms of statistics, particularly the standard tests of significance such as chi-squared: for example, '$\chi^2 = q$, which is significant at the o·ooon level', or, in other words, 'that result would only occur by chance one in z times'. Yet no truths$_4$ can be induced in this way, to attempt to employ probability theory as a means of deriving truths$_4$ from statistics is as foolish as the decision of the sociologist in Hirschi and Selvin's parable.[39]

> A quantomanic empiricist is playing Stud poker. He plays like any one else, winning sometimes, losing sometimes. Then the dealer gets four aces (showing). 'Funny!', thinks the sociologist (quickly computing the probabilities) 'that would only happen once in 54,145 hands, significant at the o·ooooi level'. So the sociologist rejects the null hypothesis (that the phenomenon occurred by chance) pulls out a gun, and shoots the dealer.

But if the Calculus itself, the mathematics of probability, is fished out of the horrible MOCK TURTLE SOUP, and disentangled from the spidery grip of positivistic and inductivistic assumptions, it can be seen for what it is. Taken by itself, the Calculus of Probability is, like any other mathematical instrument, an UNINTERPRETED AXIOMATIC SYSTEM.

As such a system, a purely formal and contentless model, the Calculus as it is now employed can be summarized in three simple propositions:[40]

1. Probability values are estimates of truth$_4$ which range from o (never true$_4$) to 1 (always true$_4$).
2. The probability value of the sum of two mutually exclusive units is the sum of the probability values of the two units considered separately.
3. Whenever the separate probability values of *all* mutually exclusive units are added together at the same ¿time?, the result must add up to 1.

These propositions may be stated more briefly thus,

Let P = 'probability'
1. $o \leq P \leq 1$
2. Where x and y are mutually exclusive units,
   $$P(x+y) = Px + Py$$

3. For any logically exhaustive set of mutually exclusive units,
   $$\Sigma P = 1$$

Thus stated, as a purely formal mathematical instrument, the Calculus of Probability can be seen for what it is, a rather tenuous rope ladder between levels of analysis. Like the rules of deductive logic, the Calculus of Probability provides a set of simple, and collectively acceptable, devices for moving from more to less, or less to more, general statements. By enabling the assignment of quantitative values to statements like 'rather unusual', 'very likely', 'most probable', 'highly improbable', 'once-in-a-blue-moon' and so on, the Calculus permits the consideration and comparison of several such tentative judgments at the same time.[41]

And further consideration of the (mathematical) features of the Calculus has led to the development of the whole gamut of probability statistics, ranging from simple, but non-arithmetic, averaging devices, through chi-squared estimations and correlation coefficients, to some of the more complicated statistical techniques which will be outlined later.

But it is essential to remember that these statistics are numerical gibberish if they are divorced from the background of taken-for-granted (mathematical) assumptions from which they have been derived. Whatever specific *content* is given to a statistical statement of probability, the *form* of the decision involved must be made on the basis of the belief that all three of the propositions comprising the basic Calculus of Probability may be regarded as true$_3$.

And, of course, it is the third proposition,

$$\Sigma P = 1$$

which sets the greatest restrictions upon the use of the Calculus, and hence of probability statistics in general. For, *unless the cases under consideration at any particular level of analysis may be properly regarded as derivable from a precisely defined and logically exhaustive set of non-overlapping (i.e. mutually exclusive) units, then none of the impressive methods and techniques of probability theory will be applicable.*

Oh dear! So far from being a solution to the problems (of attrition and relevant bias) posed by PURPOSIVE SAMPLING methods, the method of PROBABILITY SAMPLING, randomization, and the associated statistical methods of estimation, can only be employed *within* a clearly defined set of units, that is, *within* a PURPOSIVE SAMPLE.

We have been circling and circling around and around a non-existent tureen, wondering where to dip in our spoons for the best samples of a very surprising soup. But surely we should have realized before we began that, without a tureen, that SOUP is just plain *silly*!

The jury all wrote down on their slates, '*She* doesn't believe there's an atom of meaning in it,' but none of them attempted to explain the paper.

'If there's no meaning in it,' said the King, 'that saves a world of trouble, you know, as we needn't try to find any. . . .'

Chapter 15

The Amazing, Incredible Sampling Machine

Now if you are feeling that your brains have been simmered in SOUP until not *quite* done, I am not at all surprised. But I do not believe that you would be feeling any better if you had spent the last hour in the LIBRARY.

There are tomes and tomes of statistical texts to be found in there, and many of the volumes are addressed specifically to putative social scientists like ourselves. Yet most of these books are quite as absurd as the chapter that you have just been reading! For almost all of them are thinly disguised versions of the ancient legend of the GRYPHON and the MOCK TURTLE SOUP. And, in the same way, almost every undergraduate course in the social sciences devotes a very noticeable chunk of the limited ¿time? available to the awesome business of 'statistics'. But I hope that the horrors you have just encountered will have led you to the very sensible assessment that the GOLD-STAR students will have been truanting themselves from these boring classes along with those whose truancy, like my own, stemmed from rather less admirable motives.

Like every other set of decisions to be made in the ritual business of research, the questions of selecting a representative sample can only be formulated and answered within the framework of a research programme. Perhaps *you* are prepared to take for granted the spidery assumptions of positivism and inductivism which lie behind most current interpretations of statistical theory? In that case you will be content to believe the most unlikely story that there is a real GRYPHON condemned forever to the business of stirring a real SOUP so that it will continue to oblige the gamblers with surprise.

> Alice laughed. 'There's no use trying,' she said: 'one *can't* believe impossible things.'
> 'I daresay you haven't had much practice,' said the Queen. 'When I was your age, I always did it for half-an-hour a day. Why,

sometimes I've believed as many as six impossible things before breakfast.'[1]

But if you have difficulty believing in 'impossible things' I expect that you will agree with me that *in the first instance, all sets of sampling decisions must be PURPOSIVE ones*. Probability sampling and the statistical techniques whose applicability rests upon the assumption that probability sampling has been accomplished, can only be employed where the set from which the units are to be drawn has been defined clearly in terms of all relevant parameters. Thus – far from being a means of overcoming the Catch 22 of attrition and relevant bias posed by PURPOSIVE SAMPLING – *PROBABILITY SAMPLING must be relegated to the humble role of an economy measure within some form of PURPOSIVE SAMPLING method*. To select a PROBABILITY SAMPLE is merely to draw a smaller subsample of a sample selected in some purposeful way. That is to say that it is to employ certain standardized routines for selecting a subset from the set which *you* have defined as the most appropriate conglomeration of appearances on which to test your theory. Thus the only GOLD-STAR reason for drawing a PROBABILITY SAMPLE and employing statistical methods of estimation, is, quite simply, that you may save ¿time?, effort, and resources that way.[2]

Having delimited a sample, S, as a result of a series of PURPOSIVE SAMPLING decisions, the GOLD-STAR RABBIT may decide that S is too big for his purposes, that is that he does not have sufficient resources at his disposal to cope with all the data which he could produce if he were to analyse the relevant characteristics of all the units which are, *on his own definition*, included in S. In that case he will use one of the simple methods of PROBABILITY SAMPLING in order to select, or rather *unselect*, from S a subsample s, which, being thus drawn from S, may be assumed to be isomorphic with S in all conceivable ways (except, of course, that of having actually been selected from S!). When he then proceeds to estimate the probability limits of sampling variation for s with respect to S he must be careful to remember that all his statistics afford is an indication of the relationship between s and S. That is to say that probability statistics are employed merely as a means of assessing whether or not bias has crept into his sampling at this stage. However impressive these statistics may be, they tell him no more than whether or not he has made a mistake at this stage in the whole, very dicey, business of sample selection. And, though the precise limits of error in the selection of s from S can thus be calculated, the relationship between S and the theoretical universe which it has been defined to represent (U) remains, like so much else in the research process, an entirely arbitrary matter.

To summarize:

Purposive sampling · Probability sampling

U   S   s

The research assumption

$S \equiv s$

is a precise and quantitative one whose probability limits of error can be calculated reliably by the use of statistical probability theory. But it is to the problems of selecting S such that it may be assumed that

$U \equiv S$

that most of the uncertainties of sampling are attached. And probability theory and statistics can be of no help to the researcher when he is faced with this prior, and far more ¿interesting? quandary.

The very first stage in the selection of S must, of course, consist in the precise definition of the theoretical universe to which the theory under test is supposed to apply. And, as you know, to *define* a universe – or anything else for that matter – is simply to specify

(i) the relevant dimensions of variance, that is to say, *the variables in which you are ¿interested?*,

and (ii) *the range of permissible values for each defining variable.*

Now the definition of U in terms of (i) ¿interesting? variables and (ii) permissible values for (i) should be a fairly straightforward business. For you already have a complete listing of (i) in your *Research Notebook* on the page headed '*Variables to be Controlled by Selection*'. The variables which are relevant at this point are, quite simply, all those which you have already decided neither to ignore nor to control by actual measurement. And the second part of the definition of U, (ii) *the values of these variables*, should not produce any very serious problems either, though you must obviously attempt to achieve a good balance between many values and small groups and few values and large groups.

Now, if you have succeeded in defining U satisfactorily, that is in terms of (i) relevant variables, and (ii) permissible values for (i), you have by THAT SAME STROKE, provided a sampling frame for S. That is to say that you have succeeded in defining a set which may be taken to be isomorphic with, or inclusive of, your intended initial sample, S.

For example, suppose that you have a theory which is assumed to apply to SPIDERS. Now pretend that you choose to define the universe in question, U (SPIDERS), by just one variable, '*legginess*'. And suppose, also, that you have decided that there are only three ¿interesting? values for that variable, to wit: 'less than eight legs (1)', 'eight legs (2)', and

'more than eight legs (3)'. You have defined U, and you have simultaneously provided a sampling frame for S. Mind you, you will have
done both those jobs in a pretty lousy fashion. For, though your three
categories of happenings are certainly logically exhaustive, and mutually
exclusive, in that everything conceivable can be classified as (1) or (2)
or (3), and nothing conceivable could be labelled with more than one of
those values at once, you would still have a rather silly definition of
SPIDERS, and consequently, a somewhat ludicrous sampling frame for S,
a sample of SPIDERS. After all, the category (1) would include an enor-
mous and motley collection of 'live' and 'dead' appearances ranging
from bananas, typewriters, stick insects, milkmen, etc. through one-
time SPIDERS who had lost a leg or two in combat. And, while the
category (2) certainly embraces some *bona fide* SPIDERS, it might also
include hideously maimed centipedes, Siamese-Twin-Poodles and so
on. Clearly, then, the definition of U, and hence of S is rarely satisfactory if it is made in terms of a single variable (however many values
are considered in respect of that variable).

Let me therefore offer one more example of a sampling frame, in
order, at least, to take away some of the taste of SPIDERS.

Suppose that the theory under consideration is a story about the effect
of growing old on persons who have been exposed to the mindblowing
influences of sociology. The theory might be a long and complicated
one, involving all kinds of terms like 'anticipatory socialization', 'role
vacuum', 'status inconsistency', 'erotic inflation', 'verbal flatulence' and
so on, but let us not bother with the details. Suppose only that the
researcher who had the impertinence to propose and test such a sub-
versive theory with the aid of funds from the Social Science Research
Council, had made the prior research decision that the following
EXPERIMENTAL AND EXTRANEOUS VARIABLES were
relevant to the selection of his samples.

A age
B occupation
C country of residence
D type of residential area
E marital status

By the very act of listing these variables the researcher has already
begun the business of providing a precise definition of U.

Now, suppose that, realizing the impossibility of stretching his funds
to cover a vast international and intergalactic survey of sociologists and
other workers, he decides to limit his research to England and Wales.
That is, he decides to cope with the possibility of the possibly confounding influence of variable C by treating it as a constant. Now notice that,
in doing this, he is *not* – or at least should not be! – making the assump-

tion that an English and Welsh sample may be taken to be isomorphic with or 'representative of' some larger (and still undefined) universe of persons. Instead he is limiting the generality or scope of applicability of the theory itself. That is to say that, by the decision to treat C as a constant, he has committed himself to the decision to rewrite his theory as a theory 'about the effect of growing old on English and Welsh people who have been . . . etc.'.

So, having thus demoted the variable C to the status of a constant (or variable with only one relevant value), our cheeky researcher has made another leap forward towards defining U itself.

The next stage is to decide upon (ii) *the permitted values* for the remaining four variables. Say like this:

Values for A	1:	youth (under 25)
	2:	early middle age (26–30)
	3:	middle middle age (31–40)
	4:	late middle age (41–50)
	5:	antiquity (51+)
Values for B	1:	teaching sociology to undergraduates
	2:	sociological research
	3:	other undergraduate teaching (non-sociology)
	4:	other professional work involving relations of superior authority with young people
	5:	other
	6:	unemployed
Values for D	1:	London
	2:	other large city
	3:	small town
	4:	rural and maritime
Values for E	1:	lousy
	2:	medium
	3:	good
	4:	non-existent

This combination of (i) *relevant variables* and (ii) *permitted values* is now, of course, a complete definition of U. When C is treated as a constant, the five relevant variables define the logically exhaustive categories in Figure 26.

And this definition of U is also an exact statement of the sampling frame for S.

So the actual process of sample selection cannot begin until you have a sampling frame. And of course once you have such a frame you have what it takes to play the RABBITS' SAMPLING GAME.

I have found that the basic moves of the highly complicated SAMPLING GAME can best be mastered if the sport is conceived as a repeating series

A

			1 D				2 D				3 D				4 D			
			1	2	3	4	1	2	3	4	1	2	3	4	1	2	3	4
		E 1																
1		2																
		3																
		4																
		E 1																
2		2																
		3																
		4																
		E 1																
3		2																
		3																
		4																
		E 1																
4		2																
		3																
		4																

(B, on left side)

FIGURE 26

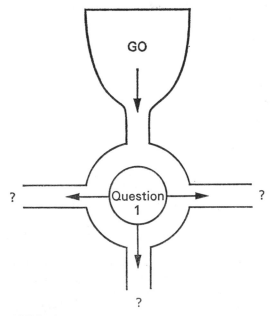

FIGURE 27

of choice situations centred around eight major considerations. I shall proceed to describe the GAME from this point of view.

Each player starts off in the position marked 'GO' and faces a series of eight ordered and interlocking questions. He must begin by asking himself QUESTION 1 and make his move according to the answer he prefers. Sometimes this move will take him directly to QUESTION 2, but sometimes not. The aim of the game is to be able to give an honest 'Yes' answer to the last question. But, as you will soon find out, if you begin to play the GAME, it is quite hard to *get* to the last question, for, in the RABBITS' SAMPLING GAME – as in snakes and ladders – one always seems to go backwards faster than forwards. For example, you may well find that, in your very first GAME you only get as far as QUESTION 3 when . . . woops! . . . you find yourself back at 'GO'.

Anyway let's have a go (see Figure 27).

Question 1: Can you be satisfied with single-variable sampling?

If, as is most unlikely in social (and slightly less unlikely in physical) science, there is only one variable defining your sampling frame, then, of course, you can happily answer 'YES' to this question. You may also feel that 'YES' is a reasonable answer if, as sometimes happens, you find that all but one of the variables comprising your initial sampling frame may be regarded for your purposes as constants rather than as variables.[3] In either case you have, by answering 'YES', begun the series of choices involved in creating a sample (or samples) by opting for a *simple-single-variable-single-stage initial-sampling-stratagem.*

There are two different ways of selecting such a sample, as we have seen in the preceding chapter. You may use the method of *homogeneous selection* or, on the other hand, you may move in the opposite ¿direction? in this GAME and opt for *heterogeneous selection* (see Figure 28).

But you may have found that the only answer which you could give to QUESTION 1 is 'NO', in which case you must reject such simple initial tactics and move straight on to QUESTION 2 (see Figure 29).

Question 2: Do you have enough information for simple purposive sampling?

Although you found that simple *single-variable* purposive sampling was not appropriate for your purposes you may still be able to use a single-stage and still relatively straightforward form of multivariable purposive sampling by selecting a *Match Sample* or a *Typological Sample*, as explained in the previous chapter. But suppose the information which you would need in order to select one of these sorts of samples is not

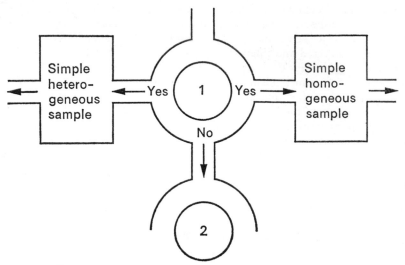

FIGURE 28

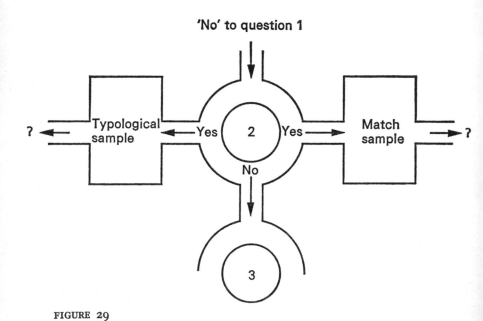

FIGURE 29

readily available to you? Suppose you find that, in order to ascertain the values of units on the relevant variables, you would have to go to ridiculous and wasteful extremes? Imagine, for example, weighing, measuring, and testing the eyesight of everyone in Leicester in order to draw a sample of Leicester-dwellers matched with regard to cubic capacity, shoe size, and myopia! So? Obviously you may often find that no form of simple or single-stage purposive sampling will strike the balance between attrition and relevant bias that you are looking for as an initial sampling stratagem.

In such circumstances you would have to answer 'NO' to *QUESTION 2*, and so move on to *QUESTION 3*.

Question 3:   Can you see a way of structural purposive sampling?

You have ruled out all the available forms of simple purposive sampling, whether single-variable or multi-variable, single-stage or multi-stage, so there is only one thing that you can do at the moment. You must consider whether or not you can devise some *other* means of defining a sample which could be regarded as isomorphic with the theoretical universe in all the respects which you have decided to be relevant, that is, in terms of all the variables defining your sampling frame. This amounts to drawing a 'structural' initial sample.

The most popular way of obtaining a structural purposive sample is by opting for quantitative or numerical isomorphism. This is, of course, the kind of sampling which is known as *Quota Sampling*, and which has been described in rather lurid detail in the previous chapter.

But sociologists have also devised a quite different approach to structural sampling. This consists in the attempt to draw a qualitative or *interactional* rather than a quantitative isomorph of the universe in question.[4]

The most commonly-used type of interactional sampling is a method which may be termed *snowball sampling*. Suppose that you wish to obtain a sample of persons from a set, the parameters of which are defined by cultural factors with no clear-cut geographical correlates. You know exactly what sort of people you are looking for but you do not know their location in ordinary taken-for-granted first-order space. Take an 'underground' group of some sort, for example, or, say, Freemasons, or pigeon-fanciers, or wife-swappers. Your problem is that you do not know where these people hang out. How are you to get hold of a sample which you can reasonably assume to be isomorphic with the set defined by your theory?

The trick of *snowball sampling* is to land up with a plausibly representative sample by starting off from an initial, limited (and, presumably,

thoroughly biased) sample, achieved by the most idiosyncratic and haphazard means. You begin by locating a very small number of the units
for which you are searching. Perhaps, for example, you spot one of the
persons you imagine yourself to be pursuing in the street and hasten
after him. Perhaps in a certain corner of a public park where 'They' are
rumoured to lurk? Or, perhaps, you answer an advertisement in a
dubious magazine, or on the door of a newsagent's; or perhaps, one day
after weeks of staring hopelessly towards the sky, you see a pigeon flying
purposefully in a certain ¿direction?.

Next? Your brilliant work as sleuth must be followed through with
the utmost diplomacy. Somehow you must gain the confidence of your
informant(s) and thus, at least minimally, infiltrate the group in
question.

You now proceed to gather a sample like a snowball gathers gob-
stoppers, or a chain-letter spawns more unwelcome litter on the door-
mat. Each initial contact is enjoined to lead you to further contacts, and
these to further contacts, and so on. For example, you may ask a willing
informant to pass a letter, or maybe even a questionnaire, or perhaps
just a telephone number, to other members. More usually, however, you
will simply employ more informal methods of inducing contacts to make
further introductions in person.

Now anyone employing this thoroughly qualitative method of drawing
a structural sample must be very careful not to pollute his sampling
technique with quantitative restrictions. *Don't* say 'Please send a copy
to 10 other . . . etc.' For you must fix no more arbitrary limits on the
snowballing process than those which are already involved in the many
practical considerations already in play. The number of further contacts
generated by each contact must be allowed to vary according to the
respondent's inclinations.

The next thing to do is to sketch a sort of rough map of the units
sampled so far. You will probably find that this is easier if you replace
the names of the respondents in the emerging sample with numerical
labels.[5] The least confusing way to do this is to number the units in
order as they become known to you, thus your first contact will come to
be known by the nickname '1' and the thirteenth as '13'. Your first
rough map will thus look something like Figure 30.

Notice that it is clear from this map that some of the units have been
implicated in the sample by more than one other unit. Thus, for example,
respondent '7' has led the researcher to a number of other respondents,
one of whom has already been included in the sample under the nickname '6' as a result of a lead from unit '2'.

Now, of course, you have nothing which could be regarded as a set
which is plausibly isomorphic with the universe to which your theory
applies. There is every reason to believe that your sample may be biased

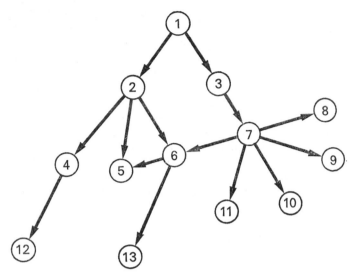

FIGURE 30

in all sorts of ways, at least some of which could be relevant from the point of view of your theory, and/or any of the rival theories which you are also considering. It seems most likely that, if you had started somewhere else entirely, you would have landed up with a quite different sample.

The only solution to this problem is more hard work. What you must do is to take each unit in your map and treat this as the starting-point for a whole new map. Thus, for example, you might begin again with unit '2' and construct a new map looking something like Figure 31.

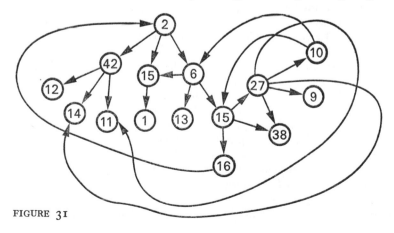

FIGURE 31

Perhaps you dislike the untidiness of this map, realizing that the units could be rearranged in a neater 'sociometric' construction.[6] But I should not waste ¿time? at this stage for you still have a lot more mapping to do.

One of the most effective ways of proceeding from an initial map to further maps is by delegating each unit in the original haphazard set to a different research worker. And, if you are fortunate enough to have the ¿time? and resources, you can also introduce a check on your developing maps by swapping your units and research workers around and starting again. Of course you *may* have to do all the dirty work yourself, in which case *you* will have to make a new start from each unit, one at a ¿time?. In either case, the more intensively each contact is exploited as a source of further contacts the better. But, of course, there is a limit to the extent to which you can replicate your maps without damaging the delicate interpersonal relations which must be maintained between researchers and respondents.

Now, if you persevere with your mapping and remapping then, *eventually*, even if each respondent is only being partially truthful$_2$, you will reach a point where less and less *new* units are turning up in the maps.[7] Then, if you keep going, you will find that you are getting practically no leads to any units which have not already been labelled with a number and filed away somewhere in your growing mound of untidy maps. Once this point has been reached it is still desirable to persevere for a while, now producing maps which are no more than differing arrangements of the units which have already been included in your emerging sample.

Once you are *thoroughly* tired of this, the next thing to do is to make a simple classification of the units thus sampled, placing each unit in one of two groups, *core units* and *peripheral units*. The core units are all those to which you were led by more than one other unit, and the peripheral units are those implicated by only one other respondent in the sample.[8]

Now you *may* have a special reason for interest in the peripheral units now defined by your mapping. In that case you will no doubt wish to extend the mapping process further by extensive sampling efforts concentrated upon the contacts generated at these points.[9] But more usually your interest in these units will cease at this point. They have served merely to mark the limits of the cultural set under study. In terms of a first-order level of meaning they are simply the families or close friends of pigeon-fanciers, wife-swappers, or whatever, people who 'know too much' to be outside the group but too little to be part of it.

Now the next stage in the tricky business of obtaining a plausible snowball sample is to check upon the extent to which your sampling is *saturated with first-order meaning*. This involves more hard work. You must proceed to each unit of (or perhaps to a carefully selected subsample of units from)[10] your sample, and question each in some way about all the other units in the set which are now known to you but which he had not mentioned himself. Does he know of them? Does he consider them to be 'members' of the 'group' in question? Somehow you have to ascertain the extent to which the sample makes sense as a real grouping to the units within it. This, like the whole business of *interactional* sampling, is pretty tricky. In some cases you *may* be able actually to show the respondents the maps, and thus check their isomorphism with first-order meanings rather directly, but there are various reasons why this will usually be quite out of the question.[11] In those cases you will have to resort to more indirect tactics.

I once overheard a conversation in a corner of a park:

ROUND-SHOULDERED PERSON:	'By the way have you ever heard of a cat called Lefty?'
OTHER:	'Lefty? Why?'
R-SP:	'Whad'y reckon to the cat?'
O:	'What do you mean?'
R-SP:	'What's his game? Where's he at?'
O:	'Why?'
R-SP:	'Well I ran into him down Gerrard's Street and, um . . . . (*I couldn't hear that bit*)
O:	'Yeah? That's cool don' worry about it man. The cat's O.K. Used to tow about with him quite a bit. He was living with Jin when she got croaked, broke him up. Old mate of Jorj's from way back. Used to do a bit of business for Chinese John (laughs). Only just come out, must've done all of four years.'
R-SP:	'S'funny, Chinky John's never mentioned him, nor Jorj.'
O:	'Why would they?'

Why indeed? I shouldn't wonder if the person with round shoulders and furrowed brow wasn't a sociologist trying to check out the first-order meaningfulness of his snowball sample.

Now you will have noticed that, if it is to be done properly, snowball sampling involves a great deal of hard work. For the outcome of all the necessary detective, diplomatic, and administrative sweat necessitated by this method is not really a *sample* at all. A successful snowball sample is not a *part* of the theoretically defined set to which the research is directed, it is the *whole* of it. Thus a valid snowball sample should really be a census of the population in question. This is, of course, all very well when the group is a small one, but when it is fairly large the method becomes seriously uneconomic. One solution is to subsample the completed sample, using probability methods, but – you will notice at once – that this may be ridiculously wasteful: to go to such lengths and then chuck most of the information away would be enough to make *me* weep. But *you* may be made of sterner stuff?

There is another reason why the snowball method may not always be the most appropriate way of obtaining a structural sample upon which to test a theory. *It may be that every unit in your theoretically defined set is not equally ¿interesting? to you.* According to the theory under test some units in the set may be more ¿interesting? than others, so you will naturally wish to draw a sample which reflects this structural inequality of ¿interest?. In this case you might be able to employ one of the more complicated forms of *interactional sampling* which may be loosely grouped together under the heading '*Key Location Sampling*'.

The point of *key location sampling* is, again, to make the maximum use of initial haphazard sampling, and to employ this thoroughly fortuitous original selection to locate a further sample which has some theoretical relevance. What you do is to use your original haphazard sample as a basis for information about the *key units* in the set in question. These *key units* will be persons who act as crucial definers or interpreters for the set. These key units may be the 'gatekeepers' of the cultural group under study, the people who, as it were, man the gates through which information flows, the interpreters of 'messages' from the 'outside world' (e.g. from the mass media). That is to say that they are respected figures whose opinions are ¿interesting? at the second-order level of meaning because they are so at the first.[12]

The selection of 'gatekeeper' samples is a favourite method with anthropologists and with sociologists ¿interested? in what are sometimes called 'community studies'. They use all kinds of systematic, or idio-syncratic, techniques to locate the gatekeepers, who may be witch-doctors or, say, the chief's son, the village priest or, say, the owner of the only wireless set for five hundred miles.

Another variation of *key location sampling* consists in the attempt to locate *crucial labellers*, those who have a disproportionate power in the matters of the definitions which people have of one another and them-selves. Here the question as to whether the sample is 'representative', in the straightforward sense of numerical isomorphism is ¿uninteresting?. The point is rather that the sampled units are being assumed to be powerful definers of the unsampled ones. Thus the sample is supposed to be representative of the theoretical universe in a rather complicated and nebulous way. Whether or not that assumption is *reasonable* under the circumstances is another question.

But, however *interactional sampling* is achieved, the questions of first-order meaningfulness and isomorphism with second-order definitions cannot be shirked. Somehow the researcher must find a means of checking the utility of his sample for the purposes in hand. And this will usually require more than a little ingenuity.[13]

So, you may or may not feel that you can give an honest 'YES' answer to *QUESTION 3*. In that case you have decided to proceed to draw a structural purposive sample which you claim to be isomorphic with the set defined by your sampling frame – either quantitatively, as with a numerical quota sample, or qualitatively, as with an interactional sample.

But what if your answer must be 'NO'?

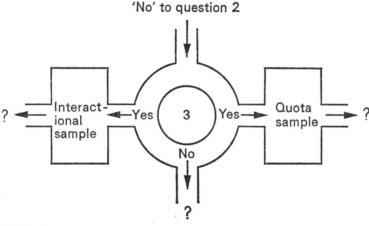

FIGURE 32

Well. I can only suggest that, under these unfortunate circumstances, you take a tea-break. By the time you have refreshed yourself you will find that you have decided to do one of three things. First, you may, perhaps very wisely, choose to give up the whole idea of testing the theory in its present state, either returning the *ANALYTICAL THEORY* to the drawing board, or abandoning the whole enterprise. Second, you may decide to brace yourself for another try. In that case you must return to 'GO' and proceed to address yourself to

QUESTION 1' all over again. For, to draw any sample at all, you must first be able to answer 'YES' to one of the first three questions in the GAME.

But once in a blue moon, a third course of action presents itself. Every so often serendipity intervenes to save the researcher from the clutches of despair. The *CONUNDRUM* of finding an adequate sample suddenly turns upon itself. The empty grin curls further yet! And warms into a secret smile. The FAIRIES come, unhoped-for; yet bidden by the moment's *PARADOX*.

So, from the vantage-point of his transcending vision, the THINKER is able to see his failure to select an adequate sample as an inevitability, given the present state of his theorizing.

But now let us consider more '*normal*' circumstances. Let us suppose that you have managed to persuade yourself that you can give an honest 'YES' answer to *QUESTION 1* or *QUESTION 2* or *QUESTION 3*: this is to say that you have succeeded in selecting one of the six types of purposive sampling around which the first three sampling decisions revolve. You are now in a position to consider a fourth question.

Question 4:   Will you try to economize by probability sampling?

If the numbers involved in your newly defined sample are small enough' and your resources adequate, then you may happily answer 'NO' to this question. And, in some cases, of course, this 'NO' will amount to a rejection of the whole notion of dealing with anything less than the whole of the real set which corresponds to the theoretical universe in question. In these cases, you will not, properly speaking, have a *sample* at all, but a *census* of an entire (theoretically defined) population.

If you have decided to forgo economizing by probability sampling, then you will proceed directly to *QUESTION 5*.

Question 5:   Are you sure that your sample is not biased?

If you are still in the GAME you must now do some checking. You must look back over your *ANALYTICAL THEORY*, the series of research decisions which followed it, and the specific considerations which led to the definition of your sampling frame. Then you must be extremely critical of the adequacy of your sampling tactics.

Of course you may never be certain that your sample is not biased at all. But, as we know, what matters is *relevant bias*. And if you cannot eliminate this then, perhaps, you may yet save your GOLD-STAR honour by turning it to your own *disadvantage*. If you cannot see a means of assuming a sample to be representative in relevant respects, then maybe you can arrange matters so that your sample can be reasonably supposed to be *biased towards the falsification of the hypotheses under test*, rather than biased in 'favour' of your theory.

If you find that you must answer 'NO' to this question then, of course, you will be in much the same position as if you had answered 'NO' to one of the first three questions. Unless serendipity intervenes, or you decide that you can stand no more and give up the fruitless SAMPLING GAME, you must go back to GO and start all over again.

But now suppose that you answered 'YES' to *QUESTION 4*.

Whether you have chosen to employ simple homogeneous, simple heterogeneous, typological, match, quota, or interactional sampling, you will now have a very clearly defined set of real units to play with. Thus you may legitimately consider the option of selecting a smaller sub-sample of units by probability methods. After all, it may be far too costly to create data in respect of *all* the units in your initial sample: thus you may have to make do with just *some* of them. But you must remember that *the selection of a cheaper subsample by probability methods will only be reasonable if you wish to take it for granted that each unit in your original sample is of equal ¿interest? from the point of view of your theory.* For probability subsampling rests on the endeavour to give each unit of the original sample an equal opportunity of inclusion in the sub-sample.[14]

There are three basic variations of *probability sampling*. But, before you can make a sensible choice between them, you will have to answer another question (see Figure 33 on page 311).

Question 6:   Is there a list of all the units in the sample to be subsampled?

Perhaps there is such a list, as there would be, say, of all the units in a properly constructed snowball sample, or as there might be if you happened to want a subsample of subscribers to the telephone network in the London area.

If this is the case then your task at this stage is a piece of cake. You can simply employ *straightforward random sampling* (using a pin, a hat, a roulette wheel, a table of random numbers, or whatever takes your fancy). Or you might use the rather more convenient method of *systematic sampling* which consists in simply picking every *n*th unit on the list (provided, of course, that the list is not arranged in any *relevant* order!).

However, if no such list is available, all is not necessarily lost. You might be able to utilize the variation of probability sampling which is known as '*area*' or '*cluster sampling*'. This type of sampling is only appropriate in the case of a set of real units with clear geographical boundaries. The method is simply to obtain an ordinary map of the geographical area in question. You then divide this map into a number of squares of equal area. The squares are then numbered in order, across and down the map and a smaller number of squares is then unselected from the whole by one of the straightforward random techniques. Sometimes this sort of sampling is done in several stages, the smaller squares being further subdivided and other subsamples selected.[15]

But *area sampling* is not quite the panacea for sampling headaches that it has sometimes been taken to be. Clearly, geographical boundaries may be thoroughly ¿uninteresting? for the purposes of a particular piece of research. Then, again, though random sampling of the subdivided areas ensures that each section of the map has an equal chance of being included in the economy subsample, it is erroneous to assume that this means that such units as, say, persons, houses or allotment gardens, *within* the sections of the map are thereby guaranteed the equal probability of selection which is necessary for genuine probability sampling. Indeed the pitfalls of *area* sampling may serve to point out a general sampling danger which consists in the transition from one sort of unit to another, e.g. from geographical area to street, to household, to person.[16] Quite often the incautious movement from one type of unit to another serves to disguise the fact that the boundaries of the universe in question have not been properly defined.[17]

Now if you have succeeded in selecting a more economical subsample from your original purposive sample, by probability methods, you must ask yourself *QUESTION 7*. This is the penultimate question in the SAMPLING GAME (look again at Figure 33, page 311).

Question 7: Are you sure that your subsample is not biased?

This question is, of course, a double-edged one. For, in considering it, you must ask yourself both whether the bias could have crept in at the initial, purposive sampling stage, *and* whether any additional bias may have resulted from the probability subsampling. Probability theory and statistical methods of estimation may be of great assistance in checking the latter but, as I have already said, they have no bearing whatsoever on the former.

Well. If you are *still* playing the GAME, you have assured yourself that you can give an honest 'YES' answer to either *QUESTION 5* or *QUESTION 7*, or, failing that, you may feel that, at least, you can give a *qualified* 'YES' to one of those questions. In the latter case you will make careful notes in your *Research Notebook* to remind yourself of the possible sources of bias in your sampling. If you decide to do this you must be sure to take these crucial notes about sampling bias into consideration

'Yes' to question 4

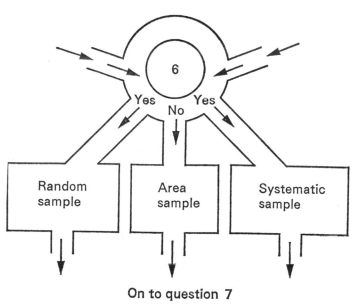

FIGURE 33

when you come to *analyse* the data generated from your sample(s), and, again, when you proceed to *draw causal conclusions from those data* and, yet again and most especially, when you come to *write up your research*, whether for publication or in your report to some sponsoring body. For, of course, any qualifications which you must make in truth$_2$ about your affirmation of *QUESTION 5* or *QUESTION 7* amount to definite limitations on the generalizability of your research results. If you are to adhere to the GOLD-STAR principles of FALSIFICATIONISM and REPLICABILITY, you must leave no room for ambiguity as far as the adequacy of your sampling is concerned.

You should now be free to consider the final question in the SAMPLING GAME.

Question 8:   Have you the all-clear?

Given that you have now decided upon sampling tactics which are reasonably adequate on theoretical grounds, do the practical, ethical and other circumstances of your actual research combine to produce a situation in which it is feasible for you to go ahead according to plan?

It seems to me that there are five factors to be considered at this stage:

BANK: the funds available for research.

EQUIPMENT: research facilities and staff.

PERMISSION: 'clearance' from the relevant authorities for entering the 'field'.

CLOCK: the ¿time? available, in terms of research manhours and schedules of happenings at the first-order level of meaning.

CONSCIENCE: the ethical issues which might arise from the selection of the intended samples.

These five considerations can be committed to memory with the aid of another silly mnemonic: *Bunnies Evade Pressing Coney-Catch*.

Now, of course, this will not be the first ¿time? that these considerations will have entered your head on the long, hard research path. Nor will it be the last. You will have occasion to mutter 'Bunnies Evade Pressing Coney-Catch' a few more times before the research is done. Financial and other facilities, the necessary access to data, and both research and first-order timetabling have naturally guided you implicitly all along; particularly, of course, when you were considering the fourth question about economizing by subsampling. And it is to be hoped that ethical considerations have not been far from your mind at any stage of the GAME, or, indeed of the whirling DERVISH DANCE which preceded it.

Funds and equipment are always limited. But it would be a most dismal view of research which led to the assumption that there is a causal connection between the extent of the resources expended upon a project and the merit and interest of the results. It goes without saying that some of the most ¿interesting? pieces of research have been carried out by single-handed workers with very little equipment, or funds. And it goes equally that some of the most turgid, inductive and empiricistic stuff has been churned out from the research buckets of the most influential and well-supported institutes, with plenty of under-bunnies to make the tea and service the computing machines. But perhaps it is worth saying that, in research, as in anything else, wastage is to be deplored. In my view it is quite scandalous to deploy funds and equipment just *because* they are available. The sort of 'Let's see what happens if . . .' or, 'Let's throw in a few questions on plum duff while we are about it', mentality in research is quite as bad as the wanton wastage of paper that is driving the owls from the oak trees.[18]

Yet, on the other hand, however large and wealthy the research unit, it is highly unlikely that you will ever have *sufficient* resources to achieve the kind of sampling that is required for any particular research purpose. Thus you will find that you must often abandon over-ambitious strategies and settle for severely qualified answers to *QUESTION 5* and/ or *QUESTION 7*.

Third, on the question of obtaining PERMISSION, or 'clearance' for entering the research 'field', you will find, of course, that the kind of clearance necessary depends upon the kind of data which you wish to employ. In some cases you will have merely to approach some formal authority, say the Home Office or a Local Education Authority. These will be in a position to grant direct permission for access to the data you want. In other cases, however, where your data are to be ¿stipulated? in a more informal way, then the business of obtaining permission will be much more difficult. Your success will depend upon the extent to which you are able to work out and play a suitable role at the level of first-order meanings. This means that you must either attempt to enter into the first-order world as an ordinary *participant* or else find some acceptable way of playing the part of an *observer* as, for example, in the case where,[19]

> an observer of a delinquent gang told the older boys he was trying to 'help the younger boys find jobs'. This was partly true in this particular case and met the need for definition at the time when the question was raised. Later, he expanded on what he was doing when they began to have more confidence in him. In another case, an observer told his young questioners he was a sociologist. The term 'sociologist' was sufficient at the time, and as the observer related later, the gang members did not know what a sociologist was, but thought they should have known, and so did not inquire further. What was important to them was that 'Bob', the observer, was a genuine 'right guy' and could be trusted.

Where the units sampled are *persons*, then, however you approach the business of gaining their trust, you will have to face the annoying possibility that your relationship with your respondents may itself be an *UNCONTROLLED EXTRANEOUS AND CONFOUNDING VARIABLE* which has the effect of *biasing* your sample in *relevant* ways. In one study of family life, for example, the researcher was a nicely spoken middle-class lady. It is hardly *surprising* that her sample of working-class families was biased in favour of those sorts of families who don't mind having nicely spoken middle-class ladies poking about in their business. Now this is not to say that the lady sociologist (who was really very well intentioned anyway) didn't acknowledge this possible source of bias in her sample. Nor, indeed, is it to say that her research was ¿uninteresting?. To the contrary. It is merely to say that no hypotheses were actually put at risk in this research and thus no light thrown upon the questions of the truth$_4$ of the ingenious theory which she outlined implicitly.[20] And, happily, subsequent researchers were ¿interested? enough in her notions to attempt to subject some of the hypotheses from her theory to test.[21] And this problem arises in the case of the postal questionnaire as well as with interview and 'participant observation' situations.

Fourth, there is the question of the limitations imposed by the *research* CLOCK. This is rather more difficult than it may seem at first. Of course there is the mundane fact that the research must often be finished by a certain date, or at least, before funds run out, or the researchers get too bored with the whole business. But then there is also the importance of ¿time? on the *first-order level*. For example, a certain public park may close fifteen minutes before sundown, after which it is inhabited by a different population; or, again, all below-the-belt operations in the men's surgical ward of Sickly General Hospital may be performed on Thursdays; or, in a sampling of children in their final year at school, there will be an optimum date for acquiring a sample which is unbiased by early leaving or systematic truancy. Such details of first-order timetables will have an obvious effect on your research deadlines for, clearly, you cannot miss such a deadline unless you are prepared to wait a day, a week, or a year for another sample. And in those cases where the research is of a 'longitudinal' character – involving the repeated generation of new data from the same units at various ¿times? – the deadlines will be all the more important, for to miss one would be to waste the data you have already recorded.

And these limitations on sampling, imposed by considerations of ¿time?, will often be compounded further because ¿time? *itself may well be ¿interesting?* from the viewpoint of your research programme. For instance, ¿time? may often be taken as a crucial EXTRANEOUS CONFOUNDING VARIABLE and, as such, it may or may not be controlled by sampling strategy. For example, it is quite plausible that hours of the day, days of the week, and phases of the year are related to *moods* (public and private) and thus that the ¿time? of recording of the data may be relevant with respect to the composition of that data.[22] Now, apart from the occasional 'panel', 'trend', and 'longitudinal' studies,[23] most sampling strategies are synchronic, that is to say that they represent first-order ¿time? as a second-order *constant* rather than as a variable. But, of course, this may not constitute an adequate control for ¿time? which *may* be related in *systematic* ways to the variables defining the sampling frame.

Occasionally, however, ¿time? is actually formulated as one of the explicit parameters defining the sampling frame. In which case the relationship between this *second-order* conception of ¿time?, real, or *first-order* ¿times?, and the limitations of the *research* CLOCK, will be further complicated.

And there are some even more complex ways in which ¿time?-considerations may enter into sampling decisions. We have already seen that causes are assumed to precede effects in ¿time? (*normally* that is!).

Yet the limits of research timing must often make do with simultaneous measurements of alleged causes and alleged effects. FAIRY TALES about causation are *asymmetric in ¿time?* but measurements are rarely so. Often this will impose no very serious problems for sampling because a rival FAIRY TALE, reversing the sequence of cause and effect in the theory under test, will be thoroughly implausible. Thus it will be unnecessary to treat it seriously. But sometimes it is precisely the direction of causation which is at issue: the major rival theory being that the 'effect' is 'in fact' the 'cause' and the 'cause' the 'effect'. Under these circumstances ¿time? may, of course, be treated as one of the variables defining the sampling frame, with all the implications this has for the associated practicalities of beating the *research* CLOCK.[24]

It is getting later all the ¿time? and you must always hurry if you are to beat the *research* CLOCK. But not *so* fast, there is the gold watch in the waistcoat pocket too! You must always find ¿time? for the final and most vital consideration that will determine whether or not you have the 'ALL CLEAR' to proceed with your sampling. Is your CONSCIENCE clear? Are you sure that your research end will justify the means, that, from an ¿ethical? point of view, it is really worth while to proceed to acquire the data you want from the sample you have decided upon? Or would such sampling create such first-order distress that no second-order questions of truth$_4$ may be weighed in the balance against it? In a study of suicidal behaviour, for example, your theoretical requirements may point to the need for an *interactional sample* of significant others of successful suicides. But whether or not you felt that you had the 'ALL CLEAR' for such sampling would, in the end, be very much a matter for your CONSCIENCE.

If you do not see the 'ALL CLEAR' in terms of all these five issues (Bunnies Evade Pressing Coney-Catch) then you must answer 'NO' to the final question in the SAMPLING GAME. Then you will be back at square one.

But perhaps you are a winner: you have decided upon a strategy and you have the ALL CLEAR to proceed?

Well, you have probably guessed that proficiency in the SAMPLING GAME depends upon practice. An experienced player will not need to approach each question slowly and cautiously, but will be able to reach decisions in a few moments as he, like the confident player of any other game, can consider several routine alternatives and their consequences all at once.

But, for novices at the SAMPLING GAME, I have devised a silly machine to speed up the play.

In order to make use of my machine you must first check that you have a *sampling frame*. You will remember that a sampling frame is precisely the same thing as an exact theoretical description of U. It is a

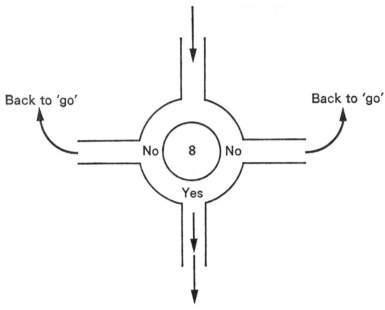

Qualified or unqualified 'Yes'
to question 5 or question 7

Back to 'go'   Back to 'go'

No (8) No

Yes

Proceed to draw sample (s)

FIGURE 34

complete definition of the theoretical universe in terms of (i) *¿interesting?
variables* and (ii) *permitted range of values for those variables.* Now,
though you are in the habit of taking it for granted, you had better also
check that there are no obvious holes in your paradigm. You must feel a
moment's confidence that there are no visible rents in the silk tissue of
unproblematic background assumptions, *BB*, *RR*, *FF* and *KK*, from
which the particular theory under test can be deduced. For, as you roll
yourself up into a ball and take a dive into the INCREDIBLE SAMPLING
MACHINE, you, like the intrepid student of the Bongy Wongy,[25] will have
nothing but your paradigm-parachute to steady you. *Ready?* (See
endpapers.)

What a sadistic device! It is very difficult indeed to escape from that
machine once you have decided to plunge into it. There are only two
ways out: you may tumble triumphantly out of the mouth, with your
nicely packaged sample(s) or, *under most extraordinary circumstances
only*, you may transcend the GAME. Whenever inspiration strikes the
prisoner of the INCREDIBLE SAMPLING MACHINE, then the AMAZING

SERENDIPITY BUZZER begins to flash like nobody's business and WOW! ZAP! KAZAM!: the player finds that he has escaped from the GAME.

So if you dare to parachute into this device, you must be prepared for the eventuality that you will be stuck in there for quite a long ¿time? On the other hand, you may prefer to play the SAMPLING GAME without the aid of my labour-saving giftnag, in which case you can, of course, leave the play at any point you like.

Now whether or not you choose actually to make some use of the INCREDIBLE SAMPLING MACHINE must be up to you. But in either case I hope that it will have served two very unsilly functions. First, it should provide a memorable way of summarizing the nine basic variations of sampling method which are currently used by social scientists.[26] It should serve particularly to remind you that the choices between these methods are based on a series of interrelated questions about the characteristics of your sampling frame and the practical circumstances surrounding your research. And it should also leave no doubts in your mind about the impropriety of consorting with the GRYPHON. For it should be clear from the diagram that the methods and techniques of probability sampling can hold no sociological SOUP on their own. These methods must, properly, be viewed as no more than convenient means of selecting more economic subsamples from prior purposive samples.

And the second, and more serious, function of the INCREDIBLE SAMPLING MACHINE is, simply, to engrave this thought upon your research memory:

THE SELECTION OF A SAMPLE IS A THOROUGHLY PRECARIOUS ENDEAVOUR

Given the large number of variables which will usually be involved, explicitly or implicitly, in the definition of U, and the inevitable inadequacy of your initial knowledge about the real worlds from which you hope to select your samples, it must be obvious that the circumstances under which honest and unqualified affirmative answers can be given to *QUESTIONS 5* and *7* will be rare indeed!

Thus the only thing that the reasonable bunny can strive to do, apart from giving up the whole idea of testing his theory at all, is to approach the business of sampling in a $truly_2$ FALSIFICATIONIST frame of mind. One way of remaining $true_2$ to this ideal is to select samples which are *biased towards the falsification of the hypothesis under test*. This involves a genuine effort to select those real units the characteristics of which are apparently least likely to reflect the patterning suggested by the theory under test.

Suppose for example I have a theory suggesting that the nurses in mental hospitals have attitudes towards their patients which result in the erosion of the basic human rights of the latter. It would be pretty easy to adopt a verificationist attitude towards sampling in order to give the appearance of having tested the theory. I could simply choose one or more mental hospitals which I knew to be the older types of establishments with authoritarian patterns of organization, and intakes even more dominantly working class than I knew to be the case throughout the country. Then I could select subsamples of patients from these hospitals by probability techniques, making a great song and dance about this stage of the sampling in the hope of disguising the obvious flaw in the initial design. Then I might use various probability statistics and come up with all sorts of 'differences' 'significant' at all sorts of incredible levels, or even at very meagre ones![27]

Well, such tactics *might* have a useful propaganda function. I might have persuaded a few other people to adopt my own suspicions about the treatment of mental patients.[28] But, of course, since I had taken practically no risks with my theory, I would have made no advance whatever towards ascertaining its truth$_4$. In order to do *that* I should really have attempted to obtain a complete census of mental hospitals (within what real universe?) classifying them according to relevant characteristics, and then selecting a sample from that frame, and, perhaps, a probability subsample thereof; or else, perhaps, I should have further multiplied the stages of sampling. But, after working all that out, I would still be faced with the final question of the SAMPLING GAME, and I might eventually have to admit to myself that I simply did not have adequate ¿time? and resources to put my plans into operation. In that case I might perhaps save my bacon (sorry, lapin) and my GOLD-STAR principles, by selecting a somewhat less adequate sample which was, none the less, biased in such a way as to make my tests *more* rather than *less* risky. I might, for example, select from the more modern institutions, picking out especially those which had recently undergone a thorough shaking-up as a result of previous allegations of cruelty to patients. Then, when I came to write up my research I would point out that, though my sample could not necessarily be regarded as *representative* (of some clearly defined universe) it was still reasonable to suppose that the evidence from this sample could be generalized to other institutions which would, after all, be assumed to be *more* rather than *less* likely to exhibit the features in question.[29]

Now, as I have already said, the PRINCIPLE OF FALSIFICATIONISM is really too vital to be left entirely to the honesty of the individual researcher. Though it may not be too much to *ask* of a RABBIT, it is perhaps too much to *expect* that he will genuinely make every attempt to destroy the theory over which he has already poured so much sweat. (If you don't believe that RABBITS sweat, roll yourself up into a furry ball and take a practice dive into the INCREDIBLE SAMPLING MACHINE!)

GOLD-STAR methodology demands that each RABBIT faces up to the possible limitations of his own falsificationist fervour. The true$_2$ GOLD-STAR bunny supplements his personal efforts to uphold the PRINCIPLE OF FALSIFICATIONISM with the risk-maximizing corollary PRINCIPLES OF REPLICABILITY AND TRIANGULATION. In these ways he can be more confident that, if he does not succeed in coping adequately with the problems of bias in his sampling, he will, at least, soon come to know about it!

Clearly adherence to the PRINCIPLE OF REPLICABILITY in sampling can best be maintained by thorough note-taking. It is essential to keep a record of every decision in the SAMPLING GAME, and of the considerations which contributed to it. If full and clear notes are kept, then even the most idiosyncratic forms of sampling (say by snowball tactics, for example) will be fully replicable. Another researcher would not, of course, acquire the *same* sample, even where the sample in question happened to be a full census of U. For all it matters at the present ¿time? Heraclitus might have said

> The second jump
> Is a different bump.

Thus no two parachutes ever land in the same ¿space? at the same ¿time?. But the point is that adequate documentation of sampling decisions may provide the means for locating further samples which are formally equivalent at the second-order level of meaning.

The pressing need for application of the PRINCIPLE OF TRIANGULATION in the uncertain circumstances surrounding sampling strategies has been well noted by several previous writers.[30] It is frequently said that *various* sampling strategies should be combined together so that the researcher has not a single sample but many samples to work with.[31]

> When obtaining data on different groups the sociologist works under the diverse structural conditions of each group: schedules, restricted areas, work tempos, the different perspectives of people in different positions, and the availability of documents of different kinds. Clearly to succeed he must be flexible in his methods and in his means for collecting data from group to group.
> The result is, of course, a variety of slices of data . . . .

But these pleas for multiple methods are somewhat confused. Various writers describe the diverse and complicated webs of data to be sampled by say 'the merger of objective, subjective, and reputational methods'.[32] But at the centre of these webs sit the same old SPIDERS. The results of the unholy alliance of positivism and inductivism are very much in evidence, even on the trendier shelves, in the LIBRARY today.

No, it is certainly not only amongst those writers with a penchant for statistics and numerical measurement that this blight has taken hold. Of all the discussions of sampling in the LIBRARY *surely* the silliest is that of Glaser and Strauss.

Here are two veteran bunnies who have in their ¿time? devised some very interesting theories. And yet, taking for granted a background of positivism and inductivism, they advocate a form of sampling which, ironically, they choose to call 'theoretical sampling'.[33]

> In theoretical sampling, no one kind of data on a category nor technique for data collection is necessarily appropriate. Different kinds of data give the analyst different views or vantage points from which to understand a category and to develop its properties; the different views we have called *slices of data*. While the sociologist may use one technique of data collection primarily, theoretical sampling for saturation of a category allows a multi-faceted investigation, in which there are no limits to the techniques of data collection, the way they are used, or the types of data acquired.

And what do these advocates of explicit inductivism, or public display of UNDERWEAR, understand by 'saturation'?[34]

> *Saturation* means that no additional data are being found whereby the sociologist can develop properties of the category. As he sees similar instances over and over again, the researcher becomes empirically confident that a category is saturated. He goes out of his way to look for groups that stretch diversity of data as far as possible, just to make certain that saturation is based on the widest possible range of data on the category.
>
> One reaches theoretical saturation by joint collection and analysis of data. . . . When one category is saturated, nothing remains but to go on to new groups for data on other categories, and attempt to saturate these new categories also. When saturation occurs, the analyst will usually find that some gap in his theory, especially in his major categories, is almost, if not completely, filled.

In other words the discoverer of 'grounded theory' looks for support for his implicit theoretical hunches in as many different appearances as possible. The so-called 'logic of ongoing inclusion' amounts to an attempt to verify emerging second-order hypotheses in terms of a mounting range of first-order meanings. Rather than providing a rationale and guide for sampling, the definition of a theoretical universe,

U, becomes the goal of the enterprise. When the researcher finds he can stretch his developing theory no further, he gets bored and gives up the SAMPLING GAME. Thus U, and in consequence the sampling frame, is defined by default at the point of saturation, that is at the margin of boredom.

Chapter 16

A Box of My Own Invention

The Hatter was the first to break the silence. 'What day of the month is it?' he said, turning to Alice: he had taken his watch out of his pocket, and was looking at it uneasily, shaking it every now and then, and holding it to his ear.

Well, it's certainly ¿time? to face the facts at last. All the ¿interesting? ones must be somehow collected together and piled up neatly in the research laboratory, there to await the proper preparations for the strange rituals of data analysis.

But you will not need to be reminded that the business of collating data is, like any other gathering operation, a paradigm-determined process.

What would you do if you wanted to go gathering nuts in May? Would you equip yourself with wellington boots[1] and a large bucket[2] and dash out and grab whatever seemed to come readily to hand? Of course not. The appearances which might reasonably be taken for nuts are by no means omnipresent, especially in May. Any putative nut-gatherer must have some implicit or explicit criteria for sorting nuts from, say, leaves, dog dirt, and tin cans alleged to be full of London fog. Ponder for a moment upon any fictitious gathering business that you care to dream up – a RABBITS' shopping spree perhaps?[3] I am sure that you will agree that there, as in any other FAIRY TALE about seeking and finding, the required units and their appropriate quantities are clearly defined by the operative intentions of the seeker. He is engaged in an ongoing process of sorting, he is selecting *this*, and not *that*, from the taken-for-granted context of ordinariness which is indicated by his *BB*, *RR*, *KK* and *FF*.

And so it is with the exhausting business of gathering '*buts*' and '*maybes*' and all the other sorts of data which social science researchers seek from their samples. For whatever kind of data a researcher believes he has obtained, he will hardly need to be told that these data did not spring from their real contexts unbidden. Nor did they leap across from FAIRYLAND of their own accord, transform themselves into 'facts and figures', and willingly pile themselves up upon his research desk. No. He did not walk into his office one morning (still musing on the strange tales of SPIDERS and MOCK TURTLE SOUP, told by the GRYPHON in the night) there to be confronted with a great heap of evidence, all ready and waiting on the desk. On the contrary, the wide-awake researcher knows that his data have resulted as much from his efforts to call them up as from the contexts in which they appear to be manifest.

Data are no more pure 'inventions' than they are simple 'discoveries'. Like all other expressions of meaning, they are products of the ongoing dialectic of expectation and recognition. The relationship between a researcher's attitude to his theory and his approach to his data is paralleled at the first-order level in the myriad reality constructions from which those data are, in another sense, to be drawn. Take the construction of the reality of a marriage, for example.[4]

> The protagonists of the marriage drama do *not* set out deliberately to re-create their world. Each continues to live in a world that is taken for granted – and keeps its taken-for-granted character even as it is metamorphosed. The new world that the married partners, Prometheuslike, have called into being is perceived by them as the normal world in which they have lived before. . . . Typically the reality that has been 'invented' within the marital conversation is subjectively perceived as a 'discovery'. Thus the partners 'discover' themselves and the world, 'who they really are,' 'what they really believe,' 'how they really feel, and always have felt, about so-and-so'. This retrojection of the world being produced all the time by themselves serves to enhance the stability of this world and at the same time to assuage the 'existential anxiety' that, probably inevitably, accompanies the perception that nothing but one's own narrow shoulders supports the universe in which one has chosen to live. If one may put it like this, it is psychologically more tolerable to be Columbus than to be Prometheus.

The relationship between a researcher and his work is more or less as precarious as that which he manages to maintain with his spouse. And just as he may find 'psychologically . . . tolerable' means of assuaging 'existential anxiety' in the latter, so it is with the former. No normal researcher would be happy with the realization that he had 'invented' his data, yet if he were true$_2$ to himself he could not deny that he had, at least, been extremely selective about his 'discoveries'. 'After all,' he might say, 'some data are simply more ¿interesting? than others!'

They certainly are! Right now there are great mounds of field-notebooks, tape-recordings, postal questionnaires (duly completed and

returned), interview records, photographs, candles, feathers,[5] bits of
paper, and what-not, sitting on desks and lurking in filing cabinets in
social science units up and down the country. Some of these data ought
not to be regarded as 'scientific evidence' at all, for they have been
collected up in a naïvely inductivist way, with no particular research
imperatives in mind. These boring bits of rubbish are thus destined for
eventual transferral from the bucket to the dustbin.[6]

But some data are ¿interesting?. They are valid and reliable evidence
on the basis of which some, albeit fleeting, guesses about truth$_4$ may be
made. In GOLD-STAR terminology, these are the data which have been
evoked by ritual methods guided by two principles: THE PRINCIPLE
OF DATA RELIABILITY, and THE PRINCIPLE OF DATA
VALIDITY.

The PRINCIPLE OF DATA RELIABILITY is one of the imperatives implied by the prior PRINCIPLE OF REPLICABILITY. For,
of course, if a researcher is to put his hypotheses to genuine test, then he
ought to be able to assure himself and his colleagues that the 'evidence'
he has is more than a product of his personal idiosyncrasies and those of
his research team. He must therefore record as much as possible of the
details of the measuring operations so that he himself, or any other
researcher, may repeat those operations. If that repetition yields different
results then the data must be assumed to be unreliable. For,[7]

> Just as a ruler which shrank or expanded materially when exposed to
> temperature changes would be useless, so would be a scale which
> yielded a different result upon each application.

The GOLD-STAR PRINCIPLE OF DATA RELIABILITY can be
stated thus:

*PRINCIPLE OF DATA RELIABILITY: It must be reasonable to
assume that each repetition of the application of the same, or supposedly
equivalent, instruments to the same units will yield similar measurements.*

Ideally, of course, the RELIABILITY of data should be established
by actual replication of the research, by the researcher himself, by
others, or by both. But no doubt the spectre of Heraclitus has already
appeared before you, and you are ahead of me in pondering on the
uncertainties of such replication, particularly where ¿time? itself must be
considered as a relevant factor in the research design. And you may
also have realized that, in some cases, one set of measurements may
actually interact upon another. Thus, for example, where the units of
analysis are persons, and a study is replicated by remeasurement of the
same population,[8]

The measurement process . . . may itself affect the outcome. If people feel that they . . . are being 'tested' and must make a good impression, or if the method of data collection suggests responses or stimulates an interest the subject did not previously feel, the measuring process may distort the . . . results.

Failing total replication, however, useful indications of the RELIABILITY of data may be obtained by alternative means. One long-popular mode of checking RELIABILITY involves a sort of minimal form of TRIANGULATION. Goode and Hatt call this technique '*Multiple Form*'. Here, 'two forms of the scale are constructed to begin with, and alternate forms are administered successively to the same sample.'

One researcher describes a very common way of using this somewhat simple-minded technique of assessing RELIABILITY.[9]

It was decided that closed schedule questions of the agree/disagree type should be used, not merely for ease of quantification but also because responses in this form were easier for the children, almost a third of whom found writing a single sentence in answer to an 'open' question a slow and agonizing process. Several separate closed instruments could therefore be administered with less stress on the children than would be produced by a single open one. This reliance on closed schedules entailed the obvious disadvantage that there is no immediate guarantee that the questions meant anything at all to the children who may have merely ticked randomly. On the other hand, the sheer duplication of indicators for the same dimension which could be achieved by this method should offset that disadvantage. For simple correlation of one supposed indicator of a phenomenon against another gives some empirical criterion of the reliability of the indicator. And it cannot be emphasised too strongly that the *only* objective criteria of success of indicators are empirical, for there is no *logical* relationship between theoretical and research language, the link between the two being merely a matter of convention or arbitrary whim.

Eight statements about social class prefaced by 'In England . . . were administered and the children were required to respond to them on a five point scale from true to false. The statements intended as indicators of the first dimension (evaluations of the legitimacy of the class structure) were as follows:

(a) If you have the brains and the determination you can *always* get on in life.
(b) Life is like a competition and the best man usually gets the prize.
(c) The only way working men can improve their lot is by sticking together against the employers.

The first two are 'negative' indicators (the response 'true' locates the respondent's imagery on the right-hand side of the continuum), while the last is 'positive' (agreement registers on the left-hand side of the continuum).

Statements designed to measure the second dimension (perception of the shape of the class structure) were as follows:

(d) You can tell with most people whether they are working class or middle class.
(e) We are all middle class really.
(f) People who work with their hands are quite different from those who sit behind a desk.
(g) There are no such things as classes nowadays.

Agreement with statements d and f indicates dichotomous perceptions and agreement with e and g indicates hierarchic perceptions.

The next stage is to disregard all those indicators which show no consistent intercorrelations with their supposed equivalent alternatives, and, assuming that the highly intercorrelated items are indeed reliable, combine these latter measures into a summary measure, or index, which will be regarded as the empirical representative, or epistemic correlate of the variable under consideration.[10]

Statements a, b and c were correlated against each other and, since the strongest (negative) correlation was between b and c these two items were selected for the index of evaluations of the class structure. Similarly statements d, e and g were selected for the index of perceptions of the shape of the class structure.

The procedure adopted for combining these indicators into indices by means of 'scores' is summarized below.

Construction of Index of Evaluations of the Class Structure

STATEMENT	RESPONSE	'SCORE'
	(True = 1 etc.)	
b	1	0
	2	1
	3	2
	4, 5	3
c	1	3
	2	2
	3	1
	4, 5	0

Scores for the two statements were added and total scores of 3–6 were considered 'High' while scores of 0–2 were designated 'Low'.

When scores for the three statements were added, total scores of 4–6 were considered 'High' while those of 0–3 were 'Low'.

Construction of Index of Perceptions of the Shape of the Class Structure

STATEMENT	RESPONSE (True = 1)	'SCORE'
d	1, 2	2
	3	1
	4, 5	0
e	1, 2	0
	3	1
	4, 5	2
g	1, 2	0
	3	1
	4, 5	2

When scores for the three statements were added, total scores of 4–6 were considered 'High' while those of 0–3 were 'Low'.[11]

However, this *'Multiple-Form'* technique of index construction does not really resolve the problems of data RELIABILITY. As Goode and Hatt have said:[12]

It is obvious that this does not completely solve the problem of first scaling effect, since, if the two forms are sufficiently correlated to measure the same continuum, then their connection may well be obvious to the subject. Further, answering any series of questions on some segment of behaviour may affect the second series of answers.

Another method of checking reliability is the *'Split-Half'* method.[13]

This measure of reliability is a modification of the multiple-form approach. One application of a scale is sufficient to secure the measure, since it treats two halves of one scale as if they were two forms, as in the multiple-form method above. The scale is divided randomly into two halves. This may be done in any way which is practical and yet assures randomization. Usually the simplest procedure is to separate the scale into two, using the odd-numbered items for one and the even-numbered for the other. This, of course, can be done only when the numbering itself has not involved a systematic principle. It is safer than comparing the first half against the second half since differential informant fatigue or cumulative item effect may lower or raise the true correlation.

Each of the two sets of items is treated as a separate scale and scored accordingly. The two subscales are then correlated and this is taken as a measure of reliability. A further step is to correct the correlation coefficient secured between the two halves by applying the Spearman-Brown prophecy formula $r_n = nr_1/[1 + (n - 1)r_1]$. This correction assumes that a scale $2n$ items long will be more reliable than a scale n items long, and since the length of the scale has been halved by dividing it into odds and evens, the full scale will have a higher reliability than would either half. Once again the coefficient should reach a high level before being taken as evidence of adequate reliability.

Yet it should be clear that this method can only be used where it is reasonable to assume that the scale hangs together in such a way that 'either half may be taken as adequately representative of the whole',[14] that is, where the data take an *interval* or *ratio* form.[15]

One method of assessing RELIABILITY which *is* appropriate for *ordinal*, though still not for *nominal*, scales, and which avoids the problem of feedback of meanings which is entailed by the methods of complete replication, 'multiple-form' and 'split-half', relies on a statistic called the *'Coefficient of Concordance'*. By using this statistic the researcher can calculate the extent to which responses to a ranking situation are patterned rather than merely haphazard.[16] And, though the patterning of responses within a group of respondents is no *guarantee* of the RELIABILITY of the data, it may be a very useful negative check. That is to say that if the data are *not* patterned, if they are merely haphazard, it would be thoroughly unreasonable to assume that they were RELIABLE. On the other hand, if the data *do* exhibit patterning (as measured by the coefficient) they could be either RELIABLE or UNRELIABLE.[17]

The available means of assessing RELIABILITY of data are, then, heavily dependent upon the types of scaling being employed. The direct techniques of correlating measures against themselves are generally only appropriate for *ratio*, or at least *interval* scales, and any methods of assessing the patterning of *ordinally* scaled data across a whole group of units (such as the 'Coefficient of Concordance') can give no *positive* assurances of data RELIABILITY. Moreover, where more than one type of scale is in use for measurement of the same item, further problems of equivalence of values will complicate the mathematics of arbitrating RELIABILITY.

But of course a more plausible basis for assessments of data RELIABILITY is provided by more radical triangulation (especially phewangulation) of research design. Thus it may often be desirable to forsake the mathematical precision, which is possible with intercorrelation of formally similar measurements, for some more *ad hoc* – perhaps qualitative – methods of assessing the agreements between data produced by entirely different methods of measurement. Thus, as well as employing different methods of measurement for *different* variables, it is always advisable to aim for a variety of instrumentation directed towards what is assumed to be the *same* variation. For RELIABILITY of *instruments* is not the same thing as RELIABILITY of *data*. Obviously the same instrument may yield measures which are RELIABLE in the sense that they are consistently bizarre. Use of several different sorts of instruments will, however, provide a better basis for judgments about the RELIABILITY of the data themselves. And, where this diversification of measurement method is achieved, more or less vague (even purely qualitative) comparisons of the ¿directions? of variation recorded by the various instruments will be much better than no comparisons at all.

Now, of course, proper attention to the PRINCIPLE OF REPLICABILITY,[18] and to the PRINCIPLE OF DATA RELIABILITY which that entails, will not guarantee that the overriding imperatives of the crucial PRINCIPLE OF FALSIFICATIONISM are given due consideration. Data may be highly RELIABLE, but still very ¿uninteresting?. For to say that data are RELIABLE is only to say that it can be fairly assumed that when similar measurements are made with respect to the same units they will yield similar results. Clearly, then, data which are UNRELIABLE will be useless, but RELIABLE data are not necessarily VALID data.[19]

> When reliability is high, validity may be either high or low, but when reliability is low validity must be low. . . . It follows that any mathematical formula which expresses validity as a direct function of reliability must be in error.

Thus if we were to set up a special GOLD-STAR DATA BRIGADE to roar around in special fire engines raiding all social science research units and ruthlessly incincrating all useless and ¿uninteresting? data,[20] we would find that the firemen would have to sort the data they found into the following categories:

		Reliable?	
		Yes	No
Valid?	Yes	A	Null class
	No	B	C

Only the Type A data would survive the raids. But how would the zealous firemen sort these from the rest?

It would, of course, be relatively easy to locate and dispose of the Cs. For, unfortunately, the scientistic paranoia of many social science researchers has led them to aim for methods of measurement which are so rigid that their RELIABILITY may readily be checked. Though they can rarely persuade themselves that the measuring instruments of the physical sciences, such as thermometers, beam balances, rulers, and what-not, are *actually* appropriate, most common or garden social scientists like to pretend that their own instruments are at least near approaches to these. Thus most research units would be able to produce some sort of plea for the RELIABILITY of quite a lot of their data.

But how could our fictitious firemen, or anyone else for that matter, tell the As from the Bs. Which data are VALID data?

Data are VALID when, and only when, they are explicitly anticipated by the researcher.[21] Only those data are VALID that are clearly specified in advance of research operations, according to the salient dimensions of the test. That is to say that, *VALID data are records of purposeful measurements of specific variations in chosen indicators.*

So only those observations which are made within the explicit framework of a series of prior research decisions meet up to the GOLD-STAR criteria of VALIDITY. Thus the shapes taken by VALID data are always prestructured by the whole series of research choices which have preceded those observations, as well as by the theory on the basis of which those appearances were premised. VALID data are thus predefined for the researcher by the researcher. He knows which variables he wishes to obtain measurements for; he has made some initial decisions about operationalization and selection of indicators; and he has chosen a sample or samples. Thus, whatever, quantitative or qualitative measurements are actually recorded as data, every scrap of VALID evidence must fall within that limited range of information which has been defined as relevant to the testing of the hypotheses under consideration.

Of course, this is not to say that there is absolutely no point in ever going around making systematic observations in the absence of any clearly defined research programme. But it is most certainly to say that observations made in that way, though they may turn out to be bases for ¿interesting? speculations and perhaps eventual theory construction, are not VALID as *evidence* when there are questions of truth$_4$ to be decided.

To believe that there are any other criteria of VALIDITY for data is just plain foolish. It is as silly as believing my story about Galileo's untimely appearance in the Observatory on the basis of the 'evidence' of a few frogs' legs, a candle, a feather and a scrap of St Thomas's manuscript. As one veteran social science researcher remarked:[22]

Surely even the younger members of our profession are sufficiently . . . [versed] . . . in social affairs to recognise that truth is a matter of social definition and that the ultimate test of the validity of any social device or procedure is how well it serves the special interests of those who use it.

Only where those special interests are made explicit in the formulation of a research programme can the problems of VALIDITY be exposed to *collective* scrutiny by a community of scientists. Thus the GOLD-STAR PRINCIPLE OF FALSIFICATIONISM requires that data be defined precisely in advance of any attempts to manipulate variables to test hypotheses. For the selection of data is a ritual operation aimed at achieving reasonable isomorphism between the theoretically predictable and the actually observable. Thus data are *always* chosen by fiat, according to parameters stipulated by the theory under test, and of course, ultimately by the whole paradigm from which that theory is derived. *So the problem of VALIDITY resolves itself into a query about the adequacy of data stipulation.* Which sorts of instruments will yield VALID data is then a question which the GOLD-STAR researcher must face *in advance* of the measurement operations themselves. And if he is uncertain about the VALIDITY of his intended measures *before* he makes them he will be none the wiser *afterwards*! Unlike RELI-ABILITY, VALIDITY can never be checked against anything other than the sequence of decisions upon which it hangs. As Lastrucci has said, the determination of VALIDITY 'must remain in the form of a categorical imperative ('By prejudice, I mean')'.[23]

But for goodness' sake don't rush off after those silly bunnies who are still running away with the impression that the problem of VALIDITY is something unique with the social sciences. If social scientists have any special problems of data VALIDITY, these do *not* arise because they, unlike the physical scientists must operate at two different levels, that is at the level of their own academic theories or FAIRY TALES on the one hand and at the level of observations or appearances on the other. Obviously physical scientists must equally face the dilemmas arising from the arbitrary division between the languages of theory on the one hand and observation on the other.[24] No theoretical concepts can ever be observed 'directly', the physicist is no more able to measure the actual parameters of real 'atoms' than the sociologist or social psychologist is able to see 'prejudice' with the naked eye. 'Atoms', like 'prejudice', are FAIRY-TALE notions; as such they are invisible at the ordinary taken-for-granted first-order level. Yet physicists or sociologists may make observations which they take to be measurable isomorphs of such theoretically described happenings.

In that sense there is nothing special, or even 'more complex' about social data when compared with physical data. As Popper has said, 'There is no doubt that the analysis of any concrete social situation is made extremely difficult by its complexity. But the same holds for any concrete physical situation.'[25]

Nor is it the case that interaction between researchers and research objects (or data) presents VALIDITY problems which are exclusive to the social scientist. It should be obvious that all sorts of VALIDITY problems may be raised when a social science researcher considers the plausibility of the hypothesis that first- and second-order levels of meaning are interactively engaged with one another during the measurement process. For, 'By singling out an individual to be tested (assuming that being tested is not a normal condition), the [typical researcher] . . . forces upon the subject a role-defining decision – What kind of a person should I be as I answer these questions or do these tasks?'[26] Reports of this source of INVALIDITY for experimental data are commonly cited.[27] But it should be clear that the same applies in the interview situation, and even with the postal questionnaire. In the latter case no researcher is actually present but his meanings must still be interpreted and responded to in terms of a first-order background of understandings.

But then, of course, the researcher may interfere with his data in many non-social science test situations as well. For example, several species of animals will not copulate if they are aware of a human audience (white-coated or not); and it is well known that even the physicist must often face the problems posed by his own interference with the objects of his study.[28]

Yet, curious though it may be, social scientists have only recently begun to pay serious attention to those sources of INVALIDITY in social data which might plausibly arise from interactions between the observers and the observed. For it is only very recently that sociologists have considered the ramifications of the highly plausible hypothesis that *second-order meanings may cause changes in first-order meanings*. Thus it is only in the last few years that two virtually opposite methods of coping with this specific VALIDITY issue have been developed: one of these, so-called *unobtrusive measurement*, is a deliberate and ingenious attempt to avoid any interaction between researchers and researched; the other, which I will call *obtrusive observation*, is an equally ingenious attempt to exploit that interaction.[29]

So, whatever forms they take, in social or any other science, the problems of VALIDITY centre upon the reasonableness of the researcher's assumption that his data can be regarded as representative manifestations of the variables involved in the test. Establishing the VALIDITY of data is thus a vitally arbitrary process. To believe that data are VALID is to believe that any reasonable person, who accepted the background of thoughts informing the research, would be prepared, at least for the ¿time? being, to accept the researcher's claim that the data he had adduced were the data he anticipated. This thoroughly *conventionalist* interpretation of the notion of VALIDITY with respect to data was expressed nicely by Galtung: 'an observation is valid if one has observed what one wants to observe.'[30]

But, of course, to say that data must be explicitly anticipated, that one must be able to convince others that he has actually found what he was looking for, is nothing to do with verificationism. If a researcher is to reach a working agreement with his colleagues about the VALIDITY of his data he must first satisfy them that these were the data stipulated by the theory itself in the context of the paradigmatic background from which it had been derived. These data are, then, measurements of a strictly predefined sort. They are values for specific variations which fall only within certain clearly stipulated ranges. But it is the actual values of those measurements, not the range of theoretically predefined possibilities, that will determine the results of the test. Will the data tend to go against the theory or not? Will the ¿directions? of variation tend to deviate from the hypothesized causal patterns? These questions are only really risky ones for the researcher who has stipulated exactly what data he is going to talk about.

Thus consideration of the crucial PRINCIPLE OF FALSIFICA-TIONISM leads to the GOLD-STAR PRINCIPLE OF DATA VALI-DITY.

PRINCIPLE OF DATA VALIDITY: Data are VALID when, and only when, they have been stipulated in advance of measurement.

Now, I hope it is clear that the way in which data are stipulated must depend upon the following:

1. Which variables are to be measured.
2. Some initial decisions about operationalization.
3. The basic modes of variable manipulation to be employed (i.e. *Physical, Mental,* or *Statistical*).
4. Sampling decisions.

And, of course, these stipulations must somehow be met in spite of the considerable limitations on the availability of data which are imposed by the hosts of practical and ethical considerations which must inevitably confront any researcher who is also a real living human being.

Now, if you still have your shopping list, your research notebook, and all the other bits and pieces you were keeping with your flask of tea and your bait, you should be properly equipped to go and get your data.

'So you will, when you've crossed the next brook,' said the White Knight. 'I'll see you safe to the end of the wood – and then I must go back, you know. That's the end of my move.'

'Thank you very much,' said Alice. 'May I help you off with your helmet?' It was evidently more than he could manage by himself: however she managed to shake him out of it at last. . . .

He was dressed in tin armour, which seemed to fit him very badly, and he had a queer-shaped little deal box fastened across his shoulders, upside down, and with the lid hanging open. Alice looked at it with great curiosity.

'I see you're admiring my little box,' the Knight said in a friendly tone. 'It's my own invention – . . . You see I carry it upside down, so that the rain can't get in.'

'But the things can get *out*,' Alice gently remarked. 'Do you know the lid's open?'

'I didn't know it,' the Knight said, a shade of vexation passing over his face.

'Then all the things must have fallen out! And the box is no use without them.' He unfastened it as he spoke, and was just going to throw it into the bushes, when a sudden thought seemed to strike him, and he hung it carefully on a tree. 'Can you guess why I did that?' he said to Alice.

Perhaps it will come in useful for something or other. Let's take a closer look.

The White Knight's open box is really a DO-IT-YOURSELF-MULTI-PURPOSE-DATA-MATRIX, and it has several mentionable uses for social scientists, as well as a few unmentionable ones. For example, one use is as a handy guide to data selection. The researcher can simply check his stipulation of data against three axes and the strange box will oblige by indicating which of the thirty-nine known types of data he is looking for.

The MATRIX also comes in handy as a guide to the LIBRARY. For it often saves ¿time? and unnecessary mistakes if one studies the ways other researchers have obtained their data. Yet, of course, research reports are not classified by librarians according to the types of data stipulated, but according to the concepts employed. So the MATRIX is stocked with references which should, at least, provide some initial clues for library searches, and careful progressive attention to the footnotes in the various books and articles classified by the MATRIX should lead to further sources of relevant information.

Another mentionable use to which the MATRIX may be put is as a tidy container in which to keep your raw or initial data once you have got it. And I am sure that you will find other mentionable and unmentionable uses for the DO-IT-YOURSELF-MULTI-PURPOSE-DATA-MATRIX. So I will say no more but simply explain how it works.

The MATRIX is constructed by considering two ¿interesting? aspects of data stipulation: first, *the definition of the unit datum*, and second, *the*

assumptions which are being made about the location of the data recorders
vis-à-vis *the initial datum universe.*

To define a unit datum is, of course, to say two things about it. It is
to *specify the dimensions of variation* which are to be examined, and it is to
state the limits of permissible variation in those dimensions, that is to
stipulate the range of values required for those variables. Thus the initial
definition of the unit datum is made along two axes:

1. The initial level of analysis
2. The initial degree of scaling

And these axes are cut by the third axis,

3. The operative assumptions about the location of the data recorders
   vis-à-vis the initial datum universe.

Let us examine each of these three axes in turn.

1. The initial level of analysis

For the purposes of classifying social science data it will be sufficient to
consider the initial level of analysis as divisible into four categories.

(i) Where the individual units are defined as 'things' the initial level
of analysis will be termed 'Tangible'.

(ii) Where the individual units are defined as 'people' the initial
level of analysis will be termed 'Personal'.

(iii) Where the individual units are defined as 'acts' the initial level
of analysis will be termed 'Behavioural'.

(iv) Where the individual units are defined as 'expressions of meaning' the level of analysis will be termed 'Processual'.

2. The initial degree of scaling

For our present purposes data may be classified along the second axis
according to three initial degrees of scaling.

At one extreme are those types of data which are to be found in a
precoded form. These data are those which will already be clearly
arranged in quantitative scales when the researcher first claps eyes upon
them. Let us call this sort of data 'Rigidly Structured'.

At the other extreme are those data which confront the researcher
initially in an arrangement which, though presumably meaningful, is not
intrinsically patterned by quantitative evaluations. Let us call these data
'Unstructured'.[31]

Then, finally, we may consider an intermediate type of data which we will call 'Loosely Structured'. These are those data which are found initially in clear-cut categories, but which are not unequivocally pre-coded as *ordinal, interval,* or *ratio* scales. Obviously this type will include data which are initially apparent as simple dichotomies (e.g. 'male', 'female') and as *nominal* scales (e.g. 'father', 'mother', 'son', etc.). But it will also include those data which are partly precoded according to at least *ordinal* scaling, but which are complicated by a 'kitchen-sink category' which does not fit into the scale. By a 'kitchen-sink category' I mean a category for everything (including the kitchen sink) which is not specifically anticipated by the other categories. For example, many items on self-administered postal questionnaires require respondents to tick one of a series of alternatives, the last of which is,

'OTHER (Please specify) . . .'

This kind of measurement will yield data which are partly structured and partly unstructured and which can, in their totality, be regarded for our present purposes as 'Loosely Structured'.

Now it should be clear that rigidly structured data on the one hand, and unstructured data on the other, present opposite problems for the researcher. Where rigid measurements are produced by his own measuring instruments rather than by those within the first-order universe of his datum, the researcher will always have to face the accusation that he has distorted his data by so categorizing them. He will have to accept the fact that by bringing his data into his operations in such a highly structured form he may have missed aspects of variation that might be highly relevant to the testing rituals which he hopes to perform. On the other hand, of course, if he is to use any numerical techniques of data analysis at all, he must *eventually* face the problems of coding his material, and thus of scaling. So accusations of bias may still be made if he opts for unstructured data, but the problem will arise at a different stage.[32]

The initial degree of scaling of data is thus classified in the DO-IT-YOURSELF-MULTI-PURPOSE-DATA-MATRIX in three categories.

(i) Rigidly Structured.
(ii) Loosely Structured.
(iii) Unstructured.

3. The operative assumptions about the location of the data recorders *vis-à-vis* the initial datum universe

The third axis of the MATRIX divides the sorts of data defined by the first two axes according to the locus of the recording apparatus with respect to the datum universe. The data recorder(s), whether they be machines or people, or complexes of both, may either be informed by the second-order perspectives of the researchers, or by the first-order perspective of an actor or actors in the world within which the measurements are to be made, or by some combination of those two.

Let us consider data as falling into four types in this respect. The location of the data recorder *vis-à-vis* the datum universe may be assumed to be one of the following:

(i) *External.*
(ii) *Internal.*
(iii) *Intrusive.*
(iv) *Obtrusive.*

Where the recorder is assumed to be *External* to the datum universe the assumption is being made that the measurements are effected, as it were, 'from outside' the phenomena or events in which they are required to be manifest, and further, that those phenomena or events are unaware of, and completely unaffected by, the measurement operation itself. For example, I think you will agree that, if I wished to measure the circumference of a group of standing stones it would be perfectly reasonable for me to make the assumption that my brand new metric tape-measure could be regarded as external to the stipulated datum.

On the other hand, where the recording apparatus is assumed to be *Internal* to the datum universe the assumption being made is that measurements are happening, or have been happening 'inside' the social world in which they are stipulated. In this case the data are recorded by men or machines, or both, which are themselves taken for granted as natural on the first-order level. Whether these data are rigidly structured, loosely structured, or unstructured, the methods of scaling or categorizing are, of course, natural outcroppings of first-order, and not of second-order, meanings.

Until rather recently, however, it was very often the case that (except for 'historical' research) the only assumption that a social scientist could reasonably make about the location of his recording apparatus was that it was neither external, nor internal, but *intrusive*. That is to say that, if he was honest, the ordinary common or garden researcher would have to admit that he usually developed instruments which were supposed to be positioned externally to the datum universe but which, because of their intrusion in the first-order reality, were themselves sources of unknown and plausibly confounding variations in that reality.

Where data were produced through straightforward experimentation, for example, it was quite obvious that the stipulated data had only been obtained at the expense of interference with the ordinary context of first-order meaning. There is thus a considerable literature on the subject of experimental interference with the measuring process.[33] For, clearly, where these sorts of variations are unknown and/or uncontrolled then the experimental data may be UNRELIABLE as well as INVALID. Suppose, for example, that an important characteristic of the experimental setting happened to be the presentation of self of a certain lady experimenter: it would be most unsurprising if replication of the study by an unattractive colleague produced startlingly different results.

But, of course, it is not only in the experiment, but also in the interview, and even in the postal questionnaire, that there must be a first-order awareness of the fact of the measurement itself. In the last case the researcher is not actually present, yet he must still communicate at the first-order level through the written word. The first-order interpretation of the nature and purposes of his research will obviously affect that research in many ways, not only influencing the ¿directions? of responses, but also determining whether or not the game will be played at all.

> ME (*opening a letter at breakfast*): Well . . . me! It's a . . . questionnaire. Someone's doing a . . . survey of . . . child-rearing practices. (*Flicking of pages and intermittent sniggers*) . . . silly . . . ! Only one thing to do with *that*! (*Promptly wipes baby's posterior thereupon.*)

Eugene Webb and his colleagues summarize the implications of the assumption that the data recorder is intrusive with respect to the datum universe.[34]

> Today, the dominant mass of social science research is based upon interviews and questionnaires. We lament this overdependence upon a single, fallible method. Interviews and questionnaires intrude as a foreign element into the social setting they would describe, they create as well as measure attitudes, they elicit atypical roles and responses, they are limited to those who are accessible and will cooperate, and the responses obtained are produced in part by dimensions of individual differences irrelevant to the topic at hand.

Finally the researcher may make the assumption that his recording apparatus is *obtrusive* with respect to the required data. Here there is a deliberate awareness of the relationship between first-order and second-order meanings. The research is actually contrived to obtrude into the reality situation in question. Thus data stipulated in this way are recorded not through first-, nor through second-order categorizations, but via an ongoing dialogue or bargaining about meaning which takes place between first- and second-order perspectives.

So, as I have defined them, VALID data are stipulated in three initial ways: according to *level of analysis, degree of scaling*, and *operative assumptions about the location of the recorders*. For the present purposes we are considering the first axis as cut into four parts (*Tangible, Personal, Behavioural, Processual*); the second into three (*Rigidly Structured,*

Loosely Structured, Unstructured), and the third into four (*External, Internal, Intrusive, Obtrusive*). Cross-classification of these three dimensions, through the DO-IT-YOURSELF-MULTI-PURPOSE-DATA-MATRIX gives forty-eight logical combinations. But, as we shall see, six of the cells in the MATRIX must be kept empty because they have been reserved for logical impossibilities. And three more cells will probably remain empty for a different reason: because the types of data that might fill them could only be got at absurd expense. This leaves thirty-nine different modes of stipulating data which are appropriate for social science purposes. Giving due consideration to the cultural impact of boring British films of the mid-twentieth-century (which, in their place, are as ¿interesting? as any other data) I shall insist on calling these thirty-nine methods of social science measurement, the THIRTY-NINE STIPS.

Until they all fell out, the THIRTY-NINE STIPS were kept in the White Knight's deal prototype of the DO-IT-YOURSELF-MULTI-PURPOSE-DATA-MATRIX, like the matrix on page 340.

Now, before we go through the MATRIX compartment by compartment, it is worth noting that the types of data defined by the various cells of the box might have been classified along many dimensions other than the three axes comprising the MATRIX. There are a whole range of differences, say between measurements of the weights of stones (STIP 1), and say videotaped recordings of conversations between deaf people and sociologists (STIP 39). But one of the most ¿interesting? of these is the variation in what might be termed the *evidential density* of the stipulated data.

By the *evidential density* of data I mean the extent to which they are saturated with second-order meaning. For the THIRTY-NINE STIPS are thirty-nine ways of stipulating data *initially*; they are thirty-nine ways of bringing 'raw' information into the research unit for processing. At one extreme these initial data may be of such a high *evidential density* that there will be very little wastage of information. Here the required data have been so precisely stipulated in terms of second-order meanings that the researcher has before him only that information which will be directly involved in his testing rituals, and nothing much else. In this case there will, of course, be few problems waiting to confront the researcher at the coding stage. The data will virtually code themselves: no major problems of interpretation and second-order categorization will remain to be resolved when the data are transcribed from the 'raw' to the 'symbolic' or coded form. So, where data are of a high *evidential density* the researcher can be satisfied that he has more or less eliminated the problems which might arise at the coding stage, and that he has found out most of what he wanted to know and little of what he didn't want to know, both speedily and economically.

Do-it-yourself-multi-purpose-data-matrix

	INITIAL LEVEL OF ANALYSIS DEFINING THE DATUM UNIT											
DEGREE OF SCALING IN INITIAL PRESENTATION OF DATA	TANGIBLE			PERSONAL			BEHAVIOURAL			PROCESSUAL		
	Rigidly structured	Loosely structured	Un-structured	Rigidly structured	Loosely structured	Un-structured	Rigidly structured	Loosely structured	Un-structured	Rigidly structured	Loosely structured	Un-structured
EXTERNAL	1	2	3	4	5	6	7	8	9	10	11	12
INTERNAL	13	14	15	16	17	18	19	20	21	22	23	24
INTRUSIVE	LOGICAL NULL-CLASSES			25	26	27	28	29	30	31	32	33
OBTRUSIVE				EMPIRICAL NULL-CLASSES			34	35	36	37	38	39

OPERATIVE ASSUMPTIONS ABOUT THE LOCATION OF THE DATA RECORDERS VIS-A-VIS INITIAL DATUM UNIVERSE

Yet where a research programme stipulates only data of high *evidential density*, many appearances might have been ¿interesting? stimuli for further speculation and theoretical development must necessarily have been evaded by the research calipers. One may zoom into a real social ¿time-space?, make the stipulated measurements speedily and RELIABLY, and zoom off again, only to find that though one has all the information required to test the specified hypotheses, one has less than enough to hold an after-dinner conversation about the situation or institution in question. Thus, perhaps, in some ways the theory has been *less* at risk than it might have been, for the researcher has been systematically shutting his eyes to all those appearances which, though seeming to contradict his theory, could none the less be ignored on the basis of a pious conviction that they were inadmissable evidence.

On the other hand, where the data stipulated are of a very low *evidential density*, the researcher will be confronted initially with a rich and fruity mess of first-order pottage which cannot speak for itself on the second-order level of meaning. Though every utterance and every gesture of a videotaped conversation may be faithfully recorded on the tape, the researcher must still, eventually, face up to the task of structuring this initial data in terms of clear-cut, unambiguous, and plausibly replicable, second-order categorizations. That is to say that if the data are to be regarded as legitimate evidence, relevant for the testing of hypotheses, they must somehow, eventually, be coded. What is relevant as evidence must somehow be selected from the context of irrelevance in which it is still embedded when it arrives upon the research desk. And, of course, every 'um' and 'ah', every 'Well, . . . I mean', every nod and every wink, has had its cost. ¿Uninteresting? data come as pricey as ¿interesting? ones. Useless data, as well as VALID and RELIABLE data, must take their share of the financial and other resources and the ¿time? available for the research.

The puzzle about the optimum degree of *evidential density* for the stipulated data is not one with which the DO-IT-YOURSELF-MULTI-PURPOSE-DATA-MATRIX is equipped to cope. For on one level that is a practical puzzle: a dilemma which must be resolved situationally by the researcher through a series of pragmatic and ethical decisions about the proper balance between the second-order imperatives of the research design on the one hand, and the practical and ethical dictates of his relationship with first-order realities on the other. Yet, on another level, this question about optimum *evidential density* for data is also a profound inquiry about the nature of perception itself. It is a query about the ways in which human beings somehow manage to figure facts in an inter-subjectively RELIABLE and extrasubjectively VALID fashion. As such it is not a puzzle for the common or garden researcher at all, it is a *CONUNDRUM.*

However hard you peer into the little deal box you won't spy a *CONUNDRUM*. But if you look hard enough you may see some ¿interesting? traces. For sometimes a *CONUNDRUM* will take the shape of a SPIDER spinning a complex web of doubt and disbelief for the education of the RABBITS!

Chapter 17

Uncertain Measures

Now let us see what else Pandora's box of social data has to offer, besides cobwebs!

The first three modes of stipulating data – STIPS 1, 2 and 3 – require measurements to be made of physical traces or residues of past happenings. These data are natural outcroppings of human activity which are, of course, assumed to exist quite independently of the researcher. They are[1]

> not specifically produced for the purpose of comparison and inference, but available to be exploited opportunistically by the alert investigator. . . . It may be helpful to discriminate between two broad classes of physical evidence, a discrimination similar to that between the intaglio and the cameo. On the one hand there are the *erosion measures*, where the degree of selective wear on some material yields the measure. . . . On the other hand, there are *accretion measures*, where the research evidence is some deposit of materials. Immediately one thinks of anthropologists working with refuse piles and pottery shards.

Data stipulated like this – that is as *tangible* phenomena to be measured by *external* instrumentation – have been largely ignored by sociological research. But such data may be highly RELIABLE and, provided that they are precisely stipulated in terms of the imperatives of the particular test situation in which they are to be employed, they have a rather special claim to VALIDITY. For, as one writer has observed, 'there is still no man who would not accept dog tracks in the mud against the sworn testimony of a hundred eye-witnesses that no dog had passed by.'[2]

Let us consider STIP 1 first. These are those sorts of erosion and accretion measures which are made in the first instance by straightforward counting, or with the aid of measuring instruments such as tape-measures, or weighing machines, which yield *rigidly structured* scales of values. For example, one might stipulate comparative weights, volumes, or areas of litter left behind after a Pop Festival, an Environmental Convention, and a gathering of Conservative Ladies. Of course, one would have to stipulate additional data to ensure the comparability of those measures. The weights, volumes, and areas could only be validly compared when appropriate steps had been taken to obtain for control purposes certain other measurements, such as the duration of the happening, the number of people present, the number of prepacked refreshments sold, and so on.

Actual examples of the use of STIP 1 are rather rare in the social science LIBRARY. But I have selected one or two suggestions from Webb and his colleagues' invaluable volume, *Unobtrusive Measures*. For example, Brown proposed to stipulate the differences between weights of food trucks entering and garbage trucks leaving a hospital ward as an index of the food intake of the patients.[3] Webb *et al.* also mention the stipulation of radio dial settings for an indicator of the popularity of radio stations.[4] Sawyer stipulated the number of empty liquor bottles in trash carted from Wellesley homes as an indicator of the consumption of liquor in that area.[5] Du Bois stipulated the number of different fingerprints on a page as an indicator of readership of an advertisement.[6] Naroll stipulated size of floor areas on archaeological sites for indicators of population size.[7] McClelland stipulated his data like this:[8]

the measure of the economic rise and fall of classical Greece was taken to be the area with which she traded, in millions of square miles, as determined by the location of vases unearthed in which her chief export commodities were transported.

And Sechrest actually wandered around trying car doors outside men's and women's blocks in a college in order to obtain his stipulated data for testing a hypothesis about the relationship between sex and the locking of car doors![9]

STIP 2 are measured in a similar fashion to STIP 1, but the initial scaling is more loosely structured. The difference between the two can perhaps be grasped best by consideration of a study stipulating both kinds of data.[10]

Mosteller conducted a shrewd and creative study on the degree to which different sections of the *International Encyclopedia of the Social Sciences* were read. He measured the wear and tear on separate sections by noting dirty edges of pages as markers, and observed the frequency of dirt smudges, finger markings, and underlining on pages. In some cases of very heavy use . . . 'dirt had noticeably changed the colour of the page so that [some articles] are immediately distinguishable from the rest of the volume'. Mosteller studied volumes at both Harvard and the University of Chicago, and went to three libraries at each institution. He even used the *Encyclopaedia Britannica* as a control.

Though the frequency of finger-marks and dirt smudges may be measured against rigid scales, clearly the assessments of the changing colour of pages involves a vaguer and less obviously mathematical kind of evaluation. The researcher measuring pages in terms of dirtiness is necessarily forcing the variation he observes into some rather loosely defined, but none the less *defined*, categories.

Another example of STIP 2 is the estimations of the shininess of areas on bronze statues where this is stipulated as an indicator of the frequency and intensity of touching and rubbing. For, of course, such measures can only be achieved through rough visual estimations: any other physical or chemical methods of analysis would destroy the statues themselves. And a final example of STIP 2 is the evaluations of the grandeur of tombstones stipulated by Durand as an indicator of social eminence.[11]

STIP 3 are similar to STIPS 1 and 2, but involve the initial selection of virtually unstructured data. The pots and pans dug up by archaeologists are data of this type, as indeed are the results of the sort of dustbinological scavenging made infamous by one A. J. Webberman, Dylanologist![12] For, provided these relics or pieces of detritus are, as it were, carted back to the research unit in their entirety, rather than measured or classed into categories on the spot, they will confront the researcher initially as STIP 3.

Though STIPS 1 to 3 vary according to the ease with which their RELIABILITY may be estimated, they present similar problems in respect of VALIDITY. For these data, like any other data, are of no intrinsic use to the researcher, their VALIDITY depends wholly on the reasonableness of the assumption that they may be taken as traces or indicators of the required variations in social meanings and behaviours. Thus, like any other data, taken *by themselves* they may be misleading. For example, Webb *et al.* make much of a suggestion that the popularity of museum exhibits could be measured by noseprinting the glass cabinets in which they are contained.[13] But, of course, it is rather dubious whether noseprints are VALID evidence of interest. Not everyone presses his nose to the glass; women and children probably do so more than men; and some people move their noses making several prints, while others, perhaps equally fascinated by the exhibit, may stand transfixed several yards away from the glass. Obviously then, STIPS 1, 2 and 3, like any other sorts of data, ought to be supplemented by data stipulated in quite different ways.[14]

The most persuasive evidence comes through a triangulation of measurement processes. If a proposition can survive the onslaught of a series of imperfect measures, with all their irrelevant error, confidence should be placed in it. Of course, this confidence is increased by minimising error in each instrument and by a reasonable belief in the different and divergent effects of the sources of error.

STIPS 4, 5 and 6 are, like the first three sorts of data, stipulated as *external* measurements, but here the level of analysis is defined as *personal* rather than *tangible*. That is to say that the units of data stipulated in this way are people rather than things.

STIP 4 is, quite simply, head-counting. Yet this may not be so simple-minded for some purposes as you may suspect. For example, suppose that you had to stipulate data to be indicative of the population density of that part of London which includes Covent Garden, the Charing Cross Road, and Piccadilly, in order to make comparisons before and after the proposed 'redevelopment' of the area. Ordinary residential measures would be thoroughly inappropriate for your purposes, as, in that part of London, almost more than anywhere else, the 'residents' and 'tourists' bear no relation to the actual dwellings there. Perhaps, then, your best bet would be to employ the following simple head-counting technique:[15]

> *Principle of the Moving Observer.* This is used to assess the numbers of individuals moving about within a given area – for example, crowds in streets. Fixed-point counting does not take account of the velocity of movement up and down a street; nor, unless points of access are all manned, does it take account of movement in and out of the area. The moving observer traverses an area in one direction counting the numbers of persons he passes – in either direction – and deducting those who overtake him. He then repeats the process traversing the area in the opposite direction. The average of the two counts gives an estimate of the average number of people in the area during the time of the counts. It is valid provided only that all individuals can be readily counted and that the passage of the observer does not influence the movements of the individuals in the area.

If you felt that this method could not be employed readily, or was, perhaps, too expensive in terms of ¿time? etc., or if you had attempted to cross-check RELIABILITY by using a number of researchers, and had found the data rather UNRELIABLE, then you might like to try another method of stipulating data for the same sort of purpose. If you were to parachute onto the top of Centre Point (no one would notice!) you could make rough estimates of the density of the crowds below from that platform. Thus situated on the monstrosity (which, needless to say, is certain to survive the efforts of the 'redevelopers') you would be able to make loosely structured measurements in the mode of STIP 5.

Finally, if you were still unsatisfied that you had obtained the stipulated data, you might use STIP 6 instead, or as well, as STIPs 4 and 5. This way you would attempt to take back to the research unit a description of the density of people in the area which was as complete as possible. This might, for example, be achieved through extensive photographing of the area from a number of different ground and aerial perspectives.[16]

The third way of defining the level of analysis for the unit datum I have called *behavioural*. Here, you will remember, the units of analysis are not the conglomerations of inorganic and organic matter which might be recognized as things or people, but the rather less evidently concrete happenings which may be apprehended as actions. It may be more difficult to pinpoint the spatio-temporal boundaries of an act than it is to, say, recognize the point at which a person ends and the chair, floor, table, and smoke-filled atmosphere begin. But it is none the less possible to observe with the naked and *external* eye, because actions are generally obvious in so far as they stand out against a background of inaction. STIPS 7, 8 and 9 are the three types of data stipulated in this way, that is as actions to be recorded by an unnoticed, or irrelevant, observer or observing apparatus.

In the case of STIP 7 the data required are to be recorded in a rigidly prestructured fashion. Thus, for example, Barch, Trumbo, and Nangle 'were interested in the degree to which turn-signalling was related to the turn-signalling behaviour of a preceding car'. They stipulated data to be recorded by a concealed roadside observer, according to the following categories:[17]

1. Presence or absence of turn signal.
2. Direction of turn.
3. Presence of another motor vehicle 100 feet or less behind the turning motor vehicle when it begins to turn.
4. Sex of drivers.

You will notice that each of these categories forms a clear and unequivocal dichotomy, thus, though no very complicated scaling is involved in the initial data stipulation, the data will none the less be very rigidly structured.

Other examples of STIP 7 in the field of traffic research are quite common.[18] STIP 7 may, of course, also be measured by machinery rather than by concealed human observers, provided the function of the devices is unknown to the persons whose actions are anticipated. Thus, for example, Schulman and Reisman equipped children with self-winding wristwatches which were actually inclusive of tiny 'acto-meters', that is devices designed to measure the amount of activity of the wearer.[19] Similarly, an interviewee's chair, a psychiatrist's couch, a motor-car seat, and other items of furniture, could all be unobtrusively wired up to record variation in the perspiration of the occupants.[20] And Cox and Marley[21] equipped furniture with a device to measure movement for a study of the effects of drugs on restlessness among patients.

STIP 8 data are initially stipulated in a less rigidly structured way. For example, estimates of the movements of crowds from an elevated perspective would fall into this category. This mode of observation would, of course, be rather similar to STIP 5, except that, in this case, the focus is on the *movement* of the crowd rather than its density and size. For example, as Galton suggested almost ninety years ago, an observer located on the stage of a theatre could make loosely structured measurements of the gross body movement of the audience.[22]

STIP 9 data are those records of behaviour which are made in an unstructured way, either by a completely unnoticed recording instrument (such as a camera, tape-recorder, etc.) or by a hidden or disguised observer. Denzin has described an interesting instance of this mode of measurement.[23]

> One of my colleagues experimented with hidden tape recorders during a field trip to Latin America. Forced to leave the major routes of transportation and travel into the mountains, he installed a transistorized tape recorder on the back of one of his pack horses. The recorder was automatically activated by a small voice microphone contained in his shirt pocket . . . the main recording devices would be installed in the investigator's automobile and could be activated at distances up to a mile away by transistorized microphones.

Videotape equipment which can be used in a completely unobtrusive way has yet to be devised. But the canny researcher might well make some use of the telephoto lens! On the other hand, of course, this surreptitious sort of observation may be undertaken with the aid of no machinery at all and only an assumedly good memory. For example, I might dress myself up as a tea-lady and, thus disguised, secretly observe the deliberations of, say, a meeting of the Associated Examining Board, or a public relations policy meeting of Rio-Tinto-Zinc. But reliance on memory must raise more doubts about the RELIABILITY of data than should be the case where mechanical recording devices are employed.

Generally speaking the use of hidden methods of observation to obtain data stipulated in these last three modes (STIPS 7, 8 and 9) is circumscribed rather strictly by the practical considerations of maintaining secrecy on the one hand, and the ethical considerations raised by that secrecy, on the other (social scientists don't tap telephones!).

In addition to tangible, personal, and behavioural levels of analysis, units of data may also be defined *processually*, that is as individual communications, rather than as things, people, or acts. Yet it should be obvious immediately that attempts to record such expressions of first-order meanings by apparatus located entirely outside the hermeneutic bounds of the reality in question are fraught with difficulty. One can imagine a Wittgensteinian postgraduate student, hidden behind a tree, making precoded records of the apparent criteria being employed by the Bongy Wongy noodle-stackers.[24] This would be STIP 10, as would, say, rigid on-the-spot classifications of conversations between workmen, made by a successfully disguised industrial sociologist. And much naïve social anthropology aims at the collation of data stipulated as STIPS 11 and 12. But such data, though not as rare as one might hope, are generally INVALID. It is simply not plausible to make the assumption that expressions of meaning can be recorded or measured in a directly external way. And, at worst, the gap between the language of the researcher and the unknown language, in terms of which he assumes his data to be structured at the first-order level, will simply be filled by his *own* first-order prejudices and assumptions, rather than by explicit second-order strategies. Though these types of data (STIPS 10, 11 and 12) are neither logical, nor unfortunately, empirical, null-classes, I suggest that they be avoided.

Now it should be clear that as the level of analysis shifts from tangible to personal to behavioural to processual, the frequency of research situations in which it is really reasonable to make the assumption that recorders will be located externally to the units to be measured tends to decrease.

So let us now have a look at the twelve forms of data which are stipulated according to the opposite sort of assumption about the location of the data recorders. STIPS 13–24 are those forms of data which, as they initially confront the researcher, are quite uncontaminated by second-order considerations. These data have been recorded, not by the researcher or any of his works, but, quite simply, and naturally, by first-order actors in the ordinary taken-for-granted context of their everyday lives. In the case of these sorts of data, then, one form of the VALIDITY problem will not trouble the researcher. He will not have to bother about whether or not second-order bias has crept into the initial collation of the stipulated data. But he must still be aware that such data are biased at the first-order level, according to the differential locations, statuses, motivations, prejudices, and other characteristics of the recorders.[25] For example, a policeman's notebook and the diary entry of an accused person will provide quite different data, but each may be equally VALID for clearly stipulated research purposes. And, of course, the problems of second-order interpretation which do not arise when STIPS 13–24 are initially recorded in a durable form, must eventually face the researcher when he comes to code his data for analysis. And this will be the case even where the initial data take a very sophisticated and authoritative form, for *no* first-order facts can speak for themselves on the second-order level.[26]

Pollner tells of a sociologist from another planet who visits Earth with a research student. The professor asks his student to carry out field-work on the subject of Earth societies. After a relatively short while, the student returns. But instead of his own report, he has brought with him bound copies of all the existing sociology journals. 'There was no need', he tells his master, 'to explore any further. For there already exist these records compiled by Earthly sociologists. They tell us all we need to know.' The professor reproves his student: 'Can't you see', he exclaims, 'that these records constitute data for analysis in the same way as do the societies themselves? For both rely on the tacit knowledge of their members and this knowledge defines the reality in ways that we must investigate.'

STIPS 13, 14 and 15 are, then, records of measurements of tangible phenomena and events which are initially compiled at the first-order level by official agencies or private individuals for their own, first-order, purposes. Examples of STIP 13 are temperature and rainfall measures compiled by the Meteorological Office, records of prices at Sotheby's, water pressures obtained from the Water Board,[27] the records of the rates of replacement of vinyl floor tiles which may be found in the main-tenance department of a museum,[28] or, say, the recorded weights and measurements of the winning marrows in Little Podsbury's annual marrow competition. An interesting example of STIP 14 which might prove useful for future social scientists is given by the estimates of environmental pollution compiled by schoolchildren in the Clean Air Research project run by the Advisory Centre for Education in conjunc-tion with the *Sunday Times* magazine in 1972. And holiday snaps of beaches, promenades, and shopping areas, and letters, diary entries and other personal descriptions of places and things may be a fruitful, if somewhat inaccessible, source of STIP 15.

In the case of STIPS 16, 17 and 18, the units of data recorded initially at the first-order level are defined as *people* rather than things. These types of evidence may be termed 'demographic data'. Where these data are initially found in a highly structured form, as are some aspects of the records of births and deaths to be found in Somerset House, they are STIP 16.[29] Where, however, the data are initially compiled in looser categories they will be STIP 17, as are, for example, the marriage records which may be found in Registry Offices.[30] And photographs of tombstones, or of parish registers, provide the unstructured data categorized in the MATRIX as STIP 18.

STIPS 19, 20, and 21 are first-order records of *acts*. Examples of STIP 19 which have sometimes been employed in educational research are school grades and examination results. Social scientists have also exploited the non-demographic forms of official statistics such as criminal statistics,[31] promotion records,[32] records of exports and imports,[33] and suicide rates.[34] But there are other forms of STIP 19 which might be appropriate for certain purposes, for example, golf cards, weight-watchers' records of calorie intake, breathalyser test results, and so on.

STIP 20 are the more loosely coded first-order records of behavioural evaluations such as school reports, sentences of courts, coroners' records, and so on. And STIP 21 are those evaluative descriptions of acts and sequences of acts which are not quantitatively structured by the initial first-order recorders. Examples are reports by probation officers and social workers, arresting officers' notebooks, and so on.

It is rather difficult to draw a clear line between STIPS 19, 20 and 21 and STIPS 22, 23 and 24. For the difference between the behavioural and processual levels of analysis only makes sense from the point of view of second-order conceptualizations. Sometimes first-order messages and records may be deliberately focused on actions rather than words, or vice versa. But more often the two levels of abstraction are tangled together in the meaningful profusion which is the real first-order world. Thus, for example, records of sales of magazines and books made by retailers or publishers may be regarded as epistemic correlates of acts (STIP 19) or of expressions of meaning (STIP 22) or both. Similarly sentences of courts may be classified as initial data of STIP 20 or of STIP 23. And radio and television broadcasts, as well as entire written documents (diaries, suicide notes, rule books, charters, manifestoes, social workers' notes, obituaries, newspapers, magazines, advertisements, Hansard, graffiti, etc.) may be regarded as either STIP 21 or as STIP 24. For what initially confronts the researcher as durable data (that is as symbols and signs recorded on paper, or acetate, or whatever) have not been selected from their natural context according to second-order criteria. Of course the researcher himself must be clear about whether he is stipulating his data in terms of a behavioural or a processual definition of the datum unit, for when he comes to structure these data in terms of second-order categories he must have some idea of what he is after. But the data themselves are not naturally ordered in terms of such distinctions, and thus the very same documents, fragments of mass media, photographs, or whatever, may be stipulated as data for rather different purposes. It is not then the initial (first-order) circumstances of their production, but the eventual (second-order) imperatives of coding and analysis which distinguishes STIPS 22–4 from STIPS 19–21. For data defined at the second-order level as internally recorded expressions of meaning are those which will be subject to the sorts of coding and analysis known as 'Content Analysis'.[35]

STIPS 13–24, then, replace the problems posed by second-order bias in initial observations and recording by those stemming from the consideration that there may be unknown and confounding sources of bias at the first-order level. For, of course, all archival records are subject to the fluctuations of selective deposit and survival. Only certain happenings are recorded at all, and the records themselves may vary in durability for one reason or another. It is a sobering thought that some of the most durably artefacts of Western consciousness are in some respects the most trivial. Yet this may, in itself, be revealing. It is a well-worn theme of science fiction writers that a metal cylinder containing a Walt Disney film is better equipped to survive the ultimate human catastrophe than any fragile pang of pain.

Now the twenty-four forms of data which we have considered so far have all been stipulated on the basis of assumptions about the location of the initial data recorder which raise no unique methodological dilemmas for the social scientist, at least not at this stage of his research. But the social scientist may make another kind of assumption about the relationship between his initial measuring operations and the measurements that they yield. The great bulk of social science research which exists today has been directed towards data produced by such instruments as the experiment, the interview, and the self-administered questionnaire. And these instruments can only be employed validly where there is a clear recognition on the part of the researcher that these devices must intrude into the consciousness of subjects and respondents at the first-order level of meaning.

It is, of course, impossible to intrude into the life-world of a feather, candle, tombstone, or discarded liquor bottle, at least with a measuring instrument. So the cross-classification of the first three divisions along the top of the MATRIX and the third group on the vertical axis will produce logical null-classes.

STIPS 25, 26, and 27 are data to be produced by *intrusive* measurements of demographically defined units. Thus population censuses and sample surveys which rely on voluntary or legally imperative statements from the population itself are of these types. Where the information required is clearly precoded, as with most censuses, we have STIP 25. Where it is more loosely coded we have STIP 26. And where it is initially unstructured it is STIP 27. This last mode of stipulating data has not been at all common in social science research, but could well prove useful in certain circumstances. For example, one might attempt to assess the density of peopling of a play area, or crash pad, or arch under Hungerford Bridge, by direct observation. In this case, in contrast to STIP 7, one would not attempt to make one's observations in an unnoticed, or even underhand, manner, but would make no bones about what it was one had come to see, and attempt to give honest answers to the inevitable questions about the uses to which the data would be put – even though such disclosures might well result in the depletion or dispersal of the population to be measured.

Apart from these various sorts of demographic data, the evidence to be measured by intrusive instrumentation may, of course, be defined initially on either a behavioural or a processual level. In the latter case the focus is on what people *say* about themselves and their worlds, whilst in the former case it is on what people actually *do* in precisely stipulated – albeit rather abnormal – circumstances.[36] Thus STIPS 28, 29 and 30 are those forms of data which are to be generated by experimental methods, whether these involve voluntary or involuntary subjects.

One of the most quoted examples of STIP 28 is Bales's set of experiments regarding group interaction which were conducted with small groups of volunteers at the Harvard Laboratory. Though the observers stayed in an adjacent room and watched the experiment through one-way mirrors, the interaction was, of course, still produced by an intrusive measurement process. For the subjects were quite aware of the fact that they were in an experimental situation. The data were coded straight away into the rigidly structured categories in Figure 35.[37] And Bales used electronic recording apparatus to check the RELIABILITY of the data coded in those categories against observations made in the mode of STIP 30.

A rather different sort of experiment in the mode of STIP 28 was carried out outside the laboratory by Gosnell.[38]

In order to measure the effect of different stimuli upon the tendency to register as a voter and to vote, the residents of twelve selected districts (of which eight were voting precincts) were divided into experimental and control groups. The stimuli were directed toward the fall presidential election (1924) and the winter aldermanic election (February, 1925). The experimental group received a mail canvass stimulus to register, before the first registration day, and the same informative notice plus a cartoon before the final registration day. Of course, the control group did not receive these. Further, specimen ballots were sent to the experimental groups before the presidential election, and a cartoon notice urging voting, together with English instructions for voting, before the aldermanic election. The control and experimental areas were matched roughly for nationality, sex ratio, economic conditions, and stimulus from the political parties. The student can see that a series of comparisons is possible within such a design. It is also clear that within the conditions stated this is a true experiment. Such a design has also been used in order to compare different techniques for eliciting answers from mailed questionnaires

354   Uncertain Measures

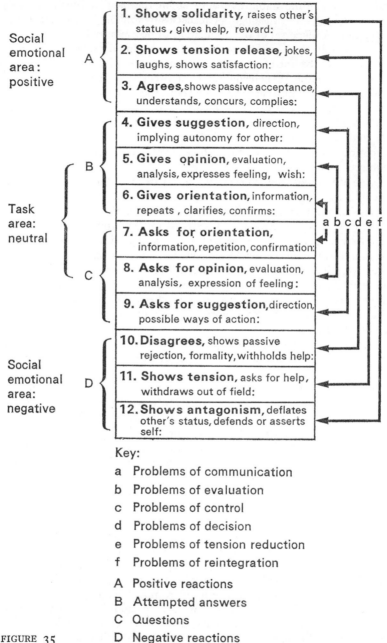

Key:

a Problems of communication
b Problems of evaluation
c Problems of control
d Problems of decision
e Problems of tension reduction
f Problems of reintegration

A Positive reactions
B Attempted answers
C Questions
D Negative reactions

FIGURE 35

(inclosure of money, use of self-addressed envelopes, double post-cards, etc.).

And many other examples of this mode of stipulating data, as well as of STIPS 29 and 30, can be found in the LIBRARY.[39]

Though it must be obvious that there will be difficulties involved in making VALID generalizations from experimental data to ordinary, natural, non-experimental propensities, the continuing utility of the experimental mode for the social scientists can, perhaps, be best appreciated by considering an imaginary piece of research. Suppose that you wished to test some hypotheses about the relationship between the cultural values propagated in schools and, say, competitiveness and co-operation as characteristics of the actual behaviour of schoolchildren. You might stipulate data of various types (say, STIPS 22–4, or, say, STIPS 31–3) as indicators of the former variables, and devise a series of comparative experiments to measure the latter variables. Thus, for example, children in various sorts of schools (say selective versus comprehensive, etc., or say, Chinese, Italian, and American) might be provided with a piece of land for gardening, and all the necessary materials and tools. The garden might be divided up amongst the children in such a way that each had his own small plot, while a larger plot was allocated for communal gardening. Various measures could then be used as indicators of the relative degrees of energy and interest of the children in the private, as compared with the communal, plots. Where the amount of ¿time? available for gardening was fixed, then, for example, STIP 28 measurements of relative ¿time? spent on the plots could be made. On the other hand, loose initial categorizations of the activity of the children could be made in the mode of STIP 29, while videotapes of the gardening children would provide data in the mode of STIP 30.[40]

The remaining three types of intrusive data, STIPS 31, 32, and 33, are those which are measured by the well-tried methods of interview and questionnaire. In the case of the interview the respondent is, of course, engaged in face-to-face interaction with the interviewer, but the self-administered questionnaire is no less intrusive, for the subject must still be aware that he is being required to respond to certain questions and that his answers will be interpreted in some way or other by the researcher.

Once a researcher has stipulated his data to be of these types, the decision between interview and questionnaire, and between rigidly structured items (STIP 31), loosely structured ones (STIP 32) and a more or less unstructured format (STIP 33) is both a theory-determined and a pragmatic one. Interviews are much more costly in terms of research ¿time? and resources than are postal questionnaires, but, on the other hand, it is generally believed that the problems of bias arising from differential willingness to co-operate in the research are greater for the postal questionnaire.[41] It is perhaps easier to ignore a missive which comes through the letter-box than an avid interviewer with his foot in the door. But there is a simple way of checking the plausibly confounding influence of variable non-response to a postal questionnaire. This is to follow-up the non-respondents with further entreaties. Data from those who respond to second or subsequent requests can then be compared with those from the original respondents, and, where no great differences are found in the patterning of these two groups of data, the tentative assumption may be made that non-response is not operating in a systematic or relevantly confounding manner.[42]

There are, however, practical circumstances in which the costlier method of the interview must be preferred to the questionnaire. Where, for example, the sample in question is assumed to be composed of persons who would have difficulty in interpreting and responding to a written document (for example, very young schoolchildren, certain classes of inmates in a mental hospital, barbiturate addicts, and people with Parkinson's disease) then there is a clear case for the interview, whether responses are to be recorded initially in rigidly precoded categories (STIP 31), or according to a loosely structured interview schedule (STIP 32), or, whether they are to be recorded verbatim with the aid of shorthand or a tape-recorder (STIP 33). And there may be theoretical as well as practical reasons for choosing the more costly method of the interview. For where the researcher is sure that his data must be STIP 33, then he will probably feel that a totally unstructured question such as, say, 'What do you think about drug addicts?' is given a spurious degree of structuring when it is presented on a written document. For one thing, people will tend to write less than they might be prepared to say, for, even if the size of the space allotted for their answers can be regarded as irrelevant, it takes more time and energy to write than to talk. Thus so-called 'unstructured' questionnaire data will probably be less rich in first-order meaning than, say, tape-recorded conversational answers.

In general the choice of degree of structuring of items in these three modes of data stipulation (31, 32, 33) should be made with full awareness of the Janus-faced dilemma of VALIDITY and BIAS. For, on the one hand, to the extent that the initial format is very rigidly structured, the responses are forced into second-order categories and thus bias may be introduced at the initial stage of data recording. But, on the other hand, to the extent that the initial format is unstructured, the possibility of bias at the later coding stage must arise.

Now, though some helpful hints for the construction of question-naires and interview schedules may be found in the LIBRARY,[43] the utility of some of these recipes is a little marred by the typical failure of commentators to distinguish between two different aspects of the instrumentation. The problems to be faced in devising a questionnaire or planning an interview fall into two broad classes. On the one hand there are problems of *instrument design*, and, on the other hand, there are problems of *instrument presentation*.

Problems of instrument design for stips 31, 32 and 33

The first kind of problems which must face the researcher who is stipulating these kinds of data are those arising from the kind of operationalization which he wishes to effect. These issues may be thought of as those arising from the *second-order* imperatives of the research. For the researcher must begin by making decisions about the instruments he wishes to employ, on the basis of his research imperatives alone. He must check his *List of Variables to be Measured*, consult his original, vague, *Notes on Operationalization*, and attempt to devise clear, if variously structured, choice situations for the respondent, which may be regarded as indicators of the variation which he wishes to measure. Sometimes the researcher will be able to draw upon the research reports in the LIBRARY, for many of the variables he wishes to measure will have been operationalized by previous workers.[44] And, even if he is firmly convinced of the INVALIDITY or UNRELIABILITY of many of these measures, he may well profit by others' mistakes.

Examples of questionnaires and interview schedules can be found in any textbook. Here are just a few which I have selected from amongst the project work on drug use carried out by our second-year undergraduate students on the Methods course at Ponders End. All these examples were stipulated for a *questionnaire* to be distributed by hand to a series of snowball samples, and these data were to be supplemented by various other modes of measurement, and also by data from different samples.

Let us begin with the rigidly structured items, STIP 31. The following instrument was devised as one of several indicators for the variable *Availability of Drugs*, which is here treated as an attribute.

It is worth noting that item A was followed by an open-schedule question (item B, STIP 33) included as a check (see page 358).

The open-schedule question was included because, though we expected the level of drug knowledge to be high for this particular sample, we considered that it was just possible that some of the respondents might be confused about the classifications of the drugs mentioned.

Another item in the rigidly structured mode of STIP 31, was the indicator of *Hedonism* (item C, page 358).

Do you think you could *normally* obtain the   YES   NO
following drugs *if* you wanted them?

Cannabis (that is Hash/Shit etc. & Grass/
Marijuana etc.)   ....

Heroin (in any form)   ....

Other Opiates (like Phiseptone, Methadone etc.;
    NOT barbiturates, amphetamines etc.)   ....

A

What other drugs *could* you normally obtain *if* you wanted
them? ....
....
....
....

B

Imagine that you have taken part in some ridiculous cornflakes
competition. You have won a cash prize. But the value of the
prize depends upon the time that you claim it. You can have
£100 now or more the longer you wait. WHEN WOULD
YOU CLAIM YOUR PRIZE?

TICK ONE ONLY

£100	£500	£2,000	£6,000	£10,000
now	in 1	in 2	in 3	in 4
	year	years	years	years
....	....	....	....	....

(CHECK THAT YOU HAVE TICKED WHAT YOU THINK YOU
WOULD BE MOST LIKELY TO ACTUALLY DO, NOT WHAT
YOU WOULD LIKE TO DO.)

C

A similar fixed-choice item, also designed to measure *Hedonism* was as follows.

Think of what you *most* enjoy doing – the very biggest buzz.
What is it? . . . .
(leave this blank if you prefer to be cool about it)

Now imagine that medical research has proved this to be extremely harmful to your health (try to imagine this even if it seems ridiculous that whatever you are thinking about could be dangerous!). Suppose that it is known for certain that if you do this *ever again* you will contract a painful terminal illness, *would you continue to do it?*

Would you continue to do it if it was known to be extremely likely that you would DIE WITHIN *TEN* YEARS?

Would you continue to do it if it was known to be extremely likely that you would DIE WITHIN *FIVE* YEARS?

TICK ONE

TICK ONE

Yes I'd *definitely*
continue   . . . .

I would *probably*
continue   . . . .

I have *mixed feelings*   . . . .

I would *probably stop*   . . . .

I would *definitely stop*   . . . .

. . . .   Yes I'd *definitely*
continue

. . . .   I would *probably*
continue

. . . .   I have *mixed feelings*

. . . .   I would *probably stop*

. . . .   I would *definitely stop*

And still another way of structuring a precoded item for ordinal scaling is shown in the following example,[45] also devised as a measure of the same variable.

Which kind of person would you rather be?   TICK ONE

Someone who doesn't let his plans for the future
stop him from enjoying the present?   . . . .
Someone who doesn't mind giving up most of his
pleasure now so that he can be sure of the future?   . . . .
How strongly do you feel about the choice you just made?
very strongly   fairly strongly   not at all strongly

. . . .

And still another type of prestructured question is exemplified by the following strategy which was suggested by one student[46] as a possible measure for the variable *Expressivity*.

'The idea is to describe a hypothetical job with the following features: (i) large salary (say, £5,000 p.a.?) (ii) short hours (say, 10 a.m. to 3 p.m., 5 days per week) (iii) certain restrictions on "expressivity" (say, necessity to wear a suit or equivalent female dress, "neat" hair, pressures to entertain boss and elderly customers in the evenings etc.)
Then we ask:

How long could you stick a job like that?

....	....	....	....	....	....	....
until retire- ment	5 years	4 years	3 years	2 years	1 year	not at all

...'

And here is a similar strategy for measuring the same variable, which was suggested by another student.[47]

'We describe two furnished flats in the same district (next door?), at the same rent and the same size. Flat A is clean and well-decorated with all mod cons but the landlady lives on the premises and restrictions include no painting or sticking anything on the walls. Flat B is tatty with no mod cons but there are absolutely no restrictions about what can be done to it or in it. Then we ask:

WHICH WOULD YOU CHOOSE? (Tick once for each flat)

	I would definitely choose this one	probably choose this	would not know	probably not this	definitely not this
Flat A	....	....	....	....	....
Flat B	....	....	....	....	....

...'

In addition to direct questions, agree/disagree type items, and the various types of choice situations shown in the above examples, STIP 31 instruments may take the form of simple rankings, like this.

'There are a lot of different things you might hope to get from a job. Below is a list of some of these. I would like you to read them through and think about them. Then I would like you to write a '1' beside the one which you think is the *most important* thing you can get from a job. When you have done that, write a '2' beside the thing which you think is the second most important and so on until you come to the number '6'.

Friendly work mates	.... (a)
Long holidays	.... (b)
A good wage	.... (c)
Chances of promotion	.... (d)
Chance to use your abilities	.... (e)
Plenty of free time	.... (f)

Now if – AND ONLY IF – the thing which *you* think is most important of all about a job was NOT in the list above, write this now:

....
....
....

Some straightforward examples of STIP 32 are provided by the following loosely structured items included as measures of *Educational Background*.

How old were you when you left school?
.... years.

What kind of school was it?
TICK NEAREST TYPE
Secondary Modern   ....
Technical   ....
Grammar   ....
Comprehensive   ....
Public School   ....
Private School   ....
Other   ....
(Please specify) ....
....
....

Have you attended any educational establishments since leaving school? Please give initials of any qualifications you got there (e.g.: GCE, HND, BSc, DipEd, etc.)

	TICK EACH YOU HAVE ATTENDED	GIVE INITIALS OF ANY QUALIFICATIONS YOU GOT THERE
School of Art, Architecture, Photography, etc.	....	....
Polytechnic or similar college	....	....
University	....	....
College of Education	....	....
Other (Explain)	....	
....		

And, finally, here are some of the unstructured (STIP 33) items which were to be included in the same questionnaire as measures of *Occupation, Identification*,[48] and *Parental Background*, respectively.

If you have a paid job, please describe it. Otherwise how would you describe your occupation? What do you think of yourself as? What do you do for bread?

WHO ARE YOU? Write down the first ten answers to the question 'Who am I?' (meaning *you*) that come into your head.

Can you describe the job your father was doing:
a. *when you were a small child?*   b. *when you left school?*

Can you describe the paid work, if any, that your mother was doing;
a. *when you were a small child?*   b. *when you left school?*

Though the above examples cover most of the most common methods of formulating items for the self-administered questionnaire, they are not intended to be regarded as exhaustive. However these should give some idea of the sort of techniques of questioning which *may* yield RELIABLE and VALID data, and I hope that you will be able to devise some other strategies.

Design of instrumentation for interview schedules, can, of course, make use of similar instrumentation. Though here the interviewer will read the questions from a card, or, perhaps, memorize the items he intends to employ.

Though, obviously, no hard and fast rules for instrument design can be set down – as the particular theoretical and practical requirements of the research will vary considerably – I suggest the following hints which may be helpful in many situations.

HINT 1 Wherever possible include at least three separate indicators for each variable. If you have only two items which yield no consistent intercorrelations, you will be entirely in the dark as to whether it is the first, or the second, or *both* which are unreliable.

HINT 2 Always have an odd number of points on a scale and, if you wish to include a 'don't know', 'mixed feelings', or 'undecided' category, place this in the *middle* of the scale. 'Kitchen-sink' categories placed at the end of questions tend to collect more debris than those which are deliberately ordered as mid-points of obvious scales – probably due to the understandable indifference of the respondent to invest unnecessary effort in the enterprise![49]

HINT 3 For precoded data (STIPS 31 and 32) aim to achieve an optimum number of points on your scales. The more categories the better, because you can always *reduce* them subsequently by collapsing categories together, but, of course, you cannot *expand* them. On the other hand, a scale of more than about seven categories may be difficult to present in a meaningful way.

As you consider these three hints you will notice that the focus of your attention is gradually shifting from the second-order to the first-order constraints on the formulation of your instruments. For one must realize that the respondents' assumed language and knowledge is as much a determinant of the form of instrumentation which will be appropriate as are the second order imperatives of the research design. So, the imperatives of *instrument design* must be tempered by the special considerations of *instrument presentation* which seem appropriate for the particular sample in question. It should be obvious that instruments which seem appropriate for one sample (say, nuns) will be useless for another (say, undergraduate students).

Problems of instrument presentation for stips 31, 32 and 33

Detailed discussions of the problems of conducting interviews and administering postal questionnaires, and of the ins and outs and dos and don'ts of wording and ordering of instruments may be found in most textbooks on survey research. So I shall simply offer a list of hints.

HINT 1 Try to maximize the motivation to respond.

(a) The most direct way in which you can persuade people to co-operate in the research is by introducing yourself, either face-to-face, or in a written letter or preamble to a questionnaire. You must state your identity and that of the organization (if any) to which you are affiliated, and you must present a persuasive and, hopefully, honest case for the research. Do not assume that the pursuit of second-order knowledge for its own sake provides a sufficient justification for your work, but be aware of the interpretations and possible applications of the study for actual first-order realities.

(b) In addition to a persuasive and honest case for your work, the potential respondents will usually also require an assurance of anonymity. They will want to know that they will not be identified personally with their answers. The usual method for coping with this problem is to allot each respondent a number, and mark his interview schedule or questionnaire with this label rather than with his name or address. Of course there will often be administrative reasons why the researcher needs to be able to pin responses down to real names and addresses (for example, for a follow-up subsample of non-respondents), but it is up to him to convince the respondents that this information will be carefully guarded.

(c) An additional point to bear in mind is that the easier you make things for the respondents the more likely they will be to co-operate. Your personal manner in the case of the face-to-face interview will, of course, be of paramount importance. And a stamped-addressed envelope included with a postal questionnaire will obviously improve the response rate considerably.

(d) The questionnaire or interview should be as short as possible. It is common knowledge amongst researchers that respondent fatigue usually sets in after about fifteen or twenty minutes, but varies according to the particular characteristics of the sample and the level of interest which can be sustained in the enterprise.

(e) In order to maintain respondents' interest in the research it is essential to word and order instruments in a palatable way. Do not group your instruments together according to your second-order perspective, but arrange things so that the respondent is led from one 'topic' to another in a way which is meaningful at the first-order level. In the case of a postal questionnaire it may be useful to divide up groups of questions with headings, like this: '*Some questions about your family*', '*Now a few questions about your work*', and so on. Thus, for example, a number of different sorts of questions (STIPS 31, 32 and 33) which are, from the researcher's point of view 'about different things' (i.e. designed to measure different variables) might be grouped together on a self-administered questionnaire under the heading '*Friends*', as on page 366.[50] Notice also that, in the case of the question about residential affiliation, the loosely structured scaling has not been ordered on the questionnaire according to the vague ordinal scaling the researchers had in mind, for such ordering might appear as prejudice on the first-order level.

(e) Try to place the most difficult items near the beginning of the questionnaire or interview – i.e. before fatigue sets in. But don't put them *right* at the beginning because this will probably throw people off their stroke.

(f) Try to avoid questions which might elicit feelings of embarrassment or guilt, remembering that what embarrasses or upsets your respondents may not be the same as what embarrasses or upsets you. If you must use questions which are dubious in this respect, order them cleverly and always follow them by open-ended items which give the poor souls a chance to 'explain themselves'. These last may produce some ¿interesting? reading but are not to be regarded as 'evidence' for anything at all, as they have not been included for the specific purpose of measuring stipulated variations. The only decent thing to do is to destroy them.[51]

HINT 2 Attempt to improve RELIABILITY through adequate presentation.

		With legal wife or husband	With virtual wife or husband	With friends	Other (Please explain)
	With parents				
	Alone				

Who do you live with?   ....

TICK AS MANY AS APPLY   ......

......

	YES	NO
a. Do you recognize the term 'head'?		....
b. What proportion of your close friends would you describe as 'heads'?		IF YOU TICKED 'NO' PLEASE GO ON TO NEXT QUESTION.

TICK NEAREST ESTIMATE

....
nearly   most   about a   a few   none
all   half

c. If you recognize this word but do not use it yourself, what do you say instead?

....

....

d. Would you *object* to being described as a 'head' yourself?

TICK ONE

....
Object   Object   No
strongly   a little   objections

(a) The most obvious way of improving RELIABILITY is to make the questions as simple to understand, and as unambiguous, as possible. Do not assume too much knowledge on the part of the respondents. But, on the other hand, consider the special characteristics of your sample and avoid the opposite error of insulting them.[52]

(b) In order to cope with the endearing human tendency to agree rather than disagree (a tendency methodologists call the 'Acquiescence Response Set'[53]) arrange positively and negatively ordered alternatives for the various indicators in some more or less random fashion.

(c) Avoid words which may be assumed to be tinged with emotion for the particular sample in question – *unless*, of course, you deliberately intend to provoke an emotional reaction.

(d) Try using questions with built-in checks on first-order meaningfulness. Like this, for example:

	strongly agree	agree	mixed feelings	disagree	strongly disagree
There is no existing cause worth giving your life for	....	....	✓	....	....
There is no existing cause worth serving a year or more in prison for	....	.. ..		✓	....
There is no existing cause worth wasting a day demonstrating for	✓	....	....	....	....

The response given to the above questions clearly indicates that the respondent either misunderstood the questions, or was deliberately mucking about. These data can, then, be seen instantly to be UNRELIABLE and must therefore also be regarded as INVALID.

This sort of RELIABILITY problem arises in a rather different form with the face-to-face interview. Consider this:

... Interviewer asks questions slightly differently with different respondents. He finds answers widely varied.

... Now he decides to standardize the interview: he tries to word the questions in precisely the same way, order them the same way and even maintain a constant tone of voice and facial expression.

... He finds that all of a sudden the answers are coming out more 'consistently'.

RELIABILITY has now increased, but has VALIDITY? It could be that the interviewer has now assumed a flat formal tone and the respondents are giving him stereotyped answers. He is not behaving like a 'real' person, so neither are they: RELIABILITY has probably increased at the *expense* of VALIDITY.

(e) Some of the problems of checking instrument RELIABILITY can often be rendered less alarming for the researcher by the judicious use of the *Pilot Survey*.

The *Pilot Survey* is often thought of as a sort of feeler, or band of advance scouts despatched ahead of the main study. But, though this may be a helpful analogy, it is, in my view, a mistake to think of pilot studies as inductive exercises on the basis of which *IMPLICIT THEO-RIES* may be derived and preliminarily verified. In my opinion the following widely respected view of the function of the pilot interview implies a wasteful application of the limited resources which must be available for the research.[54]

> After the literature has been carefully studied and experts consulted, the researcher may still have only a rather vague idea of what are the crucial elements in his problem. A pilot study may then be launched as a step preliminary to the formulation of a schedule. At this stage, all that can be formulated is an *interview guide*. Thus the researcher interviews in the field in a very nondirective fashion. The questions are structured very little and controlled only by dealing with these general areas which he has reason to think are important. During this kind of flexible interviewing, he tries to follow up every promising lead which may appear, as to meaning of phrases, embarrassing areas of inquiry, differences of response to what seems to be the same question, new areas of subject matter, etc. The researcher, then, is not putting neat hypotheses to the test at this stage but is clarifying and formulating hypotheses for a subsequent study. Not only is he uncertain as to the materials he wants to inquire about, but he may even be uncertain as to whom he wishes to interview. This stage does not usually warrant a formal sampling design, but the student must be sure that he interviews a wide variety of the various types making up the final sample to be studied. Further, he must be alert to field-sampling problems which may warn him to take precautions at the stage of formal sampling design.

Though empirical work may be undertaken usefully at the beginning of the long process of theory construction, I cannot see how the use of such obtrusive and deliberately limited instruments of observation as the interview and self-administered questionnaire can be expected to be a profitable source of inspiration. Thus, in my view, if empirical observation is to be made in an inductive – i.e. prescientific – manner, the traditional social science tools of interview and questionnaire will almost always be thoroughly inappropriate, at least in so far as they are conducted in the usual ways.[55]

Pilot surveys are not, then, play-it-as-you-go instruments for instant inductive improvisation. But they do have a clear-cut and specific function, particularly for the researcher who has stipulated data in the modes of STIPS 31, 32 and 33. Quite simply, they provide an advance check on the RELIABILITY of instruments. By running an early pilot or dummy set of interviews or questionnaires the economical researcher may check the RELIABILITY of various indicators by intercorrelation, or, say, using coefficients of concordance, or, where instruments are devised with internal checks, simply by inspecting the raw data. He may also make certain other evaluations of the adequacy and meaningfulness of the instruments at the first-order level: are certain questions left unanswered by a lot of the respondents? Do some of the open-ended questions at the end of a self-administered questionnaire elicit shorter responses than were anticipated? Perhaps the order of the items should be changed? Should the questionnaire/interview be shortened?, etc. He may thus be able to produce a more efficient interview schedule or questionnaire form for the main survey, perhaps by cutting out some of the UNRELIABLE items and slightly rearranging the others; or, perhaps, by revising his operationalization strategy rather more drastically, and actually producing some new methods of measurement. Perhaps, on the other hand, the pilot will give him confidence that his data are, at least, liable to be reasonably RELIABLE, and renew his determination to proceed with the research programme as planned.

But, of course, pilot surveys have their costs. And one of the problems raised by the research economics of the pilot is a sampling problem. For, clearly, the pilot sample must be comparable with the main sample in all relevant respects, but, given the incredible difficulties involved in obtaining most sorts of samples, one will often be loath to 'waste' a proportion of one's potential respondents by subsampling for the pilot from within the universe of the potential main sample. As always, one must simply aim for some kind of happy medium. But, of course, it must be remembered that, whatever expense is taken to establish RELIABILITY by, possibly repeated, pilot studies this will give no guarantee of the VALIDITY of the data.

Now you may well be having rather large doubts about the general VALIDITY of data stipulated as measurable in the modes of STIPS 31, 32, 33. For you may feel that, however loosely or rigidly structured they may be, such measuring instruments cannot produce data which can really be regarded as varying in those ways, *and only in those ways*, which may be assumed to be genuinely isomorphic with those of the variables defined by the theory under test.

And I am sure that the main burden of your doubt will fall upon the reasonableness of the assumption that the intrusions of the instruments themselves are irrelevant to the results which are obtained. For in the questionnaire and in the interview what is actually happening at the first-order level must always be a real dialogue which is continually being reshaped by the expectations and habitual modes of thought employed by the researchers on the one hand and the respondents on the other. Different respondents, and indeed different researchers, will play the research game in varying styles. And these stylistic variations must always be regarded as extraneous and plausibly confounding variables which are active in the measurement context. Thus the wise researcher will anticipate these variables, he will document them in detail and, wherever possible, he will attempt to control them.

As with all variables, these hypothesized effects of the measurement process itself may be controlled either by selection or by direct measurement. Thus, for example, a single highly structured self-administered questionnaire may be employed on the assumptions that the variables *emphasis, ordering, length of response*, etc. have been controlled by selection – because they have been rendered constant for all respondents (each questionnaire form looks exactly the same). In the interview situation, on the other hand, those assumptions cannot be made, and so the variables must be controlled by means of additional and independent measurements. Thus the interview data might be supplemented with information on, say, the number of times the interviewer 'probed' the respondent before the latter gave his answer, and other details, such as the way the respondent was sitting in his chair, the points at which he leaned forward, and so on.[56] But I am sure that, once you begin to speculate upon the lengths to which this line of argument can be drawn, you will realize that, again, a compromise must be reached. For, of course, the more you record the more you intrude.[57]

Recognition of the problems of bias which are necessarily involved in the stipulation of data to be measured by intrusive instrumentation brings us to the fourth and final strategy for location of recorders *vis-à-vis* the datum universe.

Some sociologists have recently turned their attention to those sorts of data which may be stipulated on the assumption that measurements are being made in an *obtrusive* manner. Rather than attempting to ignore the problems of differential interpretation and expectation of respondents and investigators – or, at best including them in the research design as extraneous and plausibly confounding variables – these writers have advocated the deliberate exploitation of the interactions between first- and second-order definitions during the measurement process itself.

Of course it is impossible to stipulate *tangible* data in an obtrusive way. And, while one may stipulate *personal*, or demographic, data for obtrusive instrumentation I cannot see why anyone would ever want to do so. The same information could be obtained more cheaply by one or more of the nine other methods (STIPS 4–6, 16–18, or 25–7). Thus obtrusive instrumentation will only be considered with regard to the last two levels of definition of the unit datum, that is *behavioural* and *processual*.

The strategy behind data STIPS 34-6 is contrived and obtrusive intervention in the first-order reality in which the observations are to be made. The researcher stipulating his data in these modes does not assume that things would have happened in much the same way if he, his assistants, and/or his machinery, were not there to observe them, nor does he attempt merely to control for the effects of their interference. Instead he employs a variation of the basic strategy of physical manipulation of variables, that is, a sort of experiment.

In its obtrusive, or 'ethnomethodological', mode the experiment is regarded as a real first-order encounter. Respondents and researchers face each other with the various paradigm-determined expectations that shape their respective worlds-taken-for-granted, and then, as in any other real-life situation, they attempt to establish a grounding of shared expectations, a working background of mutuality. The researchers are not assumed to be any less real than the respondents. Both achieve the ongoing process of mutual reality construction against an implicit, and sometimes explicit, background of a whole variety of social understandings attaching not only to their roles as researcher and respondents, but to their many other social affiliations. For it is well established sociological *KEPT KNOWLEDGE* that social interaction involves the implicit recognition of, and continual bargaining over, *latent* as well as manifest roles.[58]

> It is true that here and there we can pounce on a moment when an individual sits fully astride a single role, head erect, eyes front, but the next moment the picture is shattered into many pieces and the individual divides into different persons holding the ties of different spheres of life by his hands, by his teeth, and by his grimaces.

Like the respondents, the investigators have real prejudices and styles of sociability, some of them are aware of themselves as 'attractive young ladies', some of them are 'warm and frank', some are 'a real laugh', some are 'fatherly', some are 'prudes', some 'helpful', some 'aloof', etc. And the various understanding they bring into the situation will have been shaped by their varied biographical experiences (what-they-have-been-doing-to-whom-with-what in the real lives which preceded the experiment).

Yet this does not necessarily mean that the ethnomethodological experiment is an *informal* encounter. For the researcher is not, as in the case of STIPS 7–12, attempting to disguise the fact that he is engaged in the activity of 'doing sociological research'. On the contrary, he is openly playing the role of 'social scientist' and, just as openly, alter-casting the respondent as 'guinea pig'.[59] Thus it may well be that, even where the encounter takes place in an informal setting (such as the subject's own house, a coffee bar, etc.), a fair amount of formality must characterize his style of play. The researcher must face the fact that, if he is to maintain his credibility as a *bona fide* scientist, he must behave in some appropriate manner. But, as understandings of the nature of the activity 'doing sociological research' will presumably vary for different social locations, these should normally be regarded as empirically problematic. So, unless previous work can provide the necessary information, the researcher who is attempting to effect ethnomethodological experimentation must undertake a preliminary investigation of the social world of his destination: He must 'suss out' the norms to which he will be expected to conform.[60] On the other hand, of course, deliberate violation of those norms (for example, over- or under-formality, or, say, personal or sexual insinuations) may be the intention of the experimenter.

Clearly the stipulation of data in this manner promises some exciting possibilities for sociologists! But the cells reserved for STIPS 34, 35 and 36 in the MATRIX are empty of LIBRARY references. For the ethnomethodological experiment has never, to my knowledge, been employed by sociologists in an explicitly theory-testing, that is to say *risky*, manner. This is because 'ethnomethodological research' has always been shaped by a metatheoretic commitment to idealism on the one hand and inductivism on the other.[61] Ethnomethodologists are thus led to approach their work in a verificationist frame of mind. They reject the GOLD-STAR plea that the circumstances of theorizing are inadmissable as evidence in judgments of $truth_4$. This is quite clear in the following statement.[62]

the inseparability of theory and research is ensured by treating methodology, not as the manipulation of a set of given research techniques, as is the case in conventional sociology, but as *the processes by which a sociologist generates an abstract view of a situation*. The processes of observation, selection, interpretation, and abstraction constitute the sociologist's methods of constructing his 'theory'. In this sense, methodology comprises *how* the sociologist decides *what* social phenomena are relevant to his descriptive project at hand, and how he deals with these in developing his account or theory. Methodology, therefore, includes all the processes by which a theory is constructed. Unless we can reconstruct the processes through which the observer moves from his observations of the social world to his conceptual description of it we are in no position to evaluate this description; without this clarification our interpretation of his description has to rest on a series of taken-for-granted commonsense assumptions which allow us to implicitly assume that we 'know what the observer means'. Conventional sociology fails to treat these commonsense assumptions as problematic.

Clearly then, from a GOLD-STAR point of view, methods of ethnomethodological experimentation *as they have been used in the past* cannot be regarded as having produced VALID data. Rather they must be seen as formalized procedures for frustrating first-order expectations in the hope of frustrating sociologists to the pitch of inspiration for second-order theorizing. Whether or not all this 'needle', 'hassle', and 'hovver' is justified by the end has yet to be established.

But if ethnomethodologists are decadent and arrogant enough to conceive of themselves as existential Messiahs they will continue to couch their justifications in terms of motives which are straight out of science fiction.[63] Consider these strange words for example: 'In this sense sociology's contribution is to clarify for members their involvement in the social world.'[64] *That* is the sort of sense that comes from mistaking a jelly pie for a transcendental mushroom![65]

Yet there is no reason why ethnomethodological techniques of experimentation could *not* be used in an explicit theory-testing programme. For example, a research team with highly visible videotape machinery, or, say, closed-circuit television, could obtrude into all kinds of everyday situations and obtain recordings in respect of the actions of people who were quite aware of the fact that they had been singled out in that manner. An example of the sort of data which might be stipulated in this fashion might be, say, the actual reactions of people to the filming itself (though, if that were to be the case, it would be advisable to supplement data in the mode of STIP 36, by 'control' data in the mode of STIP 9, i.e. by recordings made with the aid of *hidden* machinery).[66]

In addition to recording reactions to the recordings themselves, ethnomethodologically inclined researchers could also devise experiments for the generation of other sorts of clearly stipulated data. This kind of theory-testing research has never been exploited properly by sociologists, who might do well to take a leaf out of the Situationists' stunt-book by devising experiments in which a cheap and easily accomplished intervention in a real-life situation might be expected to have very dramatic ramifications. Just ponder upon the possibilities of this stunt, for example.

A research assistant, dressed as Father Christmas, and carrying an empty sack, wanders into the toy department of Selfridges, just before Christmas. Another assistant in a white coat then comes in with a chair; and he is followed by others carrying various additional props, such as a set of steps covered in crepe paper. 'Father Christmas' makes himself comfortable on the chair and the other assistants announce his presence to the children and parents, before withdrawing to man their tape-recorders and notebooks. When the kids go up and sit on 'Father Christmas's' knee he asks them what they want for Christmas, telling each that he can have anything on display in the toy department. Each time he gets up and picks up a toy to present it to a child, the white-coated assistants chant 'Christmas is a time for giving'. Various data on the reactions of the kids and their parents to this strange happening can be recorded, and there is much that the resourceful researcher can squeeze out of the situation. But the stipulated data will include some more dramatic observations: the arrival of the police; the reactions of the children and parents to the spectacle of policemen taking toys back from the children to the accompaniment of the continuing chants of the research team: 'Christmas is a time for giving', etc. See what I mean?

If one could find people foolhardy enough to assist in such an experiment, the data obtained in that fashion would be valid as evidence for the testing of certain hypotheses, that is, *provided that those data were clearly and precisely stipulated in advance of the actual happening*.[67]

There are just three modes of stipulating data left in the White Knight's box of tricks, STIPS 37, 38 and 39. We may, perhaps, group these together under the rather ambiguous label 'participant observation'. But it is important to remember that researchers measuring data in these ways are not *disguised* as participants, but regard themselves, and are regarded on the first-order level, as real actors engaged in a real process of meaning construction. For the researcher who has stipulated his data to be units of meaningful expression to be measured by obtrusive instrumentation does so in explicit recognition of those first- and second-order assumptions which, he claims, 'the human observer of human beings cannot escape – having to participate in some fashion in the experience and action of those he observes'.[68]

Whether the data to be measured are regarded as rigidly structured (STIP 37), loosely structured (STIP 38), or unstructured (STIP 39), the techniques of 'participant observation' must necessarily revolve around the assumptions which the researcher makes with regard to his own role-playing, as that is reflected in the expressions of meaning which he and the other participants will create together. Thus, as Cicourel has said, 'The problem is managing one's appearance and action before others.'[69] And, of course, that management must be effected against a relevant background of both first- and second-order assumptions about the nature of the world in which it takes place. On the level of first-order meaning, then, the 'participant observer' must have adequate knowledge and skill to gain acceptance from the 'natives'. So where the datum universe is defined as a cultural segment of which the researcher actually does have ordinary, everyday, common-sense, bio-graphical knowledge, one sort of problem of participation is considerably reduced. He will know what to do, when, where and how, if he is to be awarded a normal first-order status.

But there is more to participation than protocol: expressions of meaning are very subtle and fragile involutes. There will almost always be relatively few human beings with whom one can achieve that 'rapport' or 'sympathy' which comes from the sharing of a whole paradigm of thoughts, even for a few moments of ¿time?. For it is a rare person indeed who can readily and effortlessly maintain a shared reality with more than a few close friends or family members.

Of course, veteran 'participant observers' will enjoy a fairly high degree of initial familiarity in a rather wider range of worlds than would be the case for, say, country bumpkins. Many sociologists are proud of the fact that they can make a pretty good job of making themselves at home with a variety of different sorts of people, from, say, public schoolboys to street gangs, from old-age pensioners to members of parliament, from other sociologists, to other people's wives. That is to say that clever sociologists are sophisticated in 'passing',[70] they know how to be taken for 'one of us'. They are skilled at throwing themselves into an appropriate fantasy identity and at buttressing and defending that identity with the aid of materials provided by their own real, though more than slightly rewritten, biographies.

But what of *being together*? What of real participation? What of the sort of total immersion in a meaningful mutuality which might find expression in loud and bawdy in-joking, or deep-seated insults, on the one hand, or, on the other hand, in that kind of silent emotional touching which excludes even eye contact. These cannot be played at. No amount of sophistication in role-playing can fit a sociologist for real participation. For expressions of genuine mutuality are expressions of something which transcends both the first-order and the second-order thoughts which may be taken for granted. They are expressions of love.

A rare description of loving participation is given in the following passage.[71]

There is a particular sort of intimacy between the three of us which is not of our creating and which has nothing to do with our talk, yet which is increased in our tones of voice, in small quiet turns of humor, in glances of the eyes, in ways even that I eat my food, in their knowledge how truly friendly I feel toward them, and how seriously I am concerned to have caused them bother, and to let them be done with this bother as quickly as possible. And the best in this – it will be hard to explain unless you know something of women in this civilization – is the experiencing of warmth and of intimacy toward a man and his wife at the same time (for this would seldom happen, it being the business of a wife to serve and to withdraw). I felt such an honor in her not just staying at more distance, waiting to clear up after me, but sitting near, almost equal in balance with her husband, and actually talking; and I began even through her deep exhaustion to see such pleasant and seldom warmth growing in her, in this shifted status and acceptance in it, and such a kindly and surprised current of warmth increasing through this between her husband and her, a new light and gentle novelty spreading a prettiness in her face that, beyond a first expostulation that she get back to her rest and leave me to clean off the table, I not only scarcely worried for her tiredness, or her husband's, but even somewhat prolonged the while we sat there, shamed though I was to do so, and they wakened, and warmed to talking, even while fatigue so much more heavily weighed them under, till it became in the scale of their sleeping an almost scandalously late-night conversation, in which we were all leaned toward each other in the lamplight secretly examining the growth of friendliness in one another's faces, they opening further speaking as often as I and more often: while nevertheless there stole up my quiet delight from the pit of my stomach a cold and sickening shame to be keeping them up.

Mutual worlds are created and maintained through love, just as they may be destroyed through careless intellectualism. If a researcher cannot feel himself as a human being, then, even setting aside the considerable moral implications of that failure,[72] it should be obvious from a pragmatic point of view that he will not end up with the data he wants. As an Indian villager once said to an American anthropologist: 'You may be a foreigner and we only poor villagers, but when we get to know you we will judge you as a man among other men; not as a foreigner.'[73]

And yet for the 'participant observer' the fruits of loving participation must still, somehow, be regarded at another ¿time? as mere *data*, valid at the second-order level of meaning! If he is to return to his research desk with evidence, with measures of stipulated indicators of theoretically defined variables, then the 'participant' must be an 'observer' too. The successful researcher stipulating data in these modes must, then, manage two roles, two ways of being in the real world of his data, one which makes deep demands on his heart and soul, and one which necessitates some quite extraordinary feats of intellectual chastity.

Recognizing the theoretical, practical, and moral problems posed by the competing demands of the 'participant' role on the one hand and the 'observer' role on the other, commentators on the methods and techniques of 'participant observation' have suggested that four modes of role-playing can be distinguished.[74]

Complete Participant [who] 'is or becomes a complete member of an in-group, thus sharing secret information guarded from outsiders.'

Participant as Observer . . . 'a pseudo-"Member of the Wedding".'[75]
Observer as Participant . . . 'The role may provide access to a wide range of information and even secrets may be given to the field-worker when he becomes known for keeping them, as well as for guarding confidential information. In this role the social scientist might conceivably achieve maximum freedom to gather information but only at the price of accepting maximum constraints upon his reporting.'
Complete Observer . . . 'his activities are completely public in a special kind of theoretical group where there are, by consensus, "no secrets" and "nothing sacred".'

These four types of roles are often regarded as arranged along a single continuum. Thus the polar types 'Complete Participant' and 'Complete Observer' are more or less seen as mere restrictions on the definitions of the two combination types. So it is by contrasting the roles of 'Participant as Observer' and 'Observer as Participant' with the extreme types that their nature as variations on the theme of 'participant observation' can be appreciated. But perhaps it is more helpful to think of these two types of approach to fieldwork as two of many points in social ¿time? which may be located by consideration of *two* continua. The complete participant is separated from the complete observer by differences in levels of second-order as well as of first-order awareness. And these two dimensions of consciousness will tend to pull in opposite directions. Perhaps it helps to see it like this:

Degree of first-order patterning of appearances	ROLE PLAYED WITH RESPECT TO DATUM UNIVERSE Complete participant	Degrees of second-order patterning of appearances
High ↑	Participant as Observer Observer as Participant	Low ↓
Low		High
	Complete Observer	

Yet, in my view, it is a mistake to assume that the researcher can never adopt either of the two extreme roles, that some elements of both first- and second-order patterning must *always* be at work in his perception of appearances. Rather, as it seems to me, the researcher stipulating his data in modes 37, 38 and 39 may be viewed as shifting his stance towards his data in ¿time?. So the changing relations between the researcher and the emerging universe of his datum might better be represented in the form of a sort of '¿time?-graph'.

In order to draw such a graph one must begin with the assumption that, at the ¿time? of *initial* definition of the datum universe, or 'field' as it is usually called, second-order definitional imperatives are being superimposed upon an ongoing reality which is already defined clearly at the first-order level. The 'field' may therefore be regarded, from a methodological viewpoint, as enclosed by the hedges of first-order consciousness on the one hand, and the ditches of second-order require-ments on the other (Fig. 36).

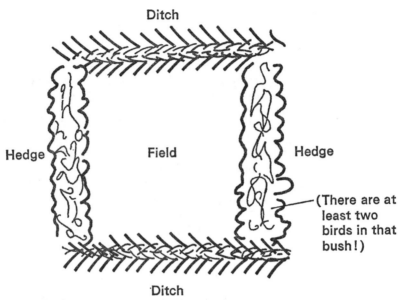

FIGURE 36

First-order consciousness increases as you move from right to left across the 'field', and second-order consciousness becomes more dominant as you move down the 'field'. But second-order consciousness can only roam within the logical ditches marking the zero limit on the one hand and the other arbitrary polar value, 'I', on the other. And, in a different way, first-order consciousness can only become real some-where between the hedgerows marking social rejection – or zero under-standing – on the one hand and unity on the other (Figure 37).

Now some of the problems and pitfalls of 'participant observation' can be illustrated by considering the motions of a hypothetical bunny RABBIT entering the 'field' through a small rabbit hole in the right-hand hedge. Let us pretend that he has been cavorting about in the field as in Figure 38.

Our hypothetical RABBIT enters the 'field' through the rabbit hole

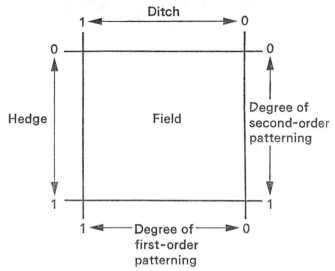

FIGURE 37

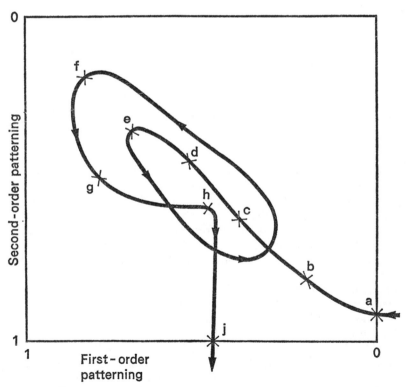

FIGURE 38

at '*a*'. At this point in ¿time? his perceptive propensities are entirely shaped by his paradigm of taken-for-granted *second-order* assumptions. He approaches his datum universe as an academic and a complete out-sider, what he sees at this point in ¿time? he sees entirely through his second-order spectacles. But, before he can do anything else at all, he must find a way of approaching the 'natives' and establishing some kind of initial entry into their world. In order to do this he must start to develop some, albeit minimal, first-order consciousness (perhaps, for example, he would need to begin by learning an entirely foreign language). As Bruyn says of this stage of 'fieldwork':[76]

> One problem in making a successful entree is effectively defining the researcher's social role. In his work *Urban Villagers*, Herbert Gans gives us some initial information on how he was able to solve this problem. He felt that he could not define his role as an 'observer' who studied the everyday lives of those with whom he came into contact, for it would make people uncomfortable and end the spontaneity of his relationships with them. He felt he could not discuss all his purposes directly with his subjects, but he could discuss some of them and have them accepted. Gans therefore described his scientific role in terms of making a historical survey of the organizations and institutions of the area, a method that was both honest and inoffensive, for such a definition was understandable and of interest to those he studied and quite compatible with his aims. In this way, he was able to function as an official researcher without producing unnecessary anxieties.

Thus, by ¿time? '*b*' the fieldworker has established some initial first-order existence, albeit in terms of some marginal social role such as 'scientist', 'historian', 'stranger', 'foreigner', or even, 'sociologist'. Now it may be that he will be content to maintain this relationship with his datum universe, stipulating his data in terms of the sorts of measure-ments that can readily be made from that sort of viewpoint. This is particularly likely to be the case where the data are to be STIP 37. Thus 'participant observation' of the compilation of official statistics and other rigidly structured data has often been made from the standpoint of minimal participation. Sociologists and officials-doing-compiling-statistics have certainly achieved an 'informal' and 'friendly' level of discussion, and reports of this kind of research reveal that it has often been characterized by much bonhomie and good humour.[77] But none the less the data thus stipulated must be assumed to differ from those which might be measured by observers who had gained a different level of acceptance from the 'natives'. This is quite clear in the following excerpt from a research publication.[78]

By this time I was fairly well known to several of the deputy district attorneys who had met me while I was looking over the shoulders of men on the public defender's staff. I suggested to the head of the public defender's office that I would like to see how 'the other half' lived. Through his recommendation, plus an extended interview with the district attorney, I was permitted to become a participant-observer in that office. After several weeks of observation in the office of the Westville district attorney, it seems important to know more about the work of the police. . . . With this in mind, I asked my 'contacts' in the prosecutor's office if it would be possible to arrange observation of the police carrying out their duties. . . . The Chief of Police was willing to entertain the idea. It is again important to emphasize that this police department regarded itself as exemplary. . . . The chief was known as a man who ran a taut ship. . . . His attitude toward the research was made up partly of cooperation and partly of the defiance of a sensitively placed public official who feels he has done a commendable job and can say, 'Go ahead and look at anything you want. Not only do we have nothing to hide in this department, but we are desirous of having our story told. We don't want a whitewash, but we do want you to be objective and truthful.' On these terms my observations of the Westville Police Department began.

But let us now pretend that our cavorting bunny RABBIT has decided to aim for fuller participation in the meaningful world of his datum universe. He will eventually move from 'b' to 'c', at which point in ¿time? he may be regarded as having attained the real status of a 'newcomer', not an outsider, as at 'b', but a potential insider.[79]

If he continues in the same ¿direction?, our exemplary researcher will soon find that he has reached point 'd' where his perceptions are already tending to be shaped more in terms of a natural first-order commitment to and belief in the native paradigm, rather than in terms of the academic frame of reference with which he initially entered the field. Perhaps we may describe his role at ¿time? 'd' as that of 'temporary member'. Thus the next significant role change might be regarded as that which will take place when, say at ¿time? 'e', he has moved even further towards the top left-hand corner of the 'field' and has really begun to 'take part in the socialization process . . . as do other true members . . . to the point where his inner experience can reflect the "unity and structure of the whole" '.[80] Let us call this stage of role-playing the stage of the '$true_2$ learner'.

Now this is the point at which many 'participant observers' begin to experience the stresses and strains of role-change. Some deliberately backtrack here, moving away from first-order commitment back towards the identity promised by the academic role. I have pretended that our imaginary 'participant observer' has withdrawn a little, but, on re-examining his dilemmas from the perspective of his research requirements, has taken a few deep breaths and rushed headlong back into the arms of the 'natives'. Thus at point 'f' he has become a whole member, a loving participant, his thoughts and feelings are in tune with those fellow human beings whom he had once intended to regard as subjects for sociological research. So it is hardly surprising that many researchers have been lost to social science at this stage of 'participant observation'. What PhD student feeling himself as a Zuni Indian, inducted as a Priest of the Bow, could wish to return to write up his 'data' for the paleface sociologists?[81] Which 'one of us' would take a last drag on the pipe and then steal off into the night to write up his field-notes?[82]

But if our imaginary RABBIT is to complete his research he must move on in ¿time? to the point 'g', that of the 'imminent migrant',[83] and thus start to draw his consciousness back towards the bottom and the right. Perhaps at some ¿time? he will reach the pitch of field-work schizo-phrenia at 'h' where he is torn apart by the conflicting ethical impera-tives of first- and second-order consciousness. Can he ever 'tell it like it is' in the sort of second-order language which must characterize valid evidence? And, if he *can*, *should* he? He will feel that there are more questions than answers. And it will be his heart, as much as his head, which is troubled.[84]

Perhaps, however, he will survive these crises to leave the field at point 'j'. But notice that this is not the same point as that at which he entered it. He can never move back to the extreme right. He will never again be able to regard as mere 'respondents', as clusters of measure-ments, as units of data, those with whom he has actually *been together* in the same world at the same ¿time?.

Chapter 18

Coder Coda

Now let us make a most unlikely assumption. Let us suppose that you have survived as a sociologist *and* produced all the stipulated data!

You have done all the shopping on the RABBITS' shopping list of *Variables to be Measured*. So you now have all the evidence required to subject your hypotheses to some genuinely risky tests, that is to make some assessments about the truth$_4$ of your theory.

But I should imagine that you are now feeling quite as queasy as was Likee-O when, after labouring for seven years, he found that he had cut off the heads of enough poppies to give such plenteous opium as to make the whole world dream for a month of Sundays.

'Wise man no smokee poppee', as the ancient lore has it. The mystic essence must be correctly extracted and prepared according to the time-honoured rituals. And, likewise, 'labbit no puttee flogs' legs in computer'. What now confronts you as a great assemblage of initial or *raw data* must somehow be translated into the form of *symbolic data*. Before you are a lot of ticks, crosses, underlinings, handwritten remarks, pieces of film, diaries, documents, photographs, tables of statistics, maps, tape-recordings, score-sheets, candles, feathers, pieces of paper, frogs' legs and goodness knows what else. Somehow this mess of measurement must be translated into a form of language which is so abstract and so simple that it can be written down clearly and unambiguously as a patterning of standardized symbols. And, since social science research usually makes use of the *STATISTICAL* method of manipulating variables, at some stage or other, it is likely that you will wish this language to be one which can be understood by a computer, counter-sorting machine, or other mechanical calculator. So you will be aiming to represent every scrap of valid evidence by some kind of series of little rectangular holes on a computer card.[1] Eventually, then, you will be able to stop worrying about the possibility of the research unit burning down and your data being destroyed. For the place in your affections originally held by your *raw data* will have been taken by a few packs of punched cards. And, since these things are infinitely reproducible, you can deposit a deck or two in the bank, keep one under your pillow at night, or even tear them up for whatever-it-is-that-people-tear-up-Hollerith-cards!

The first stage in the process of translating data from the *raw* into the *symbolic* form involves another decision. It is necessary to *define the coding units* before a *coding frame* can be devised.

Coding units, or *cases*, are not, of course, the same as datum units, and they may or may not be identical with the units sampled. These units are to be regarded as *sets of data*, that is as configurations of measurements. Thus coding units may be individual people, organizations, countries, households, books, towns, dustbins, moments, or what-have-you, and each such unit will be fully described in terms of a set of stipulated measurements, even if these be purely qualitative. For example, in a typical questionnaire survey the datum units are defined as individual measures of certain attitudes, opinions etc., and these units are grouped together into 'cases' – that is, individual respondents – which provide the basic units for both sampling and coding purposes. On the other hand, where data have been stipulated, say, via ethno-methodological experimentation, the coding units may be individual happenings, rather than people. Similarly, an entire written document may be regarded as a unit for purposes of coding. Thus specification of coding units will clearly be dependent upon the previous research decision, particularly the sampling decisions and the stipulation of data. But, at the same time, decisions about arrangements of data in sets for coding purposes must also be guided by the imperatives of the methods of *data analysis* which the researcher is anticipating.

Once coding units have been established, the *coding sheets* can be produced. A coding sheet is simply a piece of paper with eighty empty slots labelled from '1' to '80'.[2] There will be one or more coding sheets for each coding unit, and it is on these forms that the *raw* data will first appear in its new, coded, or *symbolic* state. Somehow the stipulated measurements are to be represented on these sheets in a single-digit number code. So, by the time the process called *coding* is completed, each coding sheet will look a little like this,

1. _____2_____   2. _____4_____   3. _____8_____

4. _____1_____   5. _____0_____   6. _____3_____

7. _____4_____   8. _____5_____   9. _____6_____

etc. (to '80')

And once *that* has been done the next task is to transfer this numerical data on to *computer cards*. A computer card looks like Figure 39.

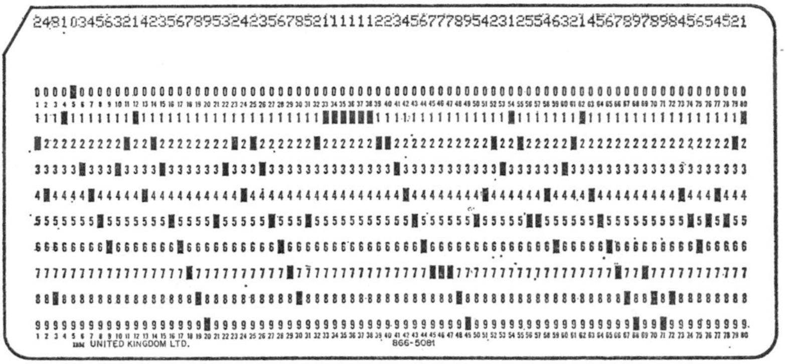

FIGURE 39

As you can see, the card has eighty spaces horizontally. These are known as *columns*, and they correspond with the eighty slots on the coding sheets. Vertically each column is divided into ten *rows* which are numbered with the digits '1–9' plus the '0'. Each unit of *symbolic data* is represented, quite simply, by a little hole in the card. Thus, for example, a '1' in the fourth slot on the *coding sheet* might refer to the observation that a particular case – i.e. person – is 'male'. This scrap of information is then represented on the computer card by a small rectangular hole in 'column' 4, 'row' 1. Thus *punching symbolic data* onto the *computer cards* from the *coding sheets* is simply a matter of making the appropriate holes in the right places. This is done with a large machine like a grotesque typewriter. They are simple, but extremely tiresome to operate. So the researcher with few moral scruples about the monetary value of other people's ¿time? will usually get someone else to do it for him.

Now, by the time *coding* and *punching* is complete you have a load of computer cards which you *must* assume to represent all the evidence stipulated as relevant to the testing of the hypotheses in question. Each card[3] now stands for a case. So here, at last, you have the deputies for which you were searching. You can never observe your variables themselves, because they cannot get out of FAIRYLAND, but here, instead, you have some very tangible things which can be manipulated in their place. You can now 'cut', 'sort', 'break', and generally 'muck about with' your packs of cards, manipulating and controlling the variables represented upon them in a manner which may well be regarded as isomorphic with the rituals of the actual physical experimenter.

But, of course, the crucial business that remains to be explained is just *how* you go about translating the *raw data* into the single-digit number code. Somehow coding must take place so that, '*all* of the relevant content [can] be analyzed in terms of *all* of the relevant categories for the problem at hand.'[4] Clearly then, the greater the degree of structuring in the presentation of the initial or *raw* data, the easier it will be to code the material. Where, on the other hand, the initial data confronts the researcher in a form which, at the second-order level, may be regarded as entirely unstructured, the business of devising and applying a coding frame will be the most delicate and difficult phase of his whole research programme. I shall therefore consider structured (that is both 'rigidly structured' and more 'loosely structured') and unstructured data separately. First, I shall discuss some straightforward techniques for creating coding frames for structured data, and the procedures for coding those data; and then I shall go on to talk about the problems involved in attempting to code unstructured data, and the vexed question of coding for so-called 'qualitative data analysis'.

Creating a coding frame for structured data

Before coding can take place you must, of course, create a *coding frame*, that is to say that you must set down the keys to the codes you intend to employ. Here is a simple procedure.

1. *List the 'questions asked' in order of asking.* Now obviously the more structured the mode of data collection the easier this will be. At one extreme they are already listed for you on a postal questionnaire; then, for example, some of your data may have been formulated in terms of questions which you imagined yourself asking yourself as you consulted various documents and records (for instance, 'How much rain fell on Mississippi in 1937?'); then, in the case of data which is very loosely structured (say the informal interview) you may have not *asked* any specific questions but simply carried on a conversation with certain questions in mind.

2. *Note by each question the variable it is designed to measure.* And, as this measurement will be one of a number of indicators selected to represent that variable you may like to give this particular indicator its own label. For example, if you are calling the variable 'Socioeconomic background' by the pet name 'SECLASS', you may label a question about father's schooling 'SECLASS: (2)', or, say, an assessment of the furniture in the front room[5] 'SECLASS: (9)', etc.

3. *Note by each question the kind of scaling that will be employed.* Notice whether you are intending nominal, ordinal, interval, or ratio scaling.

4. *Now decide upon the code.* With a completely precoded item this is, of course, straightforward. Suppose, for example, that you have a precoded question with a five-point scale of agreement:

CODE

definitely agree	1
agree	2
neither agree or disagree	3
disagree	4
definitely disagree	5

But even in such a simple case as that there are a couple of important points to bear in mind in deciding upon the coding. First, *DON'T CONFUSE YOURSELF.* Keep all the scales going the same way then you will have less to remember when it comes to data analysis, and it is *much* easier for the coders (even if the coder is you!). This is to say that if you have a lot of agreement/disagreement type items, always label the greatest degree of agreement '1' and proceed from there. Of course, you will remember that the *instruments themselves* will not all be going the same way – in fact they *should* not[6] – so sometimes '5' for one question may *mean* the exact opposite of '5' for the following question. But it is even more important to *AVOID CONFUSING THE COMPUTER.* For while *you* can make adjustments for your own stupidities and errors the computer can only do exactly as it is told. Thus you must remember that the computer may have to read your punched cards, so show it the courtesy of presenting them in a completely unambiguous way. This means that you must never punch more than one hole in each column,[7] and that you must stick to a standard interpretation of the symbol 'o'. I suggest that you reserve the zero for a real nothing, that is, for a complete blank or non-response. Do not confuse the computer by occasionally using the zero to signify something else, such as 'Don't know', 'Uncertain', 'No', 'No children', 'No education after secondary school', 'Not married', 'No previous experience', or anything else. Use the zero only for a complete blank, for no information at all.[8]

Less structured items are more difficult to code, but the general principles are the same. Here are some examples.

Example: Father's occupation

	CODE
modified Hall-Jones occupational scale, 7 categories[9]	1–7
unemployed	8
dead	9 (N.B. *not* o)

Example: School history

Question 'Have you been at *this* school ever since you left junior school? . . . Yes . . . No (*Tick One*). If you ticked 'No', write below the names of any other *secondary* schools to which you have been.'

Note that this question required a knowledge on the part of the coder of all the other schools in the area, their names and their type.

ANSWER	CODE
This school	1
Other school, same type	2
Other school, Grammar	3
Other school, Comprehensive	4
Other school, Secondary Modern	5
Other school, Private, Special	6

Example: IQ

SCHOOL RECORD OF SCORE	CODE
below 70	1
71–80	2
81–90	3
etc.	
above 131	8

(N.B. you want as much spread as possible, but you've only got 9 rows to play with; no overlap – *not* 70–80, 80–90 etc.)

5. *Now you can decide upon the arrangement of the columns.* You have worked out which rows to code various responses in, the next thing to do is to decide which columns to use for what. Obviously this is a completely arbitrary matter, and it makes no difference at all whether, for example, 'SECLASS: (7)' is punched in column 2 or in column 72. But there are a number of practical problems of arrangement of data on computer cards, and though you would certainly find these out for yourself and devise some techniques for solving them, it seems to me pointless to waste ¿time? and energy on such trifles.

So you may find the following suggestions of help.

(a) *Use the first few columns for the case number.* Obviously each coding unit, each 'case' (for example, say, each respondent) must have an identifying label which will have to be punched on the card as a number. But you can economize on columns by using meaningful case numbers. For example, in one piece of research, I was faced with coding material arranged in terms of individual children's responses to questionnaires. Each questionnaire (representing one child's views) was therefore a coding unit. There were three schools, several streams in each school, and several kids in each stream.[10] So I labelled the schools 1, 2 and 3; numbered the streams in each school from 1 (reputed to be 'top' stream); and numbered the children in register order within each stream.

My first four columns were thus coded like this:

SCHOOL   coded in column 1
STREAM   coded in column 2

CHILDREN coded in columns 3 and 4 (numbered from 01 to 35 across the two columns)

So the first child on the register in the A stream of the school called '1' had been denoted by the name '1101' and the fifteenth child in the fourth stream of the third school was nicknamed '3415' etc. But at the same time, if I wanted to select all the A stream children for some reason I'd merely have to sort the cards on column 2, selecting all those which were punched '1' on that column; and, if I wanted to select only the C stream children in school '2', I'd sort on column 1 first, then on column 2, selecting the '3's etc.

(b) *Group all the major control variables together in the columns immediately following the case number.* Thus, for example, 'sex' might be coded in column 5, residential area in column 6, an index of socioeconomic class in column 7 and so on.

(c) *Leave column 80 empty.* You'll see why in a minute.

Your data will now be grouped like this:

1–4	5–n	n–79	80
'L a b e l'	'Major control variables'	'Other variables'	➞ Empty
	(Block A)	(Block B)	

6. *Now what happens if you have more data than columns?* It may well have occurred to you that you may have more than about seventy-five separate items of information and only about seventy-five columns to fit it all in. Obviously then you *may* need *more* than one card per case. But it is *not* a simple matter of putting all the remaining information on a second card. For, in the analysis which you are going to do later, you may want to use a more primitive technique than the computer (especially when you are building indexes out of indicators), you may want to use a thing called a *counter-sorter*. This is just a great big thing with a mechanism a bit like an old-fashioned music box which runs across the pattern of holes on a particular column and drops the cards into different boxes according to which row they are punched in. If you're lucky it then counts how many cards are in each box and tells you by means of a thing like a milometer, but in my experience these rarely work, and you usually end up counting the cards yourself.

Now since you are going to be *'breaking'* (that's research jargon for selecting) on more than one variable at once, and often controlling for

a number of others as well, YOU WILL NEED ALL THE ITEMS YOU MIGHT WANT CORRELATED TOGETHER ON *ONE* CARD. It's no good saying 'We need to control for parental attitudes?' and then discovering that parental attitudes is on the other card.
So what you do is:

(a) Make out another card for each case identical with the first except for columns n-79 ('Block B').

(b) Punch 'I' in column 80 on the first card and '2' in column 80 on the second. (We now call them Card I and Card 2.)

(c) Punch the first half of Block B in on Card 2 and fill up the remainder (up to column 79) with the information there was no room for.

(d) Now take a third set of cards (again identical up to column n) and punch '3' on column 80. On this pack fill columns n-79 with the new information plus the rest of the Block B information that you didn't put on Card 2.

(Get the idea? You can obviously make dozens of cards per case if necessary.)

7. *Now get a largish hardbacked notebook and simply fill in all the above coding information* (it needs to be tough because it will get much more wear than a 'phone directory).

Try marking it out something like this:

Column	Question	Response	Notes	Code
I	(site)	Madvale loony bin		I
		Snotgrove loony bin		2
		Dementia loony bin		3
2	(ward)	Open ward		I
		Padded cells		2
3-4	(cases)	Case code on top of questionnaires		01-50
5	4*	under 18		I
		18-21		2
		22-30		3
		etc.		

*This refers to QUESTION 4 on the questionnaire which asks for age.

Repeat that whole procedure for each 'Card'. Though obviously you don't need to do it for the first 'n' columns.

Coding structured data

Once you have created your coding frame, the actual coding process for structured data is quite straightforward. Coding is simply a matter of transferring information from the *raw* state onto the coding sheets. Obviously there will be one coding sheet per computer card, so if you have decided to have more than one card per case, or coding unit, there will be more than one coding sheet for each.

Even for the more loosely structured items the coding ought to be regarded as an automatic process, so that it should be reasonable to assume that different coders will code the same information in precisely the same ways. Therefore if you are in any doubt about the unequivocality of your coding frame (particularly in the case of the more loosely structured questions) it will be desirable to check it by comparing the efforts of different coders with respect to the same information.

Punching

Provided the coding sheets are *clear* (don't write too small, block out errors clearly) punching is something that can be accomplished with speed and ease. The punching machine pushes the card to one column at a time, so that all you have to do is to focus your eyes on the appropriate column on the coding sheet, and tap the right key. Anyone can learn to touch-type on one of those machines in under half an hour. They duplicate automatically, so if you mess up column 79 you can simply duplicate the messed-up card up to column 78 and then carry on from there. Most units also have one or two 'verifiers', which are similar to the punching machines but they check rather than punch the cards. So once all your cards are punched you can repeat the process with the 'verifier' and eliminate the errors.

Let us now turn our attention to the much more thorny issues involved in the design of coding for unstructured data. Whether they be STIPS 3, 6, 9, 12, 15, 18, 21, 24, 27, 30, 33, 36 or 39, all unstructured data have one characteristic in common: they are totally uncoded when they initially confront the researcher. They are not arranged in any second-order categories at all, and hence, the stipulated indicators must somehow be rearranged into a form which *is* classifiable at the second-order level.

In the first place the researcher may find that *the choice of coding units* is a considerably more complicated matter when it is unstructured data that he is dealing with. But, of course, the choice must be made, just as some decisions about *level of definition of the units of data* must have been made in advance of the actual collation of data, indeed at the sampling stage.

Speaking specifically of STIPS 15, 18, 21 and 24, Galtung emphasizes the essential similarity of unstructured and structured data in this respect.[11]

Of course, the primary concern in choosing the unit of analysis is the theoretical or practical purpose of the study. The precise definition of the universe is as important here as everywhere else; sampling problems appear in exactly the same way. If the universe is 'everything written about something', it will usually have to be limited in four ways: precise indication of *where* (e.g., Norway), *when* (e.g., February to September 1959), what *medium* of communication (e.g., regular newspapers), and what *topic* (e.g., the invitation of Premier Khrushchev). Whether the whole universe should be taken or only a sample depends on the usual factors: size of the universe, precision needed, whether one can afford sampling errors in addition to other errors, etc. – content analysis is no different from other analyses in this regard.

As usual, the unit of analysis is that which one wants to characterize. There is no rule as to its level. It may be one single issue of a newspaper, it may be the paper *New York Times* as such in a given period, it may be editorials, it may be the headlines of editorials – it may be single movies or only scenes, it may be what is broadcast by a specific station, it may be a particular program, it may be the news and so on.

Once he has defined his units the researcher confronted by unstructured data can, like any other researcher, proceed to devise his coding frame.

Creating a coding frame for unstructured data

As with any other data, the type of classification to be effected by coding must necessarily be circumscribed by the requirements of the kind of analysis to which the data will, at last, be subjected. And, as we shall see in the following chapter, the researcher will have to decide whether he is to treat his data qualitatively or quantitatively; whether he is to consider his measures as attributes, or as variables amenable to at least nominal scaling; and whether he is to employ a frequency or a 'non-frequency' type of analysis. This is, then, simply to repeat that the researcher must be quite clear about what he has stipulated his data for, and hence what sort of categories he will be employing.

Whether you are looking at photographs, written words, videotapes, *ad hoc* descriptions of contrived happenings, or any other messes of first-order pottage, then you will have to find some unambiguous rules for coding this into second-order categories. The task is daunting indeed, but perhaps the following suggestions may be of assistance.

1. *First rearrange your data in terms of the coding units upon which you have now decided.* Thus, for example, you may cut up your videotapes

or sound recordings into units of ¿time?, newspaper editorials into column inches, happenings into 'phases', suicide notes into words, phrases, nouns, verbs, epithets, sentences, etc., diaries into days; or you might sort photographs of graffiti according to the locations in which they were found, divide up television programmes according to when they are broadcast and by which authority, etc., etc., according to whatever methods seem appropriate for your purposes.[12]

2. *Now take your list of variables to be measured and note by each variable the indicators which you intend to employ.* For example, in a programme devised to test certain hypotheses about the content of graffiti you may decide to take the mere presence or absence of derogatory labels for social or ethnic groups as an indicator of *'politicism'*. Then, again, you might choose to count the frequency of such terms in a set amount of graffiti and compare it with, say, frequency of occurrence of terms with a sexual content, or, say, names of football teams or individual players. You might make these frequency assessments by reference to the entire number of words in the messages considered, or, say, count only the nouns, or devise some other method of categorizing the graffiti for purposes of comparing this particular feature. Or, in the case of STIP 36, for example, you may choose certain bodily postures as indicators of responses to specific stimuli, perhaps even developing a Guttman-type scaling of degrees of response.[13] For instance, knitting of the brows might be considered a weaker response than, say, vigorous shaking of the head, which might in turn be considered weaker than stamping the foot or banging the chair, and all of these might finally be considered in comparison to the strongest kind of response which might be beating up the experimenter.

3. *Now note by each indicator the type of scaling to be employed.* And, where the indicators are simple attributes (that is simple dichotomies rather than scales of three or more values) note whether you are interested in mere presence or absence of the feature in question, or whether you intend counting the frequency of presence or absence in some clearly defined set of data.

4. *Now make a preliminary decision about the codes to be employed.* These codes may or may not be numerical. Thus, for example, where you have nominal scaling you may wish to use letter labels rather than numbers simply in order to emphasize the lack of ordinality of the categorization. And, where you are dealing with attributes only, you may prefer to use ticks and crosses or plus and minus signs.

Once you have your preliminary coding frame you are in a position to begin to check the unequivocality of your categories. For, where data are completely unstructured in their initial form, no previous estimations of the RELIABILITY of the data have been possible. Whereas the RELIABILITY of structured data may be estimated in advance of coding decisions, for unstructured d ta the question of RELIABILITY does not arise until the coding stage.

5. *Check the second-order RELIABILITY of your intended coding operations by employing a number of coders to code the same material with respect to your preliminary coding frame.* In this way the ambiguities of your intended categorizations will soon become visible, and by continued discussion with coders, and repeated revisions of the coding frame, you should be able to produce an eventual system of coding which may be regarded as RELIABLE in the sense that each coder will classify the same datum unit in terms of the same value as each other coder.

There is one final aspect of the tricky business of devising a coding frame for unstructured data which deserves your special consideration. This is the question of the extent to which coding procedures which have been established as RELIABLE at the second-order level may be regarded as *meaningful at the first-order level.* Does the kind of classification understood and consistently employed by your coders produce units of *symbolic data* which may reasonably be regarded as VALID indicators of the variables which you had intended to measure? Of course you can never *know*. But you can at least employ a negative check by introducing some means of estimating the *first-order* RELIABILITY of your coding methods.

6. *Check the first-order RELIABILITY of your intended coding operations by direct consultation with actual members of the datum universe within which the data were stipulated.* There are two major ways of doing this. Both require you to obtain a small sample of persons who may be regarded as natives residing within the same universe of meanings as those individuals or social groups who actually produced the artefacts, behaviour, or messages under consideration.[14] The first method involves persuading this sample to replicate the coding operations effected by your coders, and comparing the results with those of the professional coders. And the second method involves informal discussion with the sample of first-order 'judges' about the meanings of the various units of data and the criteria of selection and classification.[15]

If you succeed in producing a coding frame which seems to generate classifications of data which may be assumed to be RELIABLE both at the second- and at the first-order level, then, though your *symbolic data* may still be totally INVALID (in that you may still have failed to measure precisely what you intended to measure) your data are at least now on an equal footing with prestructured data.

Thus you can proceed to make decisions about the arrangement of the *symbolic data*. Perhaps you will wish to use computer cards, in which case you will follow the procedures for coding and punching which are outlined above for prestructured data. But perhaps all your indicators are being treated as attributes, rather than as many-valued variables, and, if you are dealing with a small number of coding units, or cases, you may prefer to use the more primitive McBee, or Cope-Chat card, which looks like Figure 40.

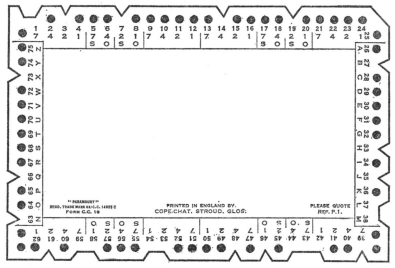

FIGURE 40

To use these cards all you need is patience, ingenuity, a pair of nail scissors, and a size '11' knitting needle. You simply take one (or more) card(s) to represent each coding unit and one of the holes around the edges of the card to represent each measurement (that is each separate indicator). For every 'positive', 'present', '+', '√' or what-have-you you cut a neat little V-shaped nick out of the card around the appropriate hole. And for each 'negative', 'absent', '—', '×', etc. you do nothing at all. Then, when you wish to analyse your data, you can select all the cases that are assigned a positive value on a specific measure by sticking the needle in, shaking the cards about a bit, and seeing which ones flutter to the floor!

So it has come to *this*? Thoughts, gestures, nuances of meaning, 'hard and heavy things', human hopes and fears, candles, feathers, and little bits of this and that, these have all been coaxed out of the contexts in which their realities inhere. And now they have been transformed into little nothings. For the purposes of the rituals of data analysis they have achieved a curious equality the one with the other. For each is now no more than a standard hole in a standard card.

Well, perhaps this is 'to make visible what to many appears as a lack of respect for human dignity and integrity. One may laugh or sneer at this attitude, but that does not change it.'[16]

Chapter 19

Statistricks!

Now that we have succeeded in transforming the results of our measuring operations into a standard numerical form we should be in a position to put our hypotheses to the test.

You will remember[1] that the *STATISTICAL* strategy for *manipulating variables to test hypotheses* is a sort of epic rewrite of the familiar logic of experimentation which is at the core of both common-sense reasoning and academic science. Where, for some reason or other, it is not possible to change the values of actual observables in order to test a hypothesis it may none the less be possible to *simulate* such manipulation by statistical rituals. Suppose, for example, that we had devised a theory from which we had derived the following hypothesis: 'The more extensive the sports coverage in a daily newspaper, the greater the popularity of that paper.'

In order to test that hypothesis by the ordinary method of *EXPERIMENTAL* manipulation of variables we would have to persuade the editor of at least one daily newspaper to vary the amount of space in the paper devoted to sport. Then we would be able to compare some measure of area of sports coverage with the daily sales figures for the newspaper(s). Obviously this would be a tricky, if not actually risible, project.[2]

A more practical strategy would involve selecting a number of newspapers by some theoretically relevant tactic, drawing a subsample of issues for each of the daily papers selected, measuring sports coverage on the sampled issues, summating these measures in some meaningful way, and comparing these data with the sales averages for certain ¿time? periods. This process of comparison would involve arranging the sampled units (issues of newspapers) in various ways according to the independent variable (sports coverage), and observing the concomitant fluctuations of the dependent variable (popularity).[3]

Perhaps it is helpful to visualize this process as an actual physical sorting activity. Imagine for the moment that we have a deserted CRICKET PITCH, a real copy of each of the sampled newspaper issues, some information about sales of the newspapers concerned, and a number of Bongy Wongese research assistants to help us with the piling up.

The sample issues are first coded according to the area in which each is covered by sport. Let us pretend that the Bongy Wongese have taken into account the fact that newspapers vary in page size and in thickness, so that they have coded the papers according to the proportion of their total area which is covered by sport. The coders have marked each sampled issue with a large red figure in the top left-hand corner, denoting its coding with respect to the variable 'sports coverage' (where this is operationally defined as the proportion of the total area covered by sport). If we suppose that they have used a ten-point scale, coding the nil-value 'o' and the top value '9', then we can see that sorting according to this variable is a simple matter. The Bongy Wongese mark out ten positions along one edge of the CRICKET PITCH and then sort the newspapers into ten piles according to the red figure in the top left-hand corner of each. Once this sorting has been done the Bongy Wongese have 'broken' the data according to the variable 'sports coverage', and revealed their *distribution* for that factor. Incidentally, this distribution could be represented in the form often known as a histogram or histograph, if a Bongy Wongese photographer were to lie flat on the grass and focus on the vertical edge of the stacks. His photograph *might* look something like Figure 41.[4]

FIGURE 41 *Side view of newspaper stacks*

Now let us suppose that 'popularity' (as measured by daily sales figures) has been ascertained from the sales records and that, once coded, this factor has also been marked on the top of each newspaper, this time by a blue figure in the top right-hand corner. The Bongy Wongese research assistants will now mark off the code values permitted for this factor along an adjacent edge of the CRICKET PITCH – as in Figure 42.

The hard-working Bongy Wongese will now begin rushing about *breaking* the data according to the second variable ('popularity') in order to test the hypothesis. Each of the original heaps will be broken up and rearranged horizontally across the pitch according to the values given by the blue figure in the top right-hand corner.

When all the sorting is finished the newspapers will be scattered across the entire CRICKET PITCH in piles of varying height. Thus another aerial photograph might look something like Figure 43.

Now I want you to tax your over-worked imagination a little further!

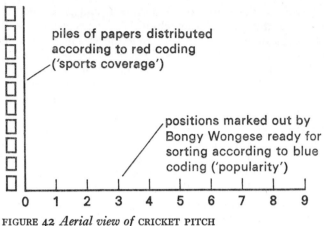

FIGURE 42 *Aerial view of* CRICKET PITCH

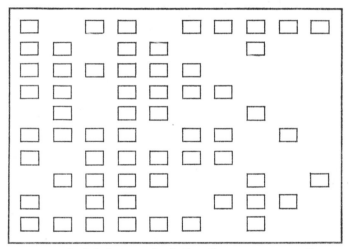

FIGURE 43 *Aerial photograph of piles of newspapers spread over*
           CRICKET PITCH

Try to imagine what the CRICKET PITCH would look like from a helicopter
in the thoroughly unusual circumstances where no errors whatsoever
had occurred in measurement or coding of data and the hypothesis
under test was *perfectly true$_4$*.[5] In these all-but-impossible circumstances
the tattoo on the grass would, of course, look like Figure 44.

Another way of expressing this very special relationship between the frequency distributions of the two sets of measurements is to say that of the one hundred logically possible combinations of red and blue figures in the top left- and right-hand corners of the newspapers only ten actually occur. And there is another formulation of the same hypothetical distribution (one to which increasing importance will be attached): this is to state that one variable is a 'perfect predictor' of the other. To say this is to say that, in this example, one could make an accurate guess of the red figure in the left-hand corner of any duly coded newspaper on the CRICKET PITCH, given knowledge only of the blue figure in the right-hand corner.

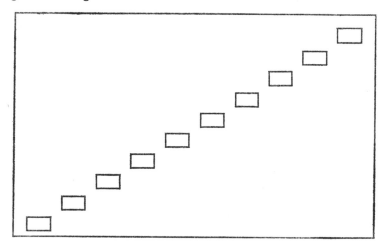

FIGURE 44 *Aerial photograph of a very unusual distribution*

It should be evident that in such circumstances one could say with great confidence that one had absolutely failed to falsify the research hypothesis that 'the more extensive the sports coverage in a daily newspaper, the greater the popularity of that paper'.

Now, the highly implausible antics of our imaginary Bongy Wongese newspaper-stackers have provided us with a very simple model of the *STATISTICAL* method of manipulating variables to test hypotheses. Whereas the *EXPERIMENTAL* method involves a process of differential *physical treatment* of groups of cases, the *STATISTICAL* method simulates this through differential *sorting procedures*. The analyst does not ask what happens to one variable when he changes the value of another, instead he deals with large numbers of cases, formulating his research inquiry in terms of questions about what happens to the distribution of values of one variable when cases are arranged with respect to their values on the other variable.

In the ordinary circumstances of research, of course, the sorting or 'breaking' into categories according to the values of variables is not done with the sample units 'themselves' (such as newspapers or, say, people) but typically with computer cards. The red and blue figures scrawled onto the newspapers by the Bongy Wongese coders in our example are thus replaced by the small rectangular holes punched on computer cards. Here, as you realize, each computer card generally bears coded data with respect to many more than two variables, so the researcher will check his coding frame to ascertain on which columns the information he requires has been punched. Having decided that, for example, he wishes to 'break column 34 against column 49', he will normally employ some mechanical or automatic assistance with the sorting rather than co-opting a band of Lilliputian Bongy Wongese for the same purpose. Thus the actual process of sorting is generally done by a counter-sorter machine or simulated entirely invisibly by an automatic computer.

Of course, the analysis of actual research data will usually be much more complicated than that model suggests. For one thing, you will remember that the number of variables involved in any particular ritual of comparison (i.e. test of a hypothesis) will only rarely be limited to two. And, for another thing, it should be clear from the arguments of the preceding chapters that comparisons of data distributions are bound to be complicated by the differences in the properties of the four types of scales that may have been produced by particular measurement and coding procedures. I expect that you also assume, *a priori*, that there will be further undreamed-of complications.[6]

But I am going to argue that, even though the basic logic of statistical analysis is necessarily obscured by the complications arising from the wide differentials that exist between types of problem situations, deductively reasonable statistical methods of reasoning about truth$_4$ always have at their core a set of tactics analogous to that portrayed in the model. However many variables are involved, whatever kinds of scales are employed, whatever assumptions are being made about the relationships between samples and the populations from which they are supposed to have been drawn, and however many tricky summation procedures intervene between the initial coding and the actual testing, the point of data analysis is always the same. The purpose of the analysis is to make standard (or 'repeatable') assessments of the truth$_4$ of hypotheses, that is to judge the extent to which relationships between groups of measurements deviate from the patterning suggested by the theory under test.

It is my argument, then, that, however complicated and impressive the statistical sums involved in a research programme, such devices are only meaningful in so far as they contribute to the all-important business of comparing the hypothesized relationships between variables with the patterning of observed value distributions of measurements made with respect to some theoretically relevant group of units.

Now it is common knowledge that statisticians are tricksters![7] So, before we delve into their SOUPY storehouse to extract a few recipes which may be useful for our particular purposes, I suggest that we get our bearings clear by fixing in our heads the image of the ten heaps of newspapers which the friendly Bongy Wongese have arranged across our imaginary test ground in a neat diagonal line (Figure 45).

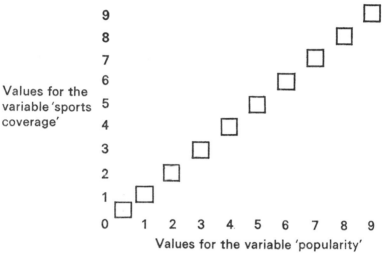

FIGURE 45

I think that when *you* think about that image you will be drawn to the conclusion that this hypothetical distribution represents an extremely harsh criterion against which to make assessments of the truth$_4$ of a hypothesis. For instance, I wonder if you consider that it would be sensible to reject the research hypothesis if the Bongy Wongese had spread the pattern in Figure 46 on the grass.

And it *may* have occurred to you that even a patterning such as that depicted by our first aerial photograph of the scattered papers (*Aerial photograph of piles of newspapers spread over* CRICKET PITCH) is hardly unequivocal evidence against the hypothesis. Indeed, even if there were a pile of papers on *each* of the one hundred possible positions marked out on the CRICKET PITCH, it could be the case that the piles along (or near to) the diagonal are noticeably *higher* than the remainder. In that case you would presumably decide that the aerial photograph is an inadequate representation of the distribution of the data with respect to the two variables under consideration. I expect that, faced with these

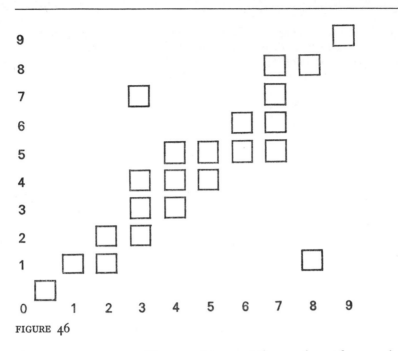

FIGURE 46

circumstances, you would proceed to *count* the numbers of papers in each pile with a view to *making some kind of assessment of the relative plausibility of two opposite judgments*:

1. That this distribution of data tends to represent a falsification of the research hypothesis;
2. That this distribution of data does not tend to represent a falsification of the research hypothesis.

Next, you would presumably set about devising some *criterion for choosing* between judgments 1 and 2 with respect to the distribution of data laid out across your test pitch. How would you judge the result of the match? Under what circumstances would you decide that, from the point of view of your theory, the data must be regarded as disobedient? What kind of patterning of data with respect to the variables under consideration would lead *you* to conclude that your hypothesis is false₄?

Well, you might dream up all kinds of tricks in order to estimate the extent to which your data seemed to straddle away from the hypothesized diagonal. But the trouble is that another UMPIRE might declare the opposite result. Then *I* might come along and agree with you. Then maybe Alice would chip in with her twopenny-worth and we'd all be thoroughly bewildered.

Obviously then it is in the interests of collective falsificationism for

RABBITS employing the *STATISTICAL* method of testing hypotheses to find some common rules, albeit arbitrary ones, by which they are all prepared to abide when making decisions about whether or not observed distributions of data tend to falsify specified research hypotheses. Whatever form such rules might take, it should be clear that they ought to involve a built-in advantage for the 'away team'.

You will remember that the test pitches used by GOLD-STAR RABBITS, and specified by such distinguished UMPIRES as Sir Karl Popper, are intentionally aslant. The GOLD-STAR spirit requires players to do their damndest to *falsify* their research hypotheses, not to verify them. So, from this point of view it is much worse for analysts of data to err on the side of judgment 2 ('That this distribution of data does *not* tend to represent a falsification of the research hypothesis') than it is for them to make the opposite kind of error.

Now you could be forgiven for supposing that it is just these kinds of rules of play which must have been in operation on the test grounds of science wherever scientists have been forced to simulate *EXPERI-MENTAL* manipulation of variables by *STATISTICAL* rituals. On the same deferential assumption, *I* went so far as to expect that courses on 'Statistics for Social Scientists', or standard textbooks on that subject, would contain the kind of rules suggested above, together with clear indications of the circumstances under which each might appropriately be applied.

Not so. Many steamy hours in the back passages of the relevant section of the LIBRARY, and seemingly interminable discussions with crackshot statisticians, have left me with the unhappy opinion that most of the statistical theory and practice, with which social (and, indeed, other) scientists are exhorted to acquaint themselves, is irrelevant to their aims *as* scientists. Statisticians are professionals' professionals. Unless they can persuade other groups of experts that they have developed, and are still developing, a craft which will be of use in actual decision-making situations, they will be out of business. Thus various theorems have been derived from the basic axioms of the Calculus of Probability with a view to their specific applications in particular fields such as, for example, medical epidemiology, decision-making in government and business, town planning, and – supposedly – academic social science. But sociologists are at last beginning to realize that the inadequacies in methodological conception and research design, which often characterize their work, have for too long been masked by the mystification of statistical legerdemain. Recently, then, the special complications created for statistical analysis by the nature of social science *data* have been given some attention. Yet I have been unable to find a single textbook on statistical methods which would make sense to a social (or other) scientist who was not prepared to fall back upon an implicitly inductive *methodology*, and hence ultimately upon a metaphysic which involved (at least residual) positivism.[8]

I shall take this opportunity to elaborate upon that prejudice!

If you look at the introductory section of any concise text purporting to cover the whole field known as 'statistics', you will find that the author divides his topic into at least two sections. He will distinguish *descriptive statistics* from *statistical inference*.

Descriptive statistics are simply summarizing procedures. The point of such techniques is merely to provide some means of rearranging the data in order to highlight its patterning with respect to the variable(s) of ¿interest?. Obvious examples of descriptive or summarizing techniques are the arithmetic mean and the equally familiar histogram or block-graph such as that represented above, and some more complicated devices will be introduced later.

Now, of course, journalists, politicians, economists, charity organizations, and various other sections of the statisticians' actual or potential clientele may often regard the production of these statistical descriptions as an end in itself. But this is rarely the case with the research scientist. For him these summarizing operations are mere preliminaries to the central scientific business of drawing *inferences* from the data.

But what do statisticians mean by 'statistical inference'? One commentator suggests that 'Statistical inference has been described as a collection of tools for making the best possible decisions in the face of uncertainty – that is, the situation where some, but not all of the (relevant) facts are in.'[9]

Other writers point out that these decisions are of two types: (i) *estimation of population parameters* and (ii) *tests of hypotheses*. The first type of problem included under the rubric '*statistical inference*', (i) *estimation of population parameters*, consists in finding criteria for assessing the probability that a specific sample was drawn from a (well-defined) population. Sometimes such techniques are combined with certain propositions derived from set theory in order to produce a method of inducing generalizations from particular sets of observations. But we have already seen that, though such a process may prove useful in the initial stages of theory formation, it has nothing to do with the GOLD-STAR methods of subjecting properly deduced hypotheses to genuinely risky tests. On the other hand, these techniques may well prove very useful to researchers wishing to check whether or not they have succeeded in selecting their desired probability subsamples *before* proceeding to test these hypotheses with respect to data drawn from those subsamples. These techniques can be found easily in any textbook so I shall not discuss them further.

Now, while you have your (haphazardly selected) textbook in your hand, glance quickly at the section on the second type of problem, (ii) *tests of hypotheses.* You may jump to the conclusion that here, at last, is the tool kit we are looking for? But unfortunately this is not the case. Problems of type (ii) are treated in the same fashion as those of type (i). Both types of problems are typically viewed by statisticians as questions about the degree of 'certainty' with which statistical generalizations may be *induced* from particular groups of data. This is to say that the business of *statistical inference* is always regarded by statisticians as a process of inferring relationships between samples and the populations from which they were supposed to have been drawn.

An example of this type of inference may be found in the 'tests of statistical significance' (such as the well-known chi-squared test) which were discussed in chapter 14, and which have been extremely popular in social science. The logic of chi-squared can be grasped readily by further reference to our deserted CRICKET PITCH and Bongy Wongese newspaper-stackers. Rather than providing a measure of the degree to which an observed distribution 'straddles away' from the hypothesized diagonal, the chi-squared test turns the problem *inside out.* Drawing on the Calculus of Probability, *and making the crucial assumption that the sampled newspapers have been drawn at random from the theoretically defined population of newspapers which they are supposed to represent,* the statistician produces an alternative theoretical distribution against which to compare the actual observations. This distribution is the *chi-squared distribution.* And, by comparing the *observed distribution* with the patterning that would be *expected on the basis of the chi-squared distribution,* the analyst estimates the degree to which the results deviate from the patterning which would have been expected 'merely by chance'. The greater the degree of deviation of observed results from those expected on the basis of the *so-called null-hypothesis* (that 'only chance is at work here') the greater the degree of confidence that the analyst has in his judgment that the null-hypothesis is falsified.

Now notice that, by turning the logic of comparison inside out in this fashion, the statistician has not only been forced to cling to the limiting assumption that the sample is properly random with respect to the population, but that he has also reversed the methodology of falsificationism. Rather than formulating his statistic as an estimation of the falsity$_4$ of his research hypothesis, he has stated it as an assessment of the probability that the *so-called null-hypothesis* is false$_4$ and, thus – taking the research hypothesis as a logical corollary of this null-hypothesis – the probability that the research hypothesis is true$_4$.

In sum, statistical 'tests of significance' which operate by comparing an observed distribution with one which 'might have been expected by chance' turn the basic logic of statistical manipulation of variables inside out, reversing the methodology of falsificationism, and producing a verificationist bias. From our point of view, then, such tests must be

considered inappropriate for purposes of hypothesis testing and, if they
have a place in our methodology, this should be limited to the preliminary
stages of theory formation where, as we have already seen, formalized
routines of induction are about as appropriate as anything else!

It should be clear, then, that only a small portion of the techniques
included in our standard statistics textbook will be useful to the social
scientist who wishes to employ the *STATISTICAL* method of
manipulating variables *to test hypotheses*. If he takes his GOLD-STAR
methodology seriously, he will not (at least at this stage) have any time
for *statistical inference* as it is normally conceived by statisticians. He is
not concerned with 'estimating population parameters' nor with those
sorts of 'tests of hypotheses' which involve comparisons of observed
patternings of data against the spurious criterion of 'chance'.

What he *does* want must surely be: *A kit of DATA PREPARATION
PROCEDURES* for summarizing the data-as-initially-coded, and
arranging it in a tidy and theoretically relevant formation *prior* to the
performance of the actual tests, plus *A bag of DECISION-RULES*, or
formulae for arbitrating the extent to which data distributions disobey
research hypotheses.

There is no available textbook which gives more than a salutary nod
in this direction.[10] We do not yet have all the equipment necessary to
make unambiguous and 'repeatable' (albeit arbitrary) assessments of the
results of every kind of match (or comparison situation) that is (logically)
possible within a falsificationist methodology of *STATISTICAL*
testing. Indeed, before such a kit-bag is available, a lot more sums will
have to be done. And, lest you assume that sums are *necessarily* boring,
I should point out that some of the required sums are of a sort which
have always been decidedly dangerous modes of passing the ¿time?.
Throughout history mathematicians who have attempted to clarify the
relationship between metaphysical involutes and their formal anaglyphs
(the so-called uninterpreted axiomatic systems) have come up against
juicy SPIDERS and heavy opposition. Only a millennium and a half ago a
lady called Hypatia got murdered by a Christian for trying to do just that
with her sums.[11] And there have been quite a few nasty scuffles since!

So perhaps you will forgive me for standing behind other people's
backs! What I offer here is merely a preliminary assemblage of second-
hand DATA PREPARATION PROCEDURES and DECISION-
RULES.

Data preparation procedures[12]

The kinds of summarizing or grouping procedures which sociologists
may require in order to prepare their data for the ritual comparisons –
or *tests* – which must be regarded as the climax of their research opera-

tions, are the standard techniques of statistical aggregation which have been described above as *descriptive statistics*.

Let us begin by visualizing the various forms in which the data will confront the researcher at this stage. The data are no longer *raw*, but coded according to the imperatives of the research design. Where they have been stipulated in modes 1–12, or 25–39, they will, of course, have been measured and coded according to second-order criteria of relevance. But where data have been stipulated in modes 13–24 they will have been arranged initially with respect to some dimensions of variance which are meaningful on the first-order level. In the latter case the *raw* data may have already been in a numerical form when first encountered by the researcher; and it may even have been arranged in the manner of a table or graph where, of course, the coding would have been a mere question of transferral of numerical symbols from one location to another.

We will start, then, by considering the most 'disorganized' form that coded data may take. Imagine that we have devised a programme of research to test the hypothesis that, for some particular group of students, *'examination performance increases with seminar attendance'*. Two sets of data or measurements are available from our sample of students: each student has been assigned a code value for the variable 'Seminar attendance', and one for the variable 'Examination performance'. For the sake of simplicity, let us pretend that 'Seminar attendance' has been operationally defined as a dichotomy, thus only two values are permitted for this variable: '1', attendance at seminars, and '2', truancy. Also for the sake of ease we shall pretend that only one indicator is being employed to represent the variable 'Examination performance' and that this is the mark gained by the students in one particular examination. Since this examination has been marked out of 100, the range of permitted values is 1–100 inclusive.[13] There are thus two sets of data:

| 2 1 2 2 1 2 1 1 |
| 2 1 1 1 |
| and so on |

| 75 42 58 62 69 47 32 51 |
| 56 59 67 69 |
| and so on |

'Seminar attendance' · *'Examination performance'*

Notice that the variable 'Seminar attendance' has been treated as a nominal dichotomy – that is, as an *attribute* – and that 'Examination performance', being a measurement in the mode of STIP 19, may be regarded as an ordinal, interval, *or* ratio scale, depending upon the kind of assumptions that we are prepared to make about the mode of conceptualization of the first-order compilers of the data, that is, the examiners.

Now, let's attempt to bring some more obvious order into the data by employing the simple descriptive device of the *Tally*, or *Non-Grouped Frequency Table*.

		No. of students
'Seminar attendance' (S)	S = 1	42
	= 2	108
		150 = total number of students in sample

		No. of students
'Examination performance' (E)	E = 100	0
	E = 99	0
	etc.	
	= 75	1
	74	0
	73	2
	72	3
	71	0
	70	0
	69	2 . . . and so on
	. .	. . .
	. .	. . .
		150 = total number of students in sample

Next, let's proceed to classify the data further by drawing up a *Grouped Frequency Table*.

'Seminar attendance', S, in the way we have measured and coded it, has only two values, but 'Examination performance' has been measured and coded against a hundred permissible values. So our data on the latter variable may perhaps be more readily compared with those on the former by grouping 'Examination performance', E, into a number of *classes* or aggregate groups. The following guidelines are suggested:

(a) Boundaries between classes should, where possible, correspond to divisions which already have some ¿interest? on either the first- or second-order levels of meaning.

(b) Classes of equal width are convenient, but not essential.[14]

Table 2 shows what our grouped frequency table for the variable E, 'Examination performance', might look like. The figures in the right-hand column show the number of students with marks up to and including the marks in that class.

In addition to *frequency* tables we may, of course, use *graphs* to describe the distribution of our data. We have already met the frequency *histogram*, or bar-graph, in the guise of a side-view photograph

TABLE 2   *Grouped frequency for the variable E*

Class[15]	Frequency	Cumulative frequency
70 and over	6	150
60–69	44	144
50–59	65	100
40–49	25	35
Under 40	10	10
	150	

of the newspaper stacks. More sophisticated techniques are represented by the frequency *polygon* and the *cumulative frequency polygon*.[16] All such graphs represent arrangements in which the values of the variable being described are displayed along one axis, usually the horizontal, and the frequencies are marked along the other axis. The distribution is thus scattered across the ¿space? defined by the two axes.

When describing the shapes of graphs, statisticians generally focus on two features: *symmetry* and *number of peaks*. They note whether the graph is symmetric about some ¿centre? or whether it is skewed (asymmetric), and they also note whether the graph exhibits one peak or several.

Now you will notice that the values on the vertical (frequency) axis of a graph will form a ratio scale, since they are produced by the arithmetic procedure of counting, but the values on the horizontal axis may represent any of the four types of scales according to the operationalization, measurement and coding of the particular variable under consideration. If it is a *nominal scale*, we can change the order of showing the values. Thus, in the example of variable S above, 1 can come before *or* after 2. If it is an *ordinal scale* then the *order* of the different values is fixed, but the ¿distances? between them are arbitrary. Only if the variable is an *interval or ratio scale* – and we shall often consider these two together in what follows – can we consider the scores as examples of the sort of numbers with which we are familiar and mathematics is concerned. You may remember that where ratio scaling is achieved all mathematical operations will be appropriate, and that, where interval scaling is employed, addition and subtraction – but not multiplication and division – are legitimate.

Suppose now that we wish to describe a distribution over the telephone, or that, as in our present quest, we wish to compare two distributions in order to test a hypothesis. We will need one or more *statistics* to *summarize* the distribution of results.

First we need a measure of *central tendency*, that is an indication of the point around which the values of our variable (let us call it E) are distributed. There are three possibilities which you may remember as 'the three *ms*' or 'middlers': mode, mean and median.

The mode is the E value under the peak. This is easy to locate, but not a statistic which is sensitive to changes in the distribution of E values away from the centre. It should also be noted that the business of establishing a mode is somewhat equivocal if there is more than one peak.

The mean, or arithmetic average, is a familiar statistic and one which is fairly easy to calculate. It has the advantage that it is based on (that is, involves the sum of) *all* the E values. But its disadvantage is that it is believed to be ¿unduly? influenced by extreme values where the distribution is asymmetric.

The median is a statistic which represents the E value of the middle unit (or case) when the observations are ranked. This may sometimes be regarded as contributing to a useful description of an asymmetric distribution.

Now distributions which have similar *m*s, that is the same 'centres' on the E-axis, may still vary considerably in their patterning with respect to E. The extent to which data are spread along the E-axis may vary independently of *m*.

So, in addition to the *m-STATISTIC*, we will need one other sort of descriptive statistic. We will also need a measure of *dispersion* or spread along the E axis. I shall refer to this sort of statistic as a *d-STATISTIC*.

The following *d-STATISTICS* are most popular:

The range is the difference between the highest and the lowest E values. It is easy to find but rather uninformative.

The quartile deviation is half the difference between the first and third quartiles, where the first quartile is the E-score of the person one quarter of the way from the lowest score when the observations are ranked, the second quartile is the median, and the third quartile is the E-score of the individual who is three quarters of the way up from the lowest score.

The standard deviation can be described as the square-root of the variation. It is calculated according to the following formula

$$\text{standard deviation} = \sqrt{\frac{\Sigma(e - \bar{E})^2}{n}}$$

where e represents *each* value of E, $\bar{E}$ represents the arithmetic *mean* of the E values, and n stands for the *number* of values of E.

The section of our kit of DATA-PREPARATION PROCEDURES which is devoted to ordinary 'descriptive statistics' is now well-stocked with everything that we shall normally need in the preliminary stages of grouping data for analysis. But it is not enough to know *how to calculate* the two sorts of statistical summaries that I have called m-STATISTICS and d-STATISTICS, *it is also essential to know when their use is* appropriate.

This you could work out for yourself very easily, given only the information presented above. But to save you ¿time? I offer a tool-tidy (Table 3).

TABLE 3 *Data-preparation procedures*

	m-STATISTICS	d-STATISTICS
Ratio and interval scales	mean median mode	standard deviation quartile deviation range
Ordinal scales	median mode	none (but it may be worth noting the 'top' and 'bottom' values)
Nominal classifications	mode	none
Nominal dichotomies	none	none

Now we have our kit of DATA-PREPARATION PROCEDURES, let us consider how we might stock our bag of *DECISION-RULES* for statistical comparisons, or *tests*.

Decision-rules

As Costner has pointed out[17] sociologists suffer 'an embarrassment of riches' when it comes to the business of assessing the relationships between pairs of variables. So many measures of association exist that we don't even *know* them all, let alone have any coherent norms to regulate the uses to which we put them. Yet, as I have said, a co-operative effort towards a genuinely falsificationist methodology of hypothesis testing *must* involve the establishment of some collectively agreeable rules.

Rules about which we are all prepared to agree must be generally judged to be both *reasonable* and *appropriate*. To say that the rules must be *reasonable* is to say that they are true₃, that is, that any reasonable person could follow their derivation, provided that he was informed of the notations being employed, and that he was familiar with the necessary algebraic, computational or, perhaps, geometric, or topological operations. To say that the rules must be *appropriate* is to make the equally trite remark that they should not be applied to decision-making situations for which they were not intended. For example, a formula prerequiring the computation of the arithmetic mean would clearly be inapplicable for comparisons involving ordinally scaled data.

We have seen that traditional *'statistical inference'* has involved a comparison of actual patterning with some hypothetical patterning that might have been expected by 'chance'. Except for those unusual research situations where such a comparison might be of explicit theoretical ¿interest?,[18] then, this group of techniques will be quite inappropriate. But, luckily, these are not the only kind of devices which statisticians have to offer.

Consider the following formula:

$$\text{'coefficient of determination'} = \left[\frac{\left[\Sigma xy - \dfrac{(\Sigma x)(\Sigma y)}{N} \right]}{\sqrt{\left[\Sigma x^2 - \dfrac{(\Sigma x)^2}{N} \right]\left[\Sigma y^2 - \dfrac{(\Sigma y)^2}{N} \right]}} \right]^2$$

This conglomeration of symbols represents a recipe for calculating the ratio of the variance of one variable, X, to the variance of another variable, Y. The denominator of this ratio is the total variance of one of the variables, and the numerator is that part of this variance which can be predicted from the other variable. *Thus the 'coefficient of determination' may be regarded as a mathematical description of the proportion of the variance of one variable which is predictable from the variance of the other.* Costner has put this (entirely mathematical) idea another way:[19]

The 'coefficient of determination' . . . indicates proportion by which 'error' (as measured by the mean of the squared deviations of actual from estimated values) is reduced as one shifts from estimating the mean of Y for all Y values (in which case 'error' is 'total variance') to predicting each Y by the regression equation (in which case 'error' is 'error variance' or variance around the regression line . . . *i.e. the hypothesised diagonal* . . .). Thus . . . *the coefficient* . . . is a measure of proportional improvement in the accuracy of estimation, that is, the proportional reduction in the error of estimation obtained by using a specified . . . variable to estimate . . . *the other* . . . variable by a specified linear prediction formula.

Here is an unequivocal test rule which does not rely in any way upon the assumptions of probability theory. It is a purely mathematical device which operates by comparing one distribution with another, *without* reference to the spurious criteron of *'Chance'*.

Perhaps, then, you will agree that we should *always* plump for the *'coefficient of determination'* as our preferred test rule, or measure of association, *if it is appropriate.* But it may be obvious to you that this statistic will *only* be appropriate where a research hypothesis, that one variable increases with another, may be interpreted as a prediction that the two variables will bear a direct *linear* relationship to one another. You may know that quadratic regression equations may be used to calculate related measures of association for tests of a hypothesized *curvilinear* relationship.[20] But these, like the *'coefficient of determination'* itself, rest upon the *crucial assumption that both variables are represented by interval or ratio scales of measurement.*

So what about those all-too-frequent situations where sociologists are faced with ordinal, and even nominal scales? The geometric analogy implied by the idea of regression is now inappropriate. The kind of ¿space? in which comparisons of patterning and ¿direction? must be made can no longer be regarded for practical purposes as an isomorph of ordinary space, as was the case with our imaginary CRICKET PITCH. Indeed, if you try to visualize a CRICKET PITCH made out of material which is both elastic *and* folded after the manner of a concertina, and which might *also* stretch and unfold in a completely unpredictable fashion, then you will have some inkling of the sort of problems which would be posed by any attempt to apply the ordinary idea of regression to ordinally scaled data. And in the case of nominal data this method of comparison would be even more ludicrous.

Well, I am glad to say that nowadays sociologists are generally aware of the limitations imposed by their crude methods of scaling, and that the emphasis on *parametric* (or linear) statistics is giving way to a renewal of interest in the development of the non-parametric devices. These, as Sidney Siegel pointed out nearly twenty years ago,[21]

> are available to treat data which are inherently in ranks as well as data whose seemingly numerical scores have the strength of ranks. That is, the researcher may only be able to say of his subjects that one has more or less of the characteristic than another, without being able to say *how much* more or less. . . If data are inherently in ranks, or even if they can only be categorised as plus or minus (more or less, better or worse), they can be treated by nonparametric methods, whereas they cannot be treated by parametric methods unless precarious and perhaps unrealistic assumptions are made.

He also noted that these methods may be used to treat data 'which are simply classificatory', that is, nominally scaled; and finally he points out that 'nonparametric statistical tests are typically much easier to learn and apply than are parametric tests'.[22]

Siegel has in fact produced a taxonomy of non-parametric tests, all nicely tagged according to whether they apply to estimations of patterning within a single sample, between two related samples, two independent samples, several related samples, or several independent samples. But, unfortunately, he does not interpret the logic of comparison in the manner suggested above, and therefore it is rather

difficult for the ordinary researcher to untangle the genuinely relevant
non-parametric statistics included in his book from the methodology of
'statistical inference', or induction, which informs – or rather *mis-
informs* – Siegel's work.

So, confronted as we are with such a glorious array of non-parametric
statistics as, for example, Goodman and Kruskal's gamma, Somers's d,
Spearman's rho, phi, tetrachoric r, Yule's Q, and the familiar chi-
squared, we are quite entitled to feel a little bewildered. How are we to
select, and choose between, the devices which permit of the *proportional-
reduction-in-error* interpretation which is essential for a falsificationist
approach? And how are we to identify, and eliminate from our bags of
tricks, all those statistics which operate by the inside-out method of
comparing observed associations with those that might have been
expected on the basis of the thoroughly spurious metaphysical criterion
of *'Chance'*?

Costner's proposals are elegantly simple:[23]

Consider the following rules and definitions. Any measure for which
such conditions can be specified can also be interpreted in propor-
tional-reduction-in-error terms, regardless of the nature of the scale
and regardless of any other feature of the data.
(a) A rule for estimating some 'characteristic' of a 'dependent' variable
from a 'characteristic' of an 'independent' variable.
(b) A rule for estimating the same 'characteristic' of the same 'dependent' variable without knowledge of the 'independent' variable.
(c) A definition of what constitutes 'error' and how 'error' shall be
measured.
(d) A definition of the measure of association that takes the form

$$\frac{\text{'P-R-E'}}{\text{measure}} = \frac{\text{Error by rule (b)} - \text{Error by rule (a)}}{\text{Error by rule (b)}}$$

In the *coefficient of determination* it is the equation for the regression
line (our hypothesized diagonal) which provides the criterion for rule (a).
The mean of the 'dependent' variable is the 'characteristic' required for
rule (b). And the definition of 'error' required by (c) is the 'variance', or
the mean of the squared deviations of actual values from the values
estimated by rules (a) and (b).

Now you will remember that the arithmetic mean is *not* an appropriate
m-STATISTIC for non-interval data. So it should be clear that
'P-R-E' measures for use with such data must replace this kind of
description of the 'characteristic' of the 'dependent' variable by some
other kind of generalization. One possibility is to employ one of the
other m-STATISTICS for rule (b). But, though the use of the mode
may be the only option in the case of nominal data, Costner suggests

another tack for the case of ordinal scales: '*to anticipate order in a given randomly drawn pair of units by some random device*'. Notice that any 'P-R-E' statistics which rely upon this method must involve assumptions which are deduceable from the Calculus of Probability. But here the use of such probability estimations seems reasonable enough, at least to me. The pairs are drawn by a *deliberately random mechanism* from a universe of units which has precise definition. That universe of units is, of course, the complete sample upon which the test is being performed, *and everything relevant is known about it*. That is to say that the analyst has a value for each of the two variables under consideration, for each unit in the sample. Here then, some derivation from the entirely formal mathematical mechanism known as the Calculus of Probability is being used in a decision-situation precisely analogous to the clearly defined game-situations for which it was originally devised, and *not* in a spurious and illegitimate attempt to infer, or *induce*, the characteristics of some (vaguely defined) set from those of some (assumedly random) subset, by way of the stop-gap metaphysic of '*chance*'!

Of those measures of association which admit of a definite 'P-R-E' interpretation, the statistics shown in Table 4 seem to offer the most promising bases for collectively agreeable decision-rules. They have been classified according to their appropriateness for arbitrating tests of hypothesized relationships between pairs of variables having the various scale characteristics.[24]

TABLE 4 *Decision-rules*

	Interval or ratio scale	Ordinal scale	Nominal classification	Nominal dichotomy
Interval or ratio scale	*coefficient of determination* (or some generalization from it)	*gamma*	*eta-squared*	*point biserial* r^2
Ordinal scale	*gamma*	*gamma*	*coefficient of predictability* OR *tau-b*	*coefficient of predictability* OR *tau-b*
Nominal classification	*eta-squared*	*coefficient of predictability* OR *tau-b*	*coefficient of predictability* OR *tau-b*	*coefficient of predictability* OR *tau-b*
Nominal dichotomy	*point biserial* r^2	*coefficient of predictability* OR *tau-b*	*coefficient of predictability* OR *tau-b*	*Yule's Q*

The necessary recipes may be found in the following sources:

FOR   *CONSULT*
gamma   Leo A. Goodman and William H. Kruskal, 'Measures of
                 association for cross-classifications', *Journal of the
                 American Statistical Association*, 49 (1954), pp. 732–64.
eta-squared   H. M. Blalock, *Social Statistics* (New York, McGraw-
                 Hill, 1960), pp. 266–7.
point biserial Helen Walker and Joseph Lev, *Statistical Inference* (New
r^2 York, Holt, 1953), pp. 261–72.
coefficient of Louis Guttman, 'An outline of the statistical theory of
predictability prediction' in Paul Horst, *The Prediction of Personal
                 Adjustment* (New York, Social Science Research Council,
                 Bulletin 48), pp. 260ff.
tau-b   Goodman and Kruskal, op. cit.
Yule's Q   James A. Davis, *Elementary Survey Analysis* (Englewood
                 Cliffs, N.J., Prentice-Hall, 1971).

It should be clear that, before any of these statistics could be adopted as bases for decision-rules for tests, the community of disputants would have to reach some arbitrary agreements about the cut-off points for the various measures of association. It would be necessary to determine values for, say, *'the coefficient of determination'*, or, say *'Yule's Q'*,[25] which could be accepted by convention as representing falsifications of research hypotheses for given variable characteristics and sample sizes. These decision-rules might then take the place of the verificationist conventions which currently attach to the essentially inductivist conceptions of 'statistical significance', 'levels of confidence', and of course 'probability' itself.

Now, *if* you accept the argument so far, *then* – I *think* – you are bound to agree that the development of *reasonable* and *appropriate* rules to regulate the decisions of tests involving more complicated kinds of comparisons than those discussed so far *must* be a (logical) possibility. Indeed, I believe that we could *each* develop the logic of comparison suggested above to the point of devising systems for comparing more than two variables, provided, of course, that we had the inclination and the mathematical ability. Indeed some useful steps have already been taken *towards* this ¿direction?.[26]

But, *as a discipline*, sociology has a long way to go. It will be some ¿time? before falsificationist conventions for the arbitration of statistical tests are established and maintained by a community of honest scientists studying the subject of *'meanings'*.

Until such time as we social scientists do have some clear rules for judging the truth$_2$ of statistical assertions we must accept that tests of hypotheses in which variables are manipulated by *STATISTICAL* rather than *PHYSICAL* ritual methods *may* be false$_2$, and that conclusions based upon them may be exaggerations or downright lies.

The, often impressive-looking, 'results' of such tests should always be taken with more than a pinch of salt. Do they 'result' from a methodologically coherent series of *repeatable* applications of *reasonable* and *appropriate* statistical decisions, such that the same results would have been obtained by *any other* competent analyst; or indeed by a suitably programmed robot? If *not* they may well be mere tricks, the sort of performances produced by conjurers intent upon fooling an audience, rather than by genuinely heroic magicians testing the reality-making potential of their FAIRY TALES.

I suggest the pejorative term 'STATISTRICKS' for such occult dishonesty and verificationist foul play. STATISTRICKS are tricks of comparison, making use of unreasonable or inappropriate statistics, or involving unstated assumptions or 'unrepeatable' grouping procedures.[27] Such figures are about as credible as bases for judging the truth$_4$ of hypotheses as would be a photograph of some ectoplasm hovering over a cricket pitch, acquired in mysterious circumstances, and accompanied by an expert's view that he was 95 per cent confident that the picture was *not* produced by a patent-elastic-summerhouse-capable-of-being-compressed-into-the-waistcoat-pocket.

How are we to avoid STATISTRICKS? Well, there are otherwise clear-headed social scientists who urge us to continue to employ the currently popular kinds of STATISTRICKS, because 'everybody does it anyway'.[28] But the heroic falsificationist, whom I hope to have depicted in this volume, is *not* a mere follower of the scientific fashions of his day. Nor is he concerned to substitute popular conjuring tricks for genuinely risky tests. If we are to emulate his GOLD-STAR role-model we *must* discontinue these practices.

Until some criteria for decision rules are established along properly falsificationist lines, then, the best that we can do is to limit ourselves to the statistics included in the above kit-bag, *and also* present our test comparisons in full detail so that readers may judge for themselves the extent to which these distributions disobey our research hypotheses. In effect, of course, this means that we must resort to the 'eyeball' method of *tabular* comparison. Tables of data should be presented comparing the frequencies of observations for each (logically) possible combination of values of the variables under consideration. Inspection of such tables may also be facilitated by the legitimate tactic of expressing these frequencies as percentages of the (horizontal or vertical) totals for the rows or columns in which they appear. As you realize, frequencies of observed values in respect of several variables (or in respect of several different indicators for one variable) may be compared in a single table. Thus, for example, the empty table-¿space? in Figure 47 could be used to test the hypothesis that 'X → Y', where the arguably confounding influence of another variable Z is to be controlled, and where measurements representing Z are available for each of the cases or units under consideration. In this example there are three permitted values for Z and five each for X and Y.

FIGURE 47

But it should be clear that the more variables you wish to consider at once the larger the ¿space? across which the same limited number of observational cases must be scattered. The point is soon reached where cell frequencies become so small that comparison no longer makes intuitive sense. This is when researchers generally start to 'collapse' their original categories, regrouping their tables in order to reduce the number of cells or shrink the ¿space? in which the comparison is to take place. Such compression or regrouping does, of course, provide further loopholes for cheats and verificationists *except where explicit details of the collapsing operations are given.*

You must allow me to raise a few more SPIDERS before letting go of this tedious thread.

You will remember that, when we discussed the questions of operationalization in general, and data stipulation in particular, we concluded that there are inherent uncertainties in the whole business of selecting measurable characteristics of appearances to represent the FAIRY-TALE entities called variables. *Triangulation,* the stipulation of several different sets of measurements for each variable, was suggested as a mitigating tactic. Several *indicators* were to be stipulated for each variable and (all or some of) these were subsequently to be combined together to produce *indexes.*

For example, the variance of variable X might be represented by five separate frequency distributions, one for each of the indicators x_1, x_2, x_3, x_4 and x_5.

Before any hypotheses relating the variation of X to some *other* variable(s) can be tested then, it will be necessary to ask whether the five sets of measurements representing X are themselves correlated in the sample. Do cases scoring higher on x_1 also tend to score higher on x_2, x_3, x_4 and x_5?

Clearly we have ten essential preliminary hypotheses to test:

x_1 varies directly with x_2
x_1 varies directly with x_3
x_1 varies directly with x_4
x_1 varies directly with x_5
x_2 varies directly with x_3
x_2 varies directly with x_4
x_2 varies directly with x_5
x_3 varies directly with x_4
x_3 varies directly with x_5
x_4 varies directly with x_5

If we do not succeed in falsifying any of these hypotheses we might feel well pleased with our measuring instruments.[29]

But suppose now that we obtain the following results:

Hypothesis	Judgment
$x_1 \propto x_2$	'FALSE!'
$x_1 \propto x_3$	'NOT OBVIOUSLY FALSE'
$x_1 \propto x_4$	'NOT OBVIOUSLY FALSE'
$x_1 \propto x_5$	'FALSE!'
$x_2 \propto x_3$	'FALSE!'
$x_2 \propto x_4$	'FALSE!'
$x_2 \propto x_5$	'FALSE!'
$x_3 \propto x_4$	'NOT OBVIOUSLY FALSE'
$x_3 \propto x_5$	'FALSE!'
$x_4 \propto x_5$	'FALSE!'

Although seven of our ten preliminary hypotheses are judged to be false$_4$, we have done nothing to shatter the credibility of the assumption that values of three of the indicators, x_1, x_3, x_4, *are* associated together in the sampled cases. In these circumstances it does not seem at all *unreasonable* to discard the indicators x_2 and x_5 as 'useless', and proceed to produce a summary score to represent the value

$$(x_1 + x_3 + x_4)$$

for each individual unit in the sample.[30] This score would then be

punched in the empty column on each computer card which had been
reserved for the *index* of X.

But notice that I have discussed only two outcomes of a set of tests
of the ten hypotheses concerning the correlations of the five separate
indicators of our variable X. What would you do in the following
situation, for example?

Hypothesis	Judgment
$x_1 \propto x_2$	'NOT OBVIOUSLY FALSE'
$x_1 \propto x_3$	'FALSE!'
$x_1 \propto x_4$	'FALSE!'
$x_1 \propto x_5$	'FALSE!'
$x_2 \propto x_3$	'NOT OBVIOUSLY FALSE'
$x_2 \propto x_4$	'FALSE!'
$x_2 \propto x_5$	'NOT OBVIOUSLY FALSE'
$x_3 \propto x_4$	'FALSE!'
$x_3 \propto x_5$	'FALSE!'
$x_4 \propto x_5$	'FALSE!'

And there are 1,021 other outcomes which are logically possible for
a five-indicator comparison!

As you have guessed, there is no presently existing set of rules to
govern such procedures. And practising researchers will agree with me
when I say that we generally choose between indicators, and sum
indicators into indices, according to the results which we *wish* to obtain.
Naturally this form of cheating would be abhorred by true$_2$ falsifica-
tionists, who would not be prepared to consider evidence from a test
which was based on 'unrepeatable' operations, that is ones which could
have turned out differently if someone else had performed them.

But if sociology can reasonably be considered to have attained the
status of a mature science then some conventions of index construction
will have been established.[31]

Let me turn now to another difficult issue, the question of the
plausibility of non-arithmetic conceptions of ¿direction?, and hence of
non-arithmetic methods of comparing one set of measurements with
another. Perhaps it is intuitively obvious to you that the basic logic of
estimating the fit between hypothesized and observed results is by no
means an *intrinsically* arithmetic one. The extent to which data distributions 'straddle away' from hypothesized diagonal ¿directions? *could* be
judged by geometric or topological operations rather than by frequency
comparisons. Ordinary geometry would, of course, be limited in
applicability to comparisons involving at least an interval level of scaling,
as is ordinary arithmetic. But there is another sort of conception of
¿space? which could provide a more useful arena for test matches
involving ordinal and perhaps even nominal data.[32]

Sometimes a peculiar kind of sociological idea of ¿space? and ¿direction? (and the notions of 'social distance' and 'sociometric proximity' which have been derived from it) can be expressed successfully by a special type of grouping operation called *sociometrics*. A whole gamut of sociometric techniques have been developed since Moreno first hit upon this idea, but, so far, the only ones which may have a place in a falsificationist research methodology are *arithmetic* generalizations based on frequency computations.[33]

The same can be said of another special kind of sociological grouping procedure which I have referred to in the above as *content analysis*. The acceptance of such analysis as evidence relevant to the test of a hypothesis must, of course, rest upon the researcher's ability to employ some standard method of judging one set of results against another. Thus, so far, the only methods which we have been able to employ in this way are those which can – *in the last analysis* – be made to boil down to frequency comparisons.[34]

'There are more of "*these*" amongst "*those*" than there are amongst "*the others*".' That is our usual form of operational interpretation for the hypothesis ' "*These*" → "*those*" '. But, clearly, the causal idea expressed by that hypothesis could be given a different sort of operational interpretation: for example, that ' "*these*" tend to move closer to "*those*" than they do to "*the others*" '. This kind of ¿direction? is almost completely unexplored by sociologists.[35]

Consideration of the terrors of this foggy realm of thought brings me to one of the most obviously SPIDERY issues involved in the attempt to test hypotheses by the *STATISTICAL* method, and one to which previous commentators have invariably felt it necessary to pay due obeisance. This is the question of the relationship between the results of statistical testing procedures and the omnipresent human tendency to assign causes to phenomena. I believe that the methodology developed in this volume leaves little room for confusion in this respect: I have stressed that causation is an essential property of theoretical relationships or FAIRY TALES, and that its connection with relationships which are actually observed between various *real-world appearances* is necessarily established by fiat. But you may still be disturbed by the emphasis which others writers place upon the business of *symmetry versus asymmetry* and its connection with so-called 'causal analysis'.

Allow me to attempt some clarification by distinguishing amongst three quite distinct ways in which these terms may be employed.

What do people mean when they say that something is asymmetric, or SKEW-IF? This sort of epithet may refer:

(i) *to a theoretical hypothesis* such as 'X → Y', which states that (the idea of) X is causally prior to (the idea of) Y, and thus that the causal hypothesis is unidirectional or irreversible:

or (ii) *to the distribution of a group of measurements* where that frequency pattern deviates from the special sort of distribution which statisticians like to call 'normal'.

or (iii) *to a measure of association* if its value varies according to whether, say, Y is compared with X, or X is compared with Y.

We have seen that all chains of theoretical generalizations, that is *all theories*, involve at least some unidirectional, irreversible, or 'asymmetric' propositions. Indeed you will probably remember that this was the reason why I urged great caution with regard to the use of mathematical *models*, or *ANALYTICAL THEORIES*, in sociology. Such models, I said, are generally symmetric while the ideas they are supposed to represent are often intrinsically SKEW-IF. But, in testing the research hypothesis that, say, 'X → Y', it is enough merely to establish whether or not X and Y *vary together* in the hypothesized ¿direction? (i.e. positively or negatively). Indeed the arguments of the preceding chapters should lead you to conclude that *any attempt to assess the empirical distribution of the two variables in order to determine causal priority* is not merely tricky,[36] but, from a deductivist viewpoint, totally unnecessary. We are not trying to 'find out' which causes which; we have already chosen a plausible causal sequence, and are now testing it against the patternings of certain (allegedly relevant) measurements. For this purpose then we may reasonably expect to employ methods of comparison which will give the same results whether X is compared with Y, or Y with X.[37]

You may have noticed that a number of other SPIDERY spectres are often raised in methodological discussions of the analysis of social science data. But it is my contention that the majority of these issues are spawned by the confused approach to *statistical inference* upon which I have been trying to put my heel.[38] I shall therefore save myself from further agony with the momentary pretence that the thing is dead.

Let me merely conclude this section by being as unfair to the straight statistician as I imagine he will be to me! I shall use the common black-magical and thoroughly dishonest practice of setting up a straw man, just for the fun of knocking him down.

SS: O.K. But you've still got the problem of statistical inference.

JF: How do you mean?

SS: Well, you might have observations on a small portion of a universe and wish to make generalizations about more of it.

JF: You mean at the theory-construction stage?

SS: Well, yes. For example, suppose that . . .

JF: (*Looks the other way and coughs rudely*)

SS: What's the matter?

JF: Oh, nothing, I was thinking of something totally irrelevant.

SS: What?

JF: Underwear! (*Creases up*)

SS: Just try and be serious. Look! I'm not interested in your bloody *sample*! I don't want statistics that tell me about things that are happening in your *sample*, I want some useful *generalizations*.

JF: You mean you want to write a theory?

SS: No, not just that, I also want to test some hypotheses. And I want to know that my results can reasonably be assumed to be similar to those that might have been obtained if I had selected my test cases *anywhere* in the universe to which my theory is supposed to apply.

JF: Yup. You want to be reasonably sure that the sampled units can be assumed to represent the unsampled ones.

SS: Quite.

JF: Um, I thought that you were supposed to work all that out *before* using probability methods of estimation?

SS: Well, look, how do you answer questions about the relationship between your sample and your theoretical universe?

JF: Not with STATISTRICKS.

SS: OK then, *how*?

JF: By theoretical fiat, that's all.

EXERCISE
Devise your own examples – and work them out!

Chapter 20

What You Will!

The computers are still at last! The measuring wand has done its work. The answering figures are conjoined in meaningful harmony. And for a moment, perhaps, we are persuaded that the facts have found a voice. (See the illustration on page 425.)

But *have* they? Is the magic done?

It is in the commonplace of our humanity that we find the promise of honesty. And, for the sociologist, the self-professed student of the science of meanings, humanity takes a baffling form. The problem is one of communication. If we have some honest ¿truths? to tell, how best can we do it?

Let me tell you a story. Once upon a time Alice had a little friend. Her name was Julienne Ford, and she was a Sociologist. She didn't know very much about anything, but what she did know she believed Very Seriously. One thing that she believed Very Seriously was that Society Ought Not To Treat Its Children So Badly. She didn't like the way the littlees got labelled by the Biggies and forced into shape to fill all the jobslots in the Horrible Machine. She overheard a lot of people talking about Comprehensivization, the new liberal painless method of branding. She didn't like it. Not at all. She wanted people to Realize that the subtler agonies are the slower poisons.

So this Silly Billy set about to try a little magic. As a matter of fact she didn't do it very well at all. But the Important Thing is that she did it. She juggled some thoughts about, produced some hypotheses from the hat, had a nasty accident with the SAMPLING MACHINE, stipulated some data, made a nuisance of herself in the process of acquiring it, coded the stuff all by herself (poor thing), punched it up with her own grimy fingernails, and played about with the computer men. Then she just opened her big mouth and spilled it all out. The lot. The Paradigm and the FAIRY TALES and the causal implications, and the moral judgments, prognoses and opinions.

And that was when the magic *began*. Bad magic.

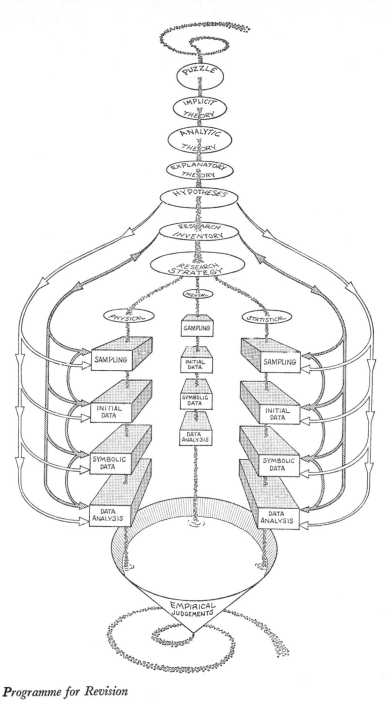

Programme for Revision

You see, what she had forgotten was that other people have opinions too! She had constructed some words and figures into the form of 'evidence' which, she claimed, was relevant to the truth$_4$ of the proposition that 'Comprehensive schools are no better than tripartite ones, and, in some respects, they may even be worse.' But what might be the fate of this 'evidence' as fodder for thought in a world in which any old fool has a right to chuck his prejudices in the air? This Silly Sociologist soon found that some Nasty Big Ears were only too ready to hear what she had to say.[1]

What is it then to be a pawnbroker of reality? When you realize that you have supplied a Tory council with, albeit feeble, ammunition in a debate about real things, what do you do? What do you do when you turn on the box and see a Nasty Biggie claiming that you have *proved* that comprehensive schools are no good? Or, again, why do you cry when you see it happening to your furry friends?

I see my brother, an eminent sociological authority on the mass media, I see him on the box. His messages are being manipulated by David Frost. He has just proved to everyone's satisfaction what they knew already: 'drug addiction is a form of sickness'. O my brother, I cry for you.[2] And you too, brothers and sisters in the newspapers, on the News at Ten, in the paperback books. We have carried our little boxes of tricks upside down and the things have got out!

Now this is not to say, as Andreski does, that 'the social sciences appear as an activity without any intrinsic mechanisms of retribution: where anybody can get away with anything.'[3] Because, of course, a lot of what we say is such obvious bullshit that no one takes us seriously for a moment. It is thoroughly big-headed of us to imagine other than that the joke is usually on us. Governments, managers, aunties, and chimney sweeps don't hang around waiting for pearls of wisdom to drop from the back ends of RABBITS. And when they do catch one they may return the compliment!

Nor is it to say that it is just because we have been doing things badly that it has all been going wrong. Andreski, for example, believes that most of his colleagues are cheats, charlatans and careerists, and that, if they only started playing the game according to the rules they could redeem themselves yet. This is to miss the point entirely.

Perhaps there are false$_2$ prophets in our ranks. Careerists, charlatans, self-appointed Black Magicians. But, you know, I doubt it. We are only human. We seek the Truth. We believe, we see. We stammer out the agonies of our souls: dddddddddddddo not adddddddjust your vision, there is a fffffffffffault in reality.

And so, desperate to get our tales told, to be rid of them, we cheat. The GOLD-STAR rules are hard. Very, very hard. They require us to make an altruistic surrender, to put behind us the desire to be right and to move with an honest urge to give the lie to our own hard-earned thoughts. Genuine falsificationism must drive us to a suicidal decision at every stage in the research game. In order to play by the rules we must first turn into poor furry masochists, thus to spin and whorl out the terrible symptoms of myxomatosis, until we dive down the plughole with the BATHWATER.

If there are any social scientists who get their questionnaires filled in at the local boozer, or who deliberately cook the figures, the laugh is on them. They have missed the Bigger Joke. The joke that sneaks up behind the counter-sorter when you are deciding where to 'make a break' in order to create an index of something or other. The joke that sets you reeling when, suddenly in the middle of an interview, you realize what you are doing. The joke that finds you tearing out your hair in the SAMPLING MACHINE, getting the sprockets and groats all clogged up in MOCK TURTLE SOUP. The joke that keeps driving you back to the beginning again, seeking rest.

There are ways and ways of cheating then. And some of them are funnier than others.

In my, obviously blighted, view the funniest of all is the one that butts you in the bunch at the moment you begin the business of communicating; when you talk about 'logic', 'validity', and 'truth', as though you can take it for granted that you know what they are; when you make statements like 'from a logical point of view', 'significant at the 0·05 level', 'it is quite clear that', etc.; *when you make like you know what you are talking about.*

Now this is so funny it is Serious.

> *ALICE:* No, Professor, I am not laughing at you. We are laughing at us.
>
> *FURRY FRIEND:* Moses supposes his toses are roses but Moses supposes erroneously for nobody's toses are poses of roses as Moses supposes his toses to be.

'But seriously though', we must share the joke. Surely the Truth must out? So how are we to do it?

Well, 'clearly', 'it seems to me', 'that it follows from the preceding arguments', 'that it is reasonable to suppose' that there is *thinking* yet to be done.

One of the ¿directions? in which I, at least, will turn my thinking is towards the question of how the student of the science of meanings is to bear the burden of responsibility inherent in the business of communication. How is he to reconcile the honesty which graces his humanity with the magical practicalities of persuasion, argument, dialogue and rhetoric?

Becker has pointed out that, from the viewpoint afforded by the presently available knowledge kept as sociology, there does appear to be a 'hierarchy of credibility'.[4] Some opinions are more influential than others. And, from this same perspective, the social structure of knowledge seems to be intimately connected with the politics of science.

None of us is big-headed enough to believe that he knows everything he needs to know. So we turn to the experts. If the box breaks down we call in the appropriate technician. If our bodies play up we put ourselves in the hands of the medical engineers. When our brains hurt we seek advice from another group of expert manipulators. If I want to be rid of my warts I go to a witch.

So, from a common-sensical point of view as well as from that of the self-conscious student of meanings, knowledge, and the technology through which it fulfils itself, appears to be *valuable*.

As you know, any value which is taken to be greater than unity but less than infinite is finite, that is to say, limited. And to say that something is limited is to say that it is, in relative terms, scarce. So the politics of science is another variant of the old legend of division and the differential distribution of power.[5] And, as many writers have pointed out, the faster the growth rate of scientific knowledge, the greater the degree of specialization and esotericism, and the more we are forced to go by the spurious authority of expertise, because we lack the energy to judge the messages for ourselves.[6]

Now, if we admit this epistemological alienation then we must accept the ethical implications of the assumption that, *just as we are sometimes prepared to take other people's words for things, so others may be willing to take ours*. Whether we like it or not, the sociologist is 'in play'. In so far as he expresses his opinions *qua* sociologist he will find that his messages carry a credibility weighting. His ¿truths? will be differentially effective on a number of counts. These perhaps include the following:

1. The reputation of the author to whom the message is attributed.
2. The intelligibility of the message in terms of the currently taken-for-granted paradigms of thought.
3. The apparent utility of the message content.

And it seems to me that these factors might operate to pattern the outcome of epistemological power conflicts both *within* a community of experts and *between* the members of that community and some wider social universe.

There are a number of ways in which sociological messages escape the rarefied realms of academia to get involved in the wider battles for knowledge and power which characterize a scientistic society.

The doing-of-research-and-offering-of-evidence is only one of these. Through the use or abuse of the rituals of science we can produce rather impressive judgments about what seem to be other people's realities.

But the burden of honesty with respect to such judgments is colossal. One can never be sure that one has performed every magical operation, including the final act of communication, in the true$_2$ GOLD-STAR spirit. For the genuine dedication of the mystic is no more common in science than it is in black magic. None of us is honestly committed to the business of destroying his own credibility.

Besides, GOLD-STAR methodology is, not to put too fine a point on it, rather long-winded! Thus there is a growing number of one-time academic sociologists who have changed their style of play entirely. Believing that it is, indeed, the spirit which counts, and knowing that they are as likely to be mistaken as anyone else, these have turned away from scientism towards 'social journalism'. Thus brilliant rhetoricians like Howard Becker follow the lead of writers like Raoul Brook and Harlan Ellison who waste no energy in argy bargy with the academic middlemen. Their slogan might well be 'we sell direct to the public'. And it certainly saves ¿time?!

So, at the moment, all that *my* thinking can lead *me* to do is to restate the opinion that it doesn't very much matter whether we sociologists adopt a scientistic or a journalistic style of rhetoric. But it seems that we must try to avoid the obvious bad faith of mixing the two. We must make a genuine effort to resist the temptation to capitalize on the authority of expertise to carry home the thrust of an argument that does not have the energy in and of itself. It is, then, a question of sorting our messages out, of devising some methods of marking the different sorts of ¿truths? which we mean them to carry.

But this is only to pinpoint another black hole. X marks the spot where the lemmings gather!

And in the meantime, Greenwich meantime, things still seem to be happening out there! It appears to us that people are tossing false$_3$ arguments and false$_4$ evidence about, making false$_2$ declarations in influential ears.

Shall we risk intervening and making matters worse?

Look at the results of our previous blunders! Magistrates believe that broken homes produce delinquents. But that information is already out of date amongst the better-read probation officers and social workers; they seek and confirm different causal sequences. Yet many of the 'best-read' of all (those who are really hip to the latest trends in paperback sociology) are, perhaps, amongst the Problem People themselves. Some of them have already disseminated the glad tidings of Labelling Theory.[7] Behold the New Rationalization! 'They have labelled me, man, I am a glass bead in their game.'

What Will Come?

We are becoming increasingly incoherent. It is impossible to think and communicate at the same ¿time?. *I* am becoming increasingly incoherent. It is impossible to think and communicate at the same ¿time?.

So I will not think at all. I will simply offer a personal opinion, a conglomeration of taken-for-granted thoughts. I have no means of knowing whether or not it is true$_4$, I cannot even say if it is true$_3$, but at least it is true$_2$. My opinion, for what it is worth, is this.

As society became more fragmented, more differentiated, as its institutions were rationalized, depersonalized and reified, so individuals became alienated, the one from the other. Not feeling unity in themselves, through one another, they sought an external explanation, or cause, for their very being. Yet they did not thereby escape their being, but only came to see it as it confronted them through appearances, external and constraining facts of life.

Now these appearances are both reassuring and confusing. Arguments break out. Conflicts arise. Blood boils, tempers rise, and little sparks fly all over the place. Many little motes are dancing in beams of darkness. But, where FAIRIES fear to tread, the fools walk in. They tell silly stories. And the stories have such curious meanings that they make us say, 'Ah, yes, *now* we understand.'

Yet there are many who would usurp the role of the Fool, and we are happy to welcome them, it makes us more comfortable to feel that we understand.

So we have inherited a mixed bag of blessings, a curious *bricolage* of thoughts into which we can dip at will and pull out something *interesting*, that is to say, something which we want to hear.

And this goes for all of us. So it is hardly surprising that we feel embarrassed every time we realize that we have got our timing wrong again. We try to manipulate other people's opinions, and we find that they are manipulating ours. We leave room for others to play the goat with our thoughts because we have not succeeded in clarifying ourselves. And, by the ¿time? we settle back in our armchairs with a sigh of relief, the things have already got out of the box. They are making havoc amongst the motes and beams. And we are too late again!

But what can it *mean* to be too late? Or even too early? As Bell and Mau have said, the real embarrassment comes from the self-conscious realization that:[8]

The level of control or the timing of release of certain information may itself importantly affect the future. The present tendency among sociologists to avoid facing this question squarely by repeating the litany of a free and open dissemination of information is understandable. It is a difficult question. One can envisage a situation in which the sociologist might behave just as public health officials do today when, fearing to cause panic and widespread disorganisation, they decide to withold certain information about the spread of a dread disease in a city.

Yet, as Germaine Greer has been known to say, arrogance may be regarded as a symptom of paranoia. Who are we to know? Who are we to say? Who are we to keep our big mouths *shut*? Does it matter what we say, or when we say it?

And so, after all that we have been through together, we are still bracketing ¿time? with interrogatives. Can we remove the brackets?

Bell and Mau suggest a way of doing so from the perspective of phenomenological sociology.[9]

Time perspectives have varied considerably during the course of human history, and the immeasurable increase in the scale of modern man's conceptions of time has given new importance to the future and added meaning to the past and present. For modern man the past is not simply shrugged off as mere history but is viewed more and more in terms of its meaning for the present and future. . . . So, also, does the emergent future have present meaning or, in a sense, 'reality' with consequences shaped by man's thoughts and expectations about alternative futures. . . . Modern man can alter his past as well as his future, although in somewhat different ways. . . histories are relative to different frames of reference, selective perceptions, assumptions, concepts, and theories that are used to organize them. . . . The sociologist can see that this is true of history, but he may have difficulty accepting the fact that it is also true of sociology. The ways in which sociologists portray the present with their sample surveys, questionnaires, interview schedules, data, and statistical analyses are also relative and result in different versions of social reality. In recent years sociological 'truths' have come, in turn, to influence the way people see themselves and their societies and, thus, have been consequential for the behaviour that emerges from such conceptions. Sociologists, who have long recognized the relativity of values, are now confronting as well the relativity of their findings and interpretations. . . . The future in important respects is as real as the past, since we know both in much the same way.

And one philosopher has stated the implication of this sort of thinking in most dramatic terms, pointing out that, if one follows this relativity through, one must consider seriously the proposition that what 'appears in the future to one observer is in the past for another. The future to us seems unreal . . . *because we cannot remember it.*'[10]

But Bell and Mau go on to suggest that, 'the future is real in the sense that images of the future exist in the present . . . expectations about the future, whether short- or long-range, may enter as a determining factor into most human behaviour.'[11]

So these authors beg to persuade us to adopt Polak's model of 'Images of the Future' as an aid to understanding the business of ¿time? from a sociological viewpoint. Look at ¿time?, they say, as if 'past', 'present' and 'future' are a simultaneity, a single point, a making moment.

But it is perhaps fortunate for the honest dualists amongst us (the rationalizers, the procrastinators, the fence-dwellers and the self-despisers) that neither Bell and Mau nor Polak himself have succeeded in thinking that particular vision of ¿time? into thought. Had they done so we would no doubt be busy constructing our ¿time-machines?, perfecting the self-conscious magic of our sociological messages, *making progress with propaganda.*[12]

But we are not! The language is Irish to us. Irish and yet still Double Dutch. The green shamrock cannot be divined with the forked wand of reason.

Polak offered a 'mystical' model of ¿time?. An image of an eye in a triangle. And yet, like the rest of us, he was condemned to *think* about it. He was doomed to rethink the legends of the future. He was fated to express them in the language of binary thought, of reason, logic, science, and power.

So, surrendering his own inspiration to the freezing channels of taken-for-granted reasonableness, he finally wrote out his *time-sum* thus:

$$1 + 2 = 3$$
Past + Present = Future

You see, he had nowhere claimed that the future exists in any other ¿time? than that which appears as *later* than the here and now. *Images* of the future abound in Polak's present, as they did in his past, but yet his story still gets told in the language of rational reconstruction, it becomes part of the scientistic FAIRY TALE of progress and advancing knowledge.

And so the triangle closed in on the eye, the visionary baby went out with the BATHWATER, and with a 'fatal movement' of the left arm, the prophet wrote the following epitaph for his orphan.[13]

In setting himself purposefully to control and alter the course of events man has been forced to deal with the concepts of value, means and ends, ideals and ideologies, as he has attempted to blueprint his own future. As long as the prophet-propitiator was acting only as a divine transmitter of messages from on high, man felt that he was accepting his ethics ready-made, with no alterations allowed. In a latter stage man staggers under the double load of not only having to construct his own future but having to create the values which will determine its design.

But surely Zarathustra will never say that! Hasn't Polak misremembered the elementary arithmetic?[14] Well, this is hardly surprising. We all know that it is extremely difficult to get your sums right when you are standing on your head!

In many ways it matters very little whether or not this student of the ancient secrets could get his metaphysical sums right. If he and his initiates wish to believe that, after all is said and done, then the future is still a *will be*, a simple sum of pasts and presents, then, perhaps, this is no one's business but their own. But may it not be that they are deliberately releasing a very nasty cat from this occult bag of tricks.

It looks to *me* as though the horrible monster is on the loose, *even in the here and now*. The idea that we have to make our futures out of the remnants of the past and the taken-for-granted facts of the present has already found expression in paperback pornography. In a book called *Future Shock*, Alvin Toffler has stated:[15]

> The rate at which man has been storing up useful knowledge about himself and the universe has been spiralling upwards for 10,000 years. . . . Francis Bacon told us that 'Knowledge . . . is power'. This can now be translated into contemporary terms. In our social setting, 'Knowledge is change' – and accelerating knowledge-acquisition, fuelling the great engine of technology, means accelerating change.

What right have *I* to call this pornography? Well, *I* judge these words degrading because, like so much other popular and academic social and science fiction, they titillate an appetite which I personally find disgusting. I would like to see this taste branded as decadent, cynical, black magical, or, in sociological jargon, *fatalistic*.[16]

Now to say that I find this kind of imagery pornographic is, of course, to admit that I am a hypocrite. For, like Mrs Whitehouse, I actually do get a buzz out of my own sense of moral outrage. I feel better when I am driven to state that Toffler's own efforts at aggravating 'future shock', will tend to deprave and corrupt. So I indulge this moral outrage by quoting another passage from his book:[17]

> Man will be able, within a reasonably short period, to redesign not merely individual bodies, but the entire human race.
> One of the more fantastic possibilities is that man will be able to

make biological carbon copies of himself. Through a process known as 'cloning' it will be possible to grow from the nucleus of an adult cell a new organism that has the same genetic characteristics of the person contributing the cell nucleus. The resultant human 'copy' would start life with a genetic endowment identical to that of the donor, although cultural differences might thereafter alter the personality or physical development of the clone.

Cloning would make it possible for people to see themselves born anew, to fill the world with twins of themselves. Cloning would, among other things, provide us with solid empirical evidence to help us resolve, once and for all, the ancient controversy over 'nature *v* nurture' or 'heredity *v* environment'. The solution of this problem, through the determination of the role played by each, would be one of the great milestones of human intellectual development. Whole libraries of philosophical speculation could, by a single stroke, be rendered irrelevant. An answer to this question would open the way for speedy, qualitative advances in psychology, moral philosophy and a dozen other fields.

This is the spiralling 'up' towards 'Progress' which the fatalists herald as an inevitability. And they urge us to come to terms with it. They beg us to accept what they themselves are prepared to take for granted: the upside-down Cosmos of MOAI; the time-theory of desperation; the inverted figure of Eros. They press upon us the thoroughly hair-raising view that we must proceed *from* the 'past' *through* the 'present', *towards* the little hole marked by our viewfinders and labelled 'future'.

Yes. I admit it again. It *is* titillating. The story of Progress and Advancing Knowledge makes fascinating bedtime reading for grown-up Jerry Corneliuses. But we remain moral censors and hypocrites at heart. These are not nice FAIRY TALES for the children.

So now that we have eaten the fruit of most of the presently available trees we have grown up as ugly giants of civilization, fuelling our own psychosomatic progeria with the wages of excess. And we are too old to get back into the Gemeinschaft garden.

We know that there is no return to innocence, no glory to be found in sentimental longings for the fondly imagined past. For if sociology has taught us anything at all it has shown that the past is as unfinished as the future. Yet the way forward into the *foreseeable* future really does not look too good for the littlees, does it?

No. Perhaps we have not forgotten that the children themselves are more optimistic. We might yet remember that, once upon a long-forgotten-time, we worked out the sum a little differently.

From the perspective of the Druids, for example, the three primary ornaments of wisdom are combined in the whole. The first 'was' love.

The second 'will be' Truth$_1$. And, in their addition the third 'is' found: courage. And so they describe the present moment in the motto 'The Truth Against The World'. This is the way they tell the Time.

$$1 \; + \; 2 \; = \; 3$$

Past + Future = Present

Yes, I agree. Their technology is too complex for our 'merely modern' taken-for-granted ways of mapping alternative futures. We can hardly begin to remember the point of alignment from which one may glimpse the child as he rides out through the gates of Time.

There are, of course, the occasional lunatics who remember the moment making the sum 'One, two, and three makes me.'[18] Generally, however, we regard this kind of flash as a portent of a nervous breakdown or other schizophrenic outburst, and either abort it before it is born into thought, or take appropriate steps to destroy it if it does escape through the birth channel of language.

There have also been courageous philosophers, anthropologists, and other thinkers who have sought to uncover the hidden structures of our present moments in the residues of meanings which make up currently taken-for-granted paradigms of thought. Feeling 'instinctively' that 'He who the invisible would find must look before him and behind', they seek to make sense out of the appearances which are the givens of our written and oral linguistic traditions. Consider, for example, the correspondences set out in the *ad hoc* Table 5.

If these words strike no chords in your memory then maybe you agree with W. S. Gilbert: 'The meaning doesn't matter if it is only idle chatter of a transcendental kind.'

'*Must* a name mean something?' Alice asked doubtfully.

'Of course it must,' Humpty Dumpty said with a short laugh: '*my* name means the shape I am – and a good handsome shape it is, too. With a name like yours, you might be any shape, almost.'

[See the illustration on page 437.]

'The question is,' said Alice, 'whether you *can* make words mean so many different things.'

'The question is,' said Humpty Dumpty, 'which is to be master – that's all.' . . .

'Impenetrability! That's what *I* say!'

'Would you tell me, please,' said Alice, 'what that means?'

'Now you talk like a reasonable child,' said Humpty Dumpty, looking very much pleased. 'I meant by "impenetrability" that we've had enough of that subject, and it would be just as well if you'd mention what you mean to do next, as I suppose you don't mean to stop here all the rest of your life.'

TABLE 5 *Humpty Dumpty's Impenetrables*

1	+ 2	= 3
Unity	Division	Opinion
Unthinkable	Thinking	Thought
Simplicity	Duality	Complexity
Thesis	Antithesis	Synthesis
Sum	Cogito	Ergo
Yes	No	Therefore
I	I/Not-I	Me
Inspiration	Reason	Recognition
Understanding	Objectivity	Commitment
Affirmation	Doubt	Inertia
Absolute	Universal	Particular
History	Ideology	Praxis
Dream	Reason	Effect
Spirit	Soul	Mind
Reality	Illusion	Shattered ear
Macrocosm	Imagination	Microcosm
Grace	Vanity	Duty
Beatrix	Lilith	Ophelia
Light	Dark	Patterned
Cosmic yawn	Sea	Silver fish
Quality	Quantity	Measure
Author	Meaning	Sentence
Child	Ancestor	Zarathustra
Sun	Moons	Earth
Love	Will	Work
Artist	Image	Creation
Siva	Kali	Scattered seed
White bird	Horned beast	Ass
Conception	Parentage	Man
Wisdom	Knowledge	Fall
Logos	Pronoia	Paranoia
Faith	Hope	Charity
Beauty	Lovers	Clay
Absorbing	Realizing	Building
Tree	Wood	Carpenter
Amgrin	Hadding	Yoked labour
Paper	Scissors	Stone
Stone	Scissors	Paper
Thor	Loki	Midgard
Oak	Ash	Thorn
Apollo	Muses	Poetic justice
Zeus	Poseidon	Cronos
Legend	Prophecy	Fulfilment
Egg	Fork	Omelette

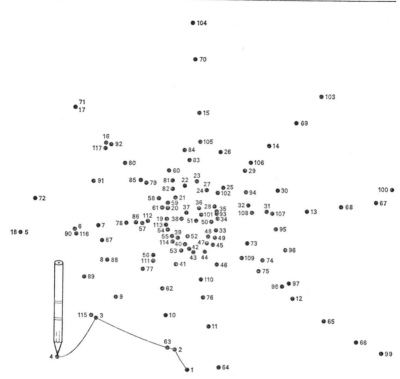

'With a name like yours you could be any shape, almost'

But it *is* more than a little hard to do anything at all when you can't seem to get the timing right.

Of one thing at least *I* am sure. We have missed the boat. *Now* what?

Shall we continue to mistake the urgent click-clack-shick of the computer-cash register for the cosmic metronome? Shall we continue to strive for Progress? Shall we improve our machinery, tighten up our methodology, perfect our silver fish to swim down the plugholes of our taken-for-granted worlds?

'ATTENTION SAID THE TENSER TENSION APPREHENSION AND DISSENSION HAVE BEGUN'

Shall we carry on flapping our ears in anticipation of the plangent twangs of ¿truth? ? Shall we go on listening *out*? *Shall* we?

I almost seem to remember . . . .

It was in the remembering that we found ourselves,[19] and our vocation. Did we remember? *Do* we?

At the back of the North Wind we can still see the earthworks as they are. Dents in the underbelly of the sky. And every stone, star, slug and social scientist has a part of the song. We *can* remember, Alice. Listen to the fairy drums! They are playing our tune. It is the song we were singing when we joined the March.

Which is the border?
The coast of all the lands?
Where score the line?
Where make the mark
Twixt thy work
And thine own hands?

Fairy days,
Fairy ways,
Fairy fears, fairy fires, fairy foes!

Sing your song!
Turn from wrong!
Sing it well!
We will tell!
You must tell!
Do it well!
For *you*
Are one among many
While many
Are they
To you
And *we*
Are one and yet many
As many are one
In
One.

Notes

10 The Light is Above

1 Barney Glaser and Anselm Strauss, *The Discovery of Grounded Theory* (London, Weidenfeld & Nicolson, 1967).
2 John Stuart Mill, *A System of Logic* (London, A. & C. Black, 1911), 3rd edn.

11 A Short Cut from A to B

1 See p. 49.
2 Cf. S. Tolman, 'A psychological model', in T. Parsons and E. A. Shils (eds), *Toward a General Theory of Action* (Harvard University Press, 1951).
3 Even if your knowledge of sociological theorizing was perfect you would obviously still have been able to anticipate only those EX-TRANEOUS VARIABLES which might be suggested from the standpoint of theories which had already been formulated, either by you or by others. The possibility would always remain that someone would devise a new theory to save the same appearances, a theory which made use of variables which had not hitherto been considered in connection with the dependent variable in question.

12 Rabbit on the Shopping List

1 See above, particularly chapter 7.
2 Adapted from Leslie Kish, 'Some statistical problems in research design', *American Sociological Review*, 24 (1959), particularly pp. 329–30.
3 Actually, however, the extent to which this was a reasonable assumption would depend upon the range and degree of variation attributed to that 'constant'.
4 A bait is a small tin box lined with greaseproof paper, generally containing either jam butties or bacon sarnies. More provident bunnies also provide themselves with a vacuum flask of strong tea.

13 Will You Join the Dance?

1 See chapters 6 and 9.
2 Adapted from Lazarsfeld's famous scheme first published in *Daedalus*, 87 (1958), pp. 99–129 and now available in May Brodbeck (ed.),

Readings in the Philosophy of the Social Sciences (New York, Macmillan, 1968).

3 Melvin Seeman, 'On the meaning of alienation', *American Sociological Review*, 24 (6) (1959), pp. 783–91. For a fairly comprehensive collection of alienation-scales which have developed out of this work, see Charles M. Bonjean, Richard J. Hill and S. Dale McLemore, *Sociological Measurement: An Inventory of Scales and Indices* (New Castle, New Hampshire, Chandler, 1967). Use index.

4 R. Blauner, *Alienation and Freedom* (University of Chicago Press, 1964).

5 This pondering might even lead to revisions of your theory. For example, consider the component '*normlessness*' which has been suggested as a constituent of '*alienation*'. This seems similar to the notion of '*anomie*' which, like '*alienation*', has wide currency in sociological thought. This observation might stimulate thought along the lines that these two conditions might be related in some interesting manner. Actually sociologists who have followed these lines of thought have ended up barking up very sticky gum trees, mainly because they have neglected to distinguish operational from theoretical notions, and to appreciate the way in which the latter are intrinsically bound up with entire theoretical frameworks.

6 See F. S. C. Northrop, *The Logic of the Sciences and Humanities* (London, Macmillan, 1947).

7 Anyone who is familiar with the substantive field of sociological research into the use of drugs should object strongly to my simplistic use of the term 'euphoriant', as this term can be misleading. For the benefit of any such pedants who have got as far as reading this footnote I offer the following definition of a 'euphoriant drug': *Any chemical substance which is consumed deliberately in order to produce some alteration in consciousness*. This definition includes drugs acting as both stimulants and depressants on the central nervous system, and is not by any means restricted to the hallucinogens. Of course, from the point of view of *someone else*'s theory, this lumping together of alcohol, nicotine, barbiturates, amphetamines, narcotics, cannabis derivatives, and other drugs might be seen as woefully inadequate.

8 Hubert M. Blalock, *Causal Inferences in Nonexperimental Research* (University of North Carolina Press, 1961), pp. 5–6 (italicization slightly revised). Blalock cites Arthur S. Eddington, *The Nature of the Physical World* (New York, Macmillan, 1933), pp. 251–5.

9 See chapter 6.

10 See chapter 16.

11 For discussions of the strategies which may be employed in accordance with the PRINCIPLE OF TRIANGULATION you might find it helpful to consult the following other texts: Norman K. Denzin, *The Research Act in Sociology* (London, Butterworth, 1970); Eugene J. Webb, Donald T. Campbell, Richard D. Schwartz and Lee Sechrest, *Unobtrusive Measures* (Chicago, Rand McNally, 1970). Use indexes.

12 The Hall-Jones scale represents one of the most useful ready-made instruments for measuring social class. Based originally on a survey of occupational prestige, it constitutes a ranking of the relative prestige attributed to various occupations by ordinary English people. As such it is clearly a more subjectively meaningful device than, say, the Registrar General's Classification which is based on nothing more than the Registrar General's own ideas about the ranking of occupa-

tions. For details of the Hall-Jones Scale see John Hall and D. Caradog Jones, 'Social grading of occupations', *British Journal of Sociology*, 1 (1950), pp. 31–55. But note that, apart from being out of date, this scale has certain other deficiencies which may make it unsuitable in certain research circumstances. See P. Wilmott and M. Young, 'Social grading by manual workers', *British Journal of Sociology*, 7 (1956), pp. 337–45. Further information on the operationalization of social class in Britain can be found in M. Kahan, D. Butler and D. Stokes, 'On the analytical division of social class', *British Journal of Sociology*, 17 (2) (1966), pp. 122–32; and see also D. Lockwood, 'Sources of variation in working class images of society', *Sociological Review*, 14 (1966), pp. 249–67.

13 See p. 177.

14 I say 'make any *further* decisions' because, of course, you have necessarily imposed some constraints on your sampling strategies already. Your *'Inventory of Variables to be Measured'* is based upon assumptions about which variables will have been controlled by your sampling, whether through *randomization* or *selection*.

15 Not a few English criminologists of the late nineteenth and early twentieth centuries carried Lombrosa's hunches to some shocking extremes. But one of the most astounding examples which has come to my notice was carried out by American social psychologists on prisoners of war. See H. S. Guetzkow and P. H. Bowman, *Men and Hunger* (Minnesota University Press, 1950).

16 See examples of the Sherifs' work in their introductory text, *An Outline of Social Psychology*, M. and C. W. Sherif (New York, Harper & Row, 1956).

17 See, for examples, S. Feshbach and R. D. Singer, 'The effects of fear arousal and suppression of fear upon social perception', *Journal of Abnormal and Social Psychology*, 55 (1957), pp. 283–8; S. Schachter, *The Psychology of Affiliation* (Stanford University Press, 1959); Nancy B. Otis and B. McCandless, 'Responses to repeated frustrations of young children differentiated according to need area', *Journal of Abnormal and Social Psychology*, 50 (1955), pp. 349–53; J. R. Davitz, 'The effects of previous training on post-frustration behaviour', ibid., 47 (1952), pp. 309–15; L. Festinger and J. M. Carlsmith, 'Cognitive consequences of forced compliance', ibid., 58 (1959), pp. 203–10.

18 Actually, of course, they didn't *'discover'* anything! For, as Carey has pointed out, observations from the later studies were 'interpreted in the light of . . . prior conclusions based on the earlier studies'. Alex Carey, 'The Hawthorne Studies: a radical criticism', *American Sociological Review*, 32 (1967).

19 F. J. Roethlisberger and W. J. Dickson, *Management and the Worker* (Harvard University Press, 1939).

20 I am thinking particularly of their lack of adequate analysis of the effects of EXTRANEOUS VARIABLES such as *method of payment* and *mode of authority*. On the first see Morris S. Viteles, *Motivation and Morale in Industry* (London, Staples, 1954), particularly p. 185. On the second, Paul Blumberg, *Industrial Democracy: The Sociology of Participation* (London, Constable, 1968), p. 25.

21 Roethlisberger and Dickson, op. cit., pp. 53–60.

22 I assure you it *can* be done! Notice that most experimental design does involve some attempts to control for the 'Hawthorne Effect'. For, by

comparing two groups, 'an experimental group' and a 'control group', which are both constant as far as the-fact-of-being-studied is concerned but varied in other respects, it is hoped that the effects of the experiment itself will be neutralized. However this may not be the case as other EXTRANEOUS VARIABLES may interact with the 'Hawthorne Effect', or that effect may interact with the EXPERIMENTAL VARIABLES, in ways unknown to the researcher.

23 Harold Garfinkel, *Studies in Ethnomethodology* (Englewood Cliffs, New Jersey, Prentice-Hall, 1967), pp. 44–53.

24 Ibid., pp. 57–60.

25 Gideon Sjoberg, *The Preindustrial City* (New York, Free Press, 1960).

26 See L. Wirth, 'Urbanism as a way of life', *American Journal of Sociology*, 44 (1938), pp. 1–24; and R. E. Park, *The City* (University of Chicago Press, 1925).

27 For examples see W. L. Kolb, 'The social structure and function of cities', *Economic Development and Cultural Change*, 3 (1954), 30–46; W. Firey, *Land Use in Central Boston* (Harvard University Press, 1947) and R. E. Dickinson, *The West European City* (London, Routledge & Kegan Paul, 1951).

28 For examples see Sjoberg, op. cit.

29 See above, pp. 121–2.

30 See above, pp. 47, 128–9.

31 See Gideon Sjoberg, 'Comparative urban sociology', in R. K. Merton, L. Broom and L. S. Cottrell (eds), *Sociology Today* (New York, Harper & Row, 1959), pp. 334–59.

32 See above, p. 000.

33 G. Santayana, *The Life of Reason* (London, Constable, revised edn, 1954), p. 399.

34 See above, p. 103, 254.

35 Cited in W. H. Walsh, *An Introduction to the Philosophy of History* (London, Hutchinson, 1951), p. 4.

36 See for example Clifford Geertz, 'Studies in peasant life: community and society', in B. J. Siegel (ed.), *Biennial Review of Anthropology* (Stanford University Press, 1962), pp. 1–41: Robert S. and Helen M. Lynd, *Middletown* (New York, Harcourt, 1929); W. Lloyd Warner and Paul S. Lunt, *The Social Life of a Modern Community* (New Haven, Yale University Press, 1941); August B. Hollingshead, *Elmtown's Youth* (New York, Wiley, 1949).

37 Gideon Sjoberg and Roger Nett, *A Methodology for Social Research* (New York, Harper & Row, 1968), p. 261.

38 Ralph H. Turner, 'The quest for universals in sociological research', *American Sociological Review*, 18 (1953), pp. 604–11; see also Sjoberg and Nett, op. cit.

39 Ibid., p. 264.

40 See Garfinkel, op. cit., pp. 116–85 where Garfinkel immerses himself in the particulars of Agnes's vagina, emerging occasionally with profound insights allegedly glimpsed therein, such as the following 'table of transition probabilities':

		At time$_2$	
		Male	*Female*
At time$_1$	*Male*	1·0	0·0
	Female	0·0	1·0

p. 117 (*sic!*)

41 See for an example, Morris Zelditch, Jr, 'Role differentiation in the nuclear family: a comparative study', in Matilda White Riley, *Sociological Research: 1 A Case Approach* (New York, Harcourt, 1963), pp. 212–23, and see also pp. 244–9.

42 'Safe' because I'm not taking many risks: you will find it difficult to test this hypothesis! (Who is a 'typical' MENTAL experimenter?)

43 See Florian Znaniecki's exposition of his method of 'analytic induction' in his *The Method of Sociology* (New York, Holt, Rinehart & Winston, 1934).

44 Sjoberg and Nett, op. cit., p. 259.

45 Ambrose Bierce, *The Enlarged Devil's Dictionary* (ed. E. Hopkins, Harmondsworth, Penguin Books, 1971).

46 More seriously, the reasoning behind this choice of term is based upon the following calculation: 'Thrice three is phew!', Peter Piper.

47 David Matza, *Becoming Deviant* (Englewood Cliffs, New Jersey, Prentice-Hall, 1969).

14 A Most Unlikely Story

1 David Willer, *Scientific Sociology: Theory and Method* (Englewood Cliffs, New Jersey, Prentice-Hall, 1967), p. 101.

2 D. O. Arnold, 'Dimensional sampling: an approach for studying a small number of cases', *American Sociologist*, 5 (2) (1970), p. 147.

3 Cf. A. Sio, 'Interpretations of slavery: the slave status in the Americas', *Comparative Studies in Society and History*, 1965.

4 Cf. Gideon Sjoberg and Roger Nett, *A Methodology for Social Research* (New York, Harper & Row, 1968), chapters 5 and 6.

5 I am ignoring the further complication of *regression to the mean* which may also be raised in this context. On this, see R. P. Althauser and Donald Rubin, 'Selection and regression to the mean' (mimeographed, Princeton University Press, 1970); R. L. Thordnike, 'Regression fallacies in the matched group experiment', *Psychometrika*, 7, pp. 85–102. And, when it is remembered that all sampling also occurs in ¿time?, further problems of regression to the mean must also be considered. See for example, Gordon Horobin, David Oldman and Bill Bytheway, 'The social differentiation of ability', *Sociology*, 1 (2) (1967), pp. 113–29.

6 Robert P. Althauser and Donald Rubin, 'The computerized construction of a matched sample', *American Journal of Sociology*, 76 (2) (1970), p. 325.

7 Ibid., p. 328.

8 Chapter 6.

9 Althauser and Rubin, op. cit.; Ronald Freedman, 'Incomplete matching in ex post facto studies', *American Journal of Sociology*, 55 (March, 1950), pp. 485–7; W. Z. Billewicz, 'The efficiency of matched samples: an empirical investigation', *Biometrics*, 21, pp. 623–43.

10 Ronald A. Fisher, *The Design of Experiments* (Edinburgh, Oliver & Boyd, 1937).

11 Beatrix Potter, *The Tale of Jeremy Fisher*.

12 Robert S. Weiss, *Statistics in Social Research* (New York, Wiley, 1968), p. 222, italics in original.

13 Ibid., p. 223.

14 W. Edwards Deming, *Sampling Design in Business Research* (New York, Wiley, 1960), p. 24.
15 E. F. Byrne, *Probability and Opinion* (The Hague, Martinus Nijhoff, 1968), p. 293.
16 Cf. Pius Servien, *Hasard et Probabilités* (Paris, 1949).
17 Thus Popper directs his attention to the problem of 'decideability': it is a question of establishing 'intervals of imprecision' and then deciding how much deviation one will tolerate within those limits.
18 Cited in Byrne, op. cit.
19 Byrne's translation from *La Science et l'Hypothèse*, 1902.
20 See Byrne, op. cit., p. 301, and Servien, op. cit.
21 Sjoberg and Nett, op. cit., p. 147.
22 Weiss, op. cit., p. 222.
23 A. R. Ilersic, *Statistics* (London, HFL Publishers, 1964) (13th edn), p. 219.
24 Actually, of course, in *reality*, they don't! There is bias deriving from the shape and folding of the tickets, the nature of the inside of the hat, the order of placing the papers in the hat, the degree of shaking of the hat, and the perspiration on the celebrity's fingertips.
25 Charles Sanders Peirce, *Collected Papers*, ed. Charles Hartshorne and Paul Weiss (Cambridge University Press, 1932), vol. 7, 126. Also cited in David Willer, *Scientific Sociology: Theory and Method* (Englewood Cliffs, New Jersey, Prentice-Hall, 1967).
26 Ibid., p. 102.
27 Byrne, op. cit., pp. 303–4.
28 Carl G. Hempel, *Philosophy of Natural Science* (Englewood Cliffs, New Jersey, Prentice-Hall, 1966), p. 68.
29 Ibid.
30 And this is even more so when computers are involved. Cf. R. S. Lee, 'Social attitudes to the computer', *Public Opinion Quarterly*, 34 (4) (1970), pp. 53–9.
31 Please see the discussion of the social communication of sociological messages in chapter 20.
32 Byrne, op. cit., p. 303.
33 P. S. de Laplace, *A Philosophical Essay on Probabilities* (trans. F. W. Truscott and F. L. Emory, New York, Dover, 1951), pp. 6–7.
34 It is interesting to consider the role of the Darwinian legend in the subsequent development of the scientistic metaphysic of *Chance*. It is at least arguable that this theory of evolution gave extra thickness to the foundation upon which a new idolatry has been based. Thus the monster *Chance* has come to usurp the throne of ultimate causation previously reserved for a, no less humorous, but certainly not mocking, Primum Mobile. For a hilarious, and thoroughly muddle-headed exposition of this new theology, see the work of that other frog, Jacques Monod.
35 Hempel, op. cit., p. 62.
36 Hanan C. Selvin, 'A critique of tests of significance in survey research', *American Sociological Review*, 22 (1957), pp. 519–27.
37 Ibid.
38 Selvin, op. cit., p. 526.
39 This is loosely remembered from Travis Hirschi and Hanan Selvin, *Delinquency Research: An Appraisal of Analytic Methods* (London, Macmillan, 1967).

40 I have tried to find a form in which to express these propositions so that, being contentless they can be interpreted from the standpoint *either* of the so-called 'logical' theory of probability, *or* of the 'statistical' or 'frequency' interpretation of the calculus. The former have, of course, been expounded by Russell and others, and the latter are made explicit in the work of A. N. Kolmogorov, *Foundations of the Theory of Probability* (New York, Chelsea Publishing, 1950) and R. A. Fisher, *The Design of Experiments* (Edinburgh, Oliver & Boyd, 1937). If, as I hope, these propositions can be read as contentless then they may also be interpreted from the standpoint of a third approach to probability which I have not discussed. This is the 'subjective' or 'personalistic' approach, discussed at some length by Michael Polanyi in his *Personal Knowledge* (London, Routledge & Kegan Paul, 1969), and by C. Perelman with L. Olbrechts-Tyteca in *New Rhetoric: Treatise on Argumentation* (University of Notre Dame Press, 1973), and made explicit as statistical theory in L. J. Savage, *Foundations of Statistics* (New York, Wiley, 1954).

41 And, of course, subsidiary theorems may be derived to cover situations in which inclusive or overlapping assessments of probabilities are to be considered simultaneously.

Perhaps it is worth pointing out that, if a reaxiomatization of the calculus were made, *starting off* with statements about *overlapping* events (which have the status of mere theorems in the standard axiomatization), then the deductive relations in the newly axiomatized calculus would need to be thought through. This would be a first problem for anyone concerned to reformulate the calculus, and taking questions about overlapping probabilities as central to his programme.

15 The Amazing, Incredible Sampling Machine

1 'In a letter to child-friend Mary Macdonald, 1864, Carroll warned: Don't be in such a hurry to believe next time – I'll tell you why – If you set to work to believe everything, you will tire out the muscles of your mind, and then you'll be so weak you won't be able to believe the simplest true things. Only last week a friend of mine set to work to believe Jack-the-giant-killer. He managed to do it, but he was so exhausted by it that when I told him it was raining (which was true) he *couldn't* believe it, but rushed out in to the street without his hat or umbrella, the consequence of which was his hair got seriously damp, and one curl didn't recover its right shape for nearly two days.' (*The Annotated Alice*, ed. Martin Gardner, p. 251, n. 5.)

2 In some ways this definition is like Cochran's, but Cochran's 'principle of specified precision at minimum cost' assumes that the selection of s from S is the *only* kind of sampling problem, and completely ignores the larger and more important class of problems involved in the selection of S itself. W. Cochran, *Sampling Techniques* (New York, Wiley, 1953), pp. 1–5.

3 That is, like the variable C (country of residence) in the gerontological sociologists' example a few pages ago.

4 The term 'interactional' or rather, 'interactive' sampling appears in Norman K. Denzin, *The Research Act in Sociology* (London, Butterworth, 1970), p. 89. I don't know whether it is original with him, but anyway, the animal is not of my own invention.

5 Obviously there is nothing intrinsically arithmetic about this use of numbers – one could use any other labels, numbers simply make convenient filing tags.

6 I shall return to the business of sociometrics in chapter 19.

7 The assumption being made here is that the inevitability of truthfulness₂ is not systematic. Though the respondents may be cagey they will rarely be conspiring *together* to give the researcher a false impression of the composition and scope of the group in question. This assumption may or may not be realistic.

8 Of course this classification is crude and arbitrary. It is tempting to go for greater numerical finesse, for example by calculating an 'Inclusion Score', or some such tally, for each unit according to the number of maps in which it appears (excluding, of course, those where it is located as a starting unit, or, say, by calculating the number of connections with other units described by those maps). Once such a score had been constructed a much finer classification than my simple dichotomy would be possible. However the dangers with this sort of quantification should be obvious, and it is essential to remember that the purpose of the enterprise is not the induction of sociometric generalizations from the set, but the selection of a sample for purposes of testing deductively valid hypotheses derived from the theory defining the set in question.

9 For example, in a theory about social marginality or one about anticipatory socialization, or, say, initiation rituals.

10 This subsample may, of course, be selected by some more complicated form of interactional sampling, say by one of those which we will be considering in a minute. Or, since you will now have a complete listing of units you may wish to select a subsample by probability methods. I shall be returning to the question of subsampling in a moment or two.

11 The necessity to maintain secrecy about the fact of the research may not be the least of these. It is only in rare cases that respondents may wish to co-operate with an overtly sociological enterprise. This is not only because many, especially 'deviant', social groups are suspicious of sociologists, but also because they are, quite understandably, disdainful of it. However, where a researcher finds himself needing to maintain secrecy about the fact, or details, of his research, he should stop to consider whether or not he does have a ¿good reason? for doing it at all! I shall return to this question later.

12 See Elihu Katz and Paul F. Lazarsfeld, *Personal Influence* (Chicago, Free Press, 1955).

13 Notice that I have discussed these structural methods of sampling as though we were implicitly assuming that these methods would only be employed where the units in question are *persons*. This was an oversimplification. There will be circumstances under which you might attempt methods formally analogous with these in the process of selecting other sorts of units (see chapter 17).

14 Additionally, you may wish to complicate matters further by drawing a subsample by some variant of the key location methods discussed above. This might, indeed, be your only reasonable course where each unit of your original sample could not be assumed to be equally ¿interesting? in respect of the subsampling.

15 See for more details, pp. 222–5 of William J. Goode and Paul K. Hatt, *Methods in Social Research* (New York, McGraw-Hill, 1952).

16 This danger involves the *ecological fallacy*, which issue will be raised again.

17 Indeed, I suspect that it is the use of area sampling in this way which has generally been responsible for the silly attempts by empirically minded researchers to set about drawing probability samples in the absence of prior purposive decisions. It is easy to fall into the comfortable belief that the boundaries of a theoretical universe have the same epistemological status as fences, streets, and the edges of maps.

18 I refer to the 'wise old owl' who was watching us through one eye in chapter 4.

19 See Severyn T. Bruyn, *The Human Perspective in Sociology* (Englewood Cliffs, New Jersey, Prentice-Hall, 1966), pp. 203–4.

20 Elizabeth Bott, *Family, and Social Network* (London, Tavistock, 1957).

21 See J. Aldous and M. A. Strauss, 'Social networks and conjugal roles: a test of Bott's hypothesis', *Social Forces*, 44 (4) (1966), pp. 576ff.

22 Office workers may well be more cheerful and pleasantly disposed towards others on Fridays than on Mondays; everyone doing day work is likely to be more tired in the evening than earlier in the day; and, as Durkheim pointed out, the time of year also bears a plausible causal relationship with the emotions.

23 For some examples of method, see Paul F. Lazarsfeld, Ann K. Pasanella and Morris Rosenberg, *Continuities in the Language of Social Research* (New York, Free Press, 1972), pp. 321ff.

24 And this consideration is particularly interesting where the hypotheses under test involve what are sometimes known as '*structural effects*'. For example, you may have a theory which states for example, working-class children are more likely to land up in the 'D' stream of a comprehensive school. Another proposition of your theory may claim that 'D' stream children are much more likely to get involved in so-called deviant countercultural gangs at school than are kids in other streams. Thus you have the problem of separating the 'structural effect' of 'D' stream placing from the 'individual' contributions of working-class socialization patterns. Clearly ¿time? may become a crucial variable in such a situation. Further issues raised by the problems of sampling in ¿time? are well covered in Eugene J. Webb *et al.*, *Unobtrusive Measures* (Chicago, Rand McNally, 1970), pp. 135–8.

25 See above, pp. 151–2.

26 I hope that it is at least a little more digestible than some of the other devices which are presently available. See for example Johan Galtung, *Theory and Methods of Social Research* (London, Allen & Unwin, 1967), p. 56, 'A diagram of different types of sampling'.

27 Um.

28 But this propaganda would, presumably, backfire the moment any other reasonable person spotted and publicized the sampling deficiency.

29 This tactic owes something to Peirce's strategy: begin with the hypothesis that is most likely to be falsified.

30 See for examples, Denzin, op. cit., p. 95, Webb *et al.*, op. cit.; and Barney Glaser and Anselm Strauss, *The Discovery of Grounded Theory* (London, Weidenfeld & Nicolson, 1967).

31 Glaser and Strauss, op. cit., pp. 65–6.

32 Ibid., p. 61.

33 Ibid.

34 Ibid.

16 A Box of My Own Invention

1 See above, pp. 14, 57.
2 See above, p. 40.
3 See above, pp. 235, 240.
4 Peter L. Berger and Hansfried Kellner, 'Marriage and the construction of reality', *Diogenes*, 46 (1964), republished in Hans Peter Dreitzel (ed.), *Recent Sociology*, *No 2* (Collier-Macmillan, 1970), pp. 63–4.
5 See above, p. 97.
6 See above, p. 269.
7 William J. Goode and Paul K. Hatt, *Methods in Social Research* (New York, McGraw-Hill, 1952), p. 235.
8 C. Sellitz, M. Jahoda, M. Deutsch and S. W. Cook, *Research Methods in Social Relations* (New York, Holt, 1959), p. 97. See also Eugene J. Webb *et al.*, *Unobtrusive Measures: Nonreactive Research in the Social Sciences* (Chicago, Rand McNally, 1970), p. 13, where the above is cited; D. T. Campbell, 'Factors relevant to the validity of experiments in social settings', *Psychological Bulletin*, 54 (1957), pp. 297–312.
9 Julienne Ford, *Social Class and the Comprehensive School* (London, Routledge & Kegan Paul, 1970), pp. 145–6.
10 See above, p. 247.
11 Ford, op. cit. The procedure used follows that of James A. Davis, 'Locals and cosmopolitans in American graduate schools', *International Journal of Comparative Sociology*, 2 (1961), pp. 212–23.
12 Goode and Hatt, op. cit., p. 236.
13 Ibid.
14 Ibid.
15 See above, pp. 179–83.
16 For an explanation of the derivation and use of this statistic see Allen L. Edwards, *Statistical Methods for the Behavioral Sciences* (New York, Holt, Rinehart & Winston, 1954), pp. 402–3, and J. C. Simms and R. D. Collins, 'Sociological research applications of an algorithm for the coefficient of concordance', *American Sociologist*, 4 (4) (1969), pp. 321–4.
17 And, of course, nothing at all has been said yet about the vexed question of VALIDITY. Any bunny responsible for a statement like this one ought to be skinned alive: 'Coefficients of the order of 0·6 and 0·7 were obtained and so the operationalization was considered to be valid'! Ford, op. cit., p. 75.
18 See above, pp. 245.
19 Irwin Deutscher, 'Looking backward: case studies on the progress of methodology in sociological research', *American Sociologist*, 4 (1969), p. 36.
20 I have borrowed the images from Ray Bradbury's novel, *Fahrenheit 451* ('the temperature at which book-paper catches fire and burns').
21 Cf. Lakatos: 'indeed, for the sort of Popperian empiricism I advocate, the only relevant evidence is the evidence anticipated by a theory', in Imre Lakatos and Alan Musgrave (eds), *Criticism and the Growth of Knowledge* (Cambridge University Press, 1970), p. 123.
22 Richard T. La Piere, 'Comment on Irwin Deutscher's "Looking Backward"', *American Sociologist*, 4 (1969), pp. 41–2.

23 Carlo L. Lastrucci, 'Looking forward: the case for hard-nosed methodology', *American Sociologist*, 5 (3) (1970).
24 See, for example Hubert M. Blalock, *Causal Inferences in Nonexperimental Research* (University of North Carolina Press, 1961), especially p. 5.
25 Karl R. Popper, *The Poverty of Historicism* (London, Routledge & Kegan Paul, 2nd edn, 1960).
26 Webb *et al.*, op. cit., p. 16.
27 Ibid., p. 17; and see the discussion of the famous Hawthorne Experiments above, pp. 248–9.
28 I refer, of course, to the 'Heisenberg Uncertainty Principle' which is based on the assumption that instruments used to measure the velocity and position of an electron inevitably affect the actual readings.
29 These strategies will be discussed in detail below.
30 Johan Galtung, *Theory and Methods of Social Research* (London, Allen & Unwin, 1967), p. 29.
31 However, it should be obvious that *all* data are structured in some way. Thus there is no such thing as genuinely unstructured data. But, none the less, some data confront the researcher initially in a form which *appears to him* to lack manifest patterning, because *he* is unable to apply the first-order categorization in terms of which the data are generated.
32 The precision, and hence the riskiness of the testing methods available will, of course, increase with the rigidity of the scaling technique. Ratio scales will, in this sense, be preferable to interval scales which will be preferable to ordinal scales which will be preferable to nominal ones. This is simply because the more 'mathematical' the scaling the more 'mathematical' can be the methods of arbitrating the tests. I will return to this point in the following chapters.
33 See, for some examples, Donald T. Campbell and Julian C. Stanley, 'Experimental and quasi-experimental designs for research on teaching', in N. L. Gage (ed.), *Handbook of Research on Teaching* (Chicago, Rand McNally, 1963), chapter 5; Robert Rosenthal, *Experimenter Effects in Behavioral Research* (New York, Appleton-Century-Crofts, 1966); Neil Freidman, *The Social Nature of Psychological Research* (New York, Basic Books, 1967); Martin T. Orne, 'On the social psychology of the psychological experiment: with special reference to demand characteristics and their implications', *American Psychologist*, 17 (1962), pp. 776–83; and Norman K. Denzin, *The Research Act in Sociology* (London, Butterworth, 1970), pp. 154–60.
34 Webb *et al.*, op. cit., p. 1.

17 Uncertain Measures

1 Eugene J. Webb, Donald T. Campbell, Richard D. Schwartz, Lee Sechrest, *Unobtrusive Measures: Nonreactive Research in the Social Sciences* (Chicago, Rand McNally, 1970), p. 36.
2 W. L. Prosser, *Handbook of the Law of Torts* (St Paul, 1964), p. 216, cited in Webb *et al.*, op. cit., p. 5. No *man* may be, but perhaps I am not the only lunatic who would accept *both*!
3 J. W. Brown, unpublished manuscript cited in Webb *et al.*, op. cit., p. 38.

4 Ibid., p. 39.
5 Ibid., p. 41.
6 C. N. Du Bois, 'Time Magazine's fingerprints study', *Proceedings: 9th Conference, Advertising Research Foundation* (New York, 1963), cited in Webb *et al.*, op. cit., p. 40.
7 R. Naroll, *Data Quality Control* (New York, Free Press, 1962), cited in Webb *et al.*, op. cit., p. 40.
8 D. C. McClelland, *The Achieving Society* (New York, Van Nostrand, 1961), p. 117 and quoted in Webb *et al.*, op. cit., p. 41.
9 L. Sechrest, in Webb *et al.*, op. cit., p. 40.
10 Ibid., p. 38. They are quoting F. Mosteller, 'Use as evidenced by an examination of wear and tear on selected sets of E.SS', in K. Davis *et al.*, 'A study of the need for a new encyclopedic treatment of the social sciences', 1955 (unpublished).
11 J. Durand, 'Mortality estimates from Roman tombstone inscriptions', *American Journal of Sociology*, 65 (1960), pp. 365–73. And see also W. L. Warner, *The Living and the Dead* (Yale University Press, 1959), who also stipulated some rigid measurements of tombstones (i.e. some STIP 1).
12 A. J. Webberman, self-styled 'Dylanologist'. Since his thoroughly mean-minded attempts to categorize the contents of Bob Dylan's dustbins, he has, unfortunately, gone on to grub about in the detritus of certain other prominent public figures such as Muhammad Ali.
13 Webb *et al.*, op. cit., pp. 45–6 and footnote on p. 46.
14 Ibid., p. 3.
15 T. L. Burton and G. E. Cherry, *Social Science Techniques for Planners* (London, Allen & Unwin, 1970), p. 100.
16 Notice that great care would have to be taken to ensure appropriate sampling in ¿time? for all three of these methods.
17 A. M. Barch, D. Trumbo and J. Nangle, 'Social setting and conformity to a legal requirement', *Journal of Abnormal and Social Psychology*, 55 (1957), pp. 396–8, cited in Webb *et al.*, op. cit., p. 127.
18 See, for examples and for further references, G. W. Blomgren, T. W. Scheuneman and J. L. Wilkins, 'Effects of exposure to a safety poster on the frequency of turn signalling', *Traffic Safety*, 7 (1963), pp. 15–22.
19 Webb *et al.*, op. cit., p. 43.
20 The physical principle employed would be that exploited by Scientologists in the design of an instrument called the 'E-meter' which they use for 'auditing'.
21 G. H. Cox and E. Marley, 'The estimation of motility during rest or sleep', *Journal of Neurology, Neurosurgery and Psychiatry*, 22 (1959), pp. 57–60.
22 F. Galton, *Hereditary Genius* (1870), cited in Webb *et al.*, op. cit., p. 60; but see also his 'The measure of fidget', in *Nature*, 32 (1885), pp. 174–5, and 'Statistical inquiries into the efficacy of prayer', *Fortnightly Review*, 12 (1872), pp. 125–35.
23 Norman K. Denzin, *The Research Act in Sociology* (London, Butterworth, 1970), p. 286; and see Kai T. Erikson, 'A comment on disguised observation in sociology', *Social Problems*, 14 (4) (1967).
24 See above, p. 151.
25 Naroll, op. cit. See also 'Two solutions to Galton's Problems', *Philosophy of Science*, 28 (1961), pp. 15–39 and 'On bias of exotic data', *Man*, 25 (1963), pp. 24–6.

26 Paul Filmer, Michael Philipson, David Silverman and David Walsh, *New Directions in Sociological Theory* (New York, Collier-Macmillan, 1972), p. 8.

27 Cf. J. Mabley, 'Mabley's report', *Chicago American*, 22 January 1963, p. 3.

28 Private communication cited in Webb *et al.*, op. cit., p. 36.

29 See R. M. Marsh, 'Formal organization and promotion in preindustrial society', *American Sociological Review*, 26 (1961), pp. 547–56 and Ping-ti Ho, *Studies on the Population of China, 1368–1953* (Harvard University Press, 1959): both of these employed this sort of data in combination with other types.

30 S. Winston, 'Birth control and sex-ratio at birth', *American Journal of Sociology*, 38 (1932), pp. 225–31.

31 On the problems involved in stipulating criminal statistics as data see particularly Aaron V. Cicourel, *The Social Organization of Juvenile Justice* (New York, Wiley, 1968), pp. 26–9; and see Kitsuse and Cicourel, 'A note on the uses of official statistics', *Social Problems*, (1963).

32 Marsh, op. cit.; Ping-ti Ho, op. cit.

33 McClelland, op. cit.

34 Emile Durkheim, *Suicide* (London, Routledge & Kegan Paul, 1969); Jack D. Douglas, *The Social Meanings of Suicide* (Princeton University Press, 1967).

35 I shall return to the problems of analysing these sorts of data below.

36 Cf. Irwin Deutscher, 'Words and deeds: social science and social policy', *Social Problems*, 13 (1966), pp. 235–54; H. Blumer, 'Sociological analysis and the variable', *American Sociological Review*, 21 (1956), pp. 683–90.

37 R. F. Bales, *Interaction Process Analysis* (New York, Addison Wesley, 1950).

38 W. J. Goode and Paul K. Hatt, *Methods in Social Research* (New York, McGraw-Hill, 1952). The experiment described here is reported in H. F. Gosnell, *Getting Out the Vote* (University of Chicago Press, 1927).

39 For further references consult the following: Donald T. Campbell and Julian C. Stanley, 'Experimental and quasi-experimental designs for research on teaching', in N. L. Gage (ed.), *Handbook of Research on Teaching* (Chicago, Rand McNally, 1963); Ronald A. Fisher, *The Design of Experiments* (Edinburgh, Oliver & Boyd, 1937); L. Festinger, 'Laboratory experiments', in L. Festinger and D. Katz (eds), *Research Methods in the Behavioral Sciences* (New York, Holt, Rinehart & Winston, 1953), pp. 136–72; B. Kaplan, *The Conduct of Inquiry: Methodology for Behavioral Science* (San Francisco, Chandler, 1964).

40 Cf. the experiment conducted in Russia reported by C. Washburne, 'The good and bad in Russian education', *New Era*, 9 (1928), pp. 8–12, and cited in Webb *et al.*, op. cit., p. 135.

41 See C. A. Moser, *Survey Methods in Social Investigation* (London, Heinemann, 1958).

42 I say 'tentative' because, of course, it may still be the case that non-respondents differ in important respects from the respondents, including those who were initially unwilling to co-operate.

43 See Clyde H. Coombs, 'Theory and methods of social measurement', in L. Festinger and D. Katz (eds), op. cit. (1953), chapter 11; A. V.

Cicourel, op. cit., chapter 4; Margaret Stacey, op. cit., chapters 5 and 6; Goode and Hatt, op. cit., chapter 11; John Madge, *The Tools of Social Science* (London, Longman, 1953), chapter 4.

44 Particularly useful in this respect is the inventory compiled by Charles M. Bonjean, Richard J. Hill and S. Dale McLemore, *Sociological Measurement: An Inventory of Scales and Indices* (New Castle, New Hampshire, Chandler, 1967).

45 After Ralph Turner, *The Social Context of Ambition* (San Francisco, Chandler, 1964).

46 Kevin Buckley.

47 Jeanette Kellner.

48 See Manford H. Kuhn and Thomas S. McPartland, 'An empirical investigation of self-attitudes', *American Sociological Review*, 19 (February 1954), pp. 68–76, and cf. Carl J. Couch, 'Self-attitudes and degree of agreement with immediate others', *American Journal of Sociology*, 63 (March 1958), pp. 491–6.

49 But, cf. A. Sicinski, ' "Don't know" answers in cross national surveys', *Public Opinion Quarterly*, 34 (1) (1970), pp. 126–9; L. Bogart, 'No Opinion, D.K., and Maybe NO Answers', ibid., 31 (1967), pp. 331–45. And consult also Cannel and Axelrod, 'The respondent reports on the interview', *American Journal of Sociology*, 1965.

50 Also from the above-mentioned student project.

51 Incidentally, there may be other circumstances in which tact demands the collection of information which is useless from a theory-testing point of view. For example, in a questionnaire survey of school-children where the required sample are to have been resident in the U.K. for a set number of years, and children are to be approached in class groups, recent immigrant children must obviously be given questionnaires and required to fill them in in exactly the same way as the long-standing natives. The information will, however, be simply destroyed.

52 Thus, for example, a sample of research scientists, or of, say, school teachers, might be insulted by a too simplistic questionnaire design. A reasonable response rate might be elicited from such a sample by the inclusion of rather complicated questionnaires, for example, requiring the estimation of percentages or the direct use of a precode numerical scale. Cf. also the comments on 'high status' respondents in Peter K. Manning, 'Problems in interpreting interview data', *Sociology and Social Research*, 51 (1967), pp. 303–16.

53 See L. J. Chapman and D. T. Campbell, 'The effect of acquiescence response set upon relationships among the F scale, ethnocentricism and intelligence', *Sociometry*, 22 (1959), pp. 153–61; G. E. Lenski and J. C. Leggett, 'Caste, class and deference in research interview', *American Journal of Sociology*, 65 (1960), pp. 463–7.

54 Goode and Hatt, op. cit., pp. 145–6. And cf. R. F. Sletto, 'Pretesting of questionnaires', *American Sociological Review*, 5 (1940), pp. 193–200.

55 For good measure I shall repeat the crucial point that descriptive reports produced by preliminary empirical observations are not data in the sense in which that word is defined here. They may be food for further thought, but they are not *evidence*, and hence have nothing to do with questions of truth$_4$.

56 Cicourel, *Method and Measurement in Sociology*, chapter 5, and cf. . L. Kahn and C. F. Cannell, *The Dynamics of Interviewing* (New

York, Wiley, 1957), and H. Hyman *et al.*, *Interviewing in Social Research* (University of Chicago Press, 1954).

57 Thus it is often desirable to attempt to control some of these factors by randomization rather than by measurement. For example, by rotating blocks of questions to mitigate the possible effects of informant fatigue etc.

58 See Erving Goffman, *Encounters* (New York, Bobbs-Merrill, 1961), also cited in Denzin, op. cit., p. 143.

59 Actually many of Garfinkel's experimental designs do involve a false presentation of self on the part of experimenters. But I find these methods more than a little distasteful. See for example the experiment in which subjects were enjoined to ask intimate personal advice from a 'trainee student counsellor' (the experimenter) and given 'yes' or 'no' answers which had been prescheduled in a random sequence! See *Studies in Ethnomethodology* (Englewood Cliffs, New Jersey, Prentice-Hall, 1967), pp. 79–96.

60 This is the sort of situation which does call for genuinely exploratory research, not as a putative inductive enterprise with the hope of achieving theorization, but simply as a means of *collating* the appearances in relation to certain questions of ¿interest?.

61 See above, pp. 157–61.

62 Paul Filmer *et al.*, op. cit., p. 79.

63 An excellent and prophetic description of this kind of sociological morality can be found in C. S. Lewis's appraisal of the sociologist, Mark, in his novel *That Hideous Strength.*

64 Filmer *et al.*, op. cit., p. 156.

65 See above, pp. 58–79 and p. 158.

66 It might even be possible to employ records which have already been compiled by media agencies in much the same way. These would, of course, be STIP 21 rather than STIP 39. I have in mind particularly the now defunct television programme called 'Candid Camera', and a horrendous piece of film made by newsmen in Northern Ireland. In this latter (which gained an award as a piece of newsfilm, but should rather have resulted in the dishonourable dismissal of all the men responsible) an army bomb-disposal unit was seen defusing a bomb, not more than five yards from a growing group of women and children. The commentator remarked that it was not normal to carry out bomb-disposal work without prior evacuation of the area. But no one seemed to realize that, without the cameras, the crowds would not have been there. Sadly, in Belfast, bomb-disposal is rather common, television cameras are still an event.

67 It need hardly be said that it is not only the precise stipulation of the data which requires careful planning! I know of more than one case of this sort of experimentation which has landed the experimenter in front of a singularly unamused magistrate.

68 Herbert Blumer, Foreword to Severyn T. Bruyn, *The Human Perspective in Sociology* (Englewood Cliffs, New Jersey, Prentice-Hall, 1966), p. vi.

69 Cicourel, *Method and Measurement in Sociology*, p. 42.

70 Erving Goffman, *Stigma* (Englewood Cliffs, New Jersey, Prentice-Hall, 1963).

71 From James Agee and Walker Evans, *Let us Now Praise Famous Men* (Boston, Houghton Mifflin, 1960), and reproduced in David Bray-

brooke (ed.), *Philosophical Problems of the Social Sciences* (London, Macmillan, 1965), p. 81.

72 I am thinking of such wanton intellectualism as the filming of hitherto 'undiscovered' 'tribes', or the creation of discontent amongst individuals who had never thought about such notions as, say, 'powerlessness', 'meaninglessness', 'isolation', 'self-estrangement', etc. until the meddling sociologist appeared on the scene.

73 Gerald D. Berreman, *Behind Many Masks* (monograph, Ithaca, Cornell University, 1962), p. 8. Cited in Bruyn, op. cit., p. 204.

74 Buford Junker, cited in Raymond L. Gold, 'Roles in sociological field observations', *Social Forces*, 36 (1958), p. 217. See also Cicourel, *Method and Measurement in Sociology*, pp. 43–9, and Bruyn, op. cit., pp. 15–22.

75 Junker's description of this role is rather odd and doesn't seem to me to hang together very well. But he has in mind a different sort of datum stipulation altogether, one in which the researcher is acting in 'bad faith' by misrepresenting himself to his subjects in some respect.

76 Bruyn, op. cit., pp. 202–3. Bruyn is referring to H. Gans, *Urban Villagers* (New York, Free Press, 1962).

77 See, for example, Aaron V. Cicourel, *The Social Organization of Juvenile Justice* (New York, Wiley, 1968).

78 Jerome H. Skolnick, *Justice Without Trial* (New York, Wiley, 1967), p. 32.

79 Cf. Robert W. Janes, 'A note on the phases of the community role of the participant observer', *American Sociological Review*, 26 (1961), pp. 446–50.

80 Bruyn, op. cit., p. 21.

81 This apparently happened to a Ph.D. student of Robert Redfield's, see Bruyn, op. cit., p. 230.

82 Yet some do seem to manage somehow. I know of a lady anthropologist who kept her field-notebook under the pillow of the bed she shared with a Caribbean fisherman.

83 Janes, op. cit.

84 Some of these questions are raised in the following literature: Howard S. Becker, 'Problems of inference and proof in participant observation', *American Sociological Review*, 23 (1958), pp. 652–9; Arthur J. Vidich, 'Participant observation and the collection and interpretation of data', *American Journal of Sociology*, 60 (1955); Morris Schwartz and Charlotte Schwartz, 'Problems in participant observation', *American Journal of Sociology*, 60 (1955); S. M. Miller, 'The participant observer and over-rapport', *American Sociological Review*, 17 (1952), pp. 97–9; V. L. Oleson and E. W. Whittaker, 'Role-making in participant observation: processes in the researcher-action relationship', *Human Organization*, 26 (1967), pp. 273–81; and Daniel S. Claster and Howard Schwartz, 'Strategies of participation in participant observation', *Sociological Methods and Research*, vol. 1 (1) (August 1972), and this also contains an excellent bibliography for further reading.

18 Coder Coda

1 Although it is, obviously, possible to punch the *'symbolic data'* straight onto magnetic tape from the coding sheets, I consider that the Hollerith card is a more flexible, durable and accessible intermediary.

These cards can be read directly by the computer, transcribed onto magnetic tape by the computer, or used in a mechanical counter-sorter. You will find that there are many operations which can be performed as speedily on the old-fashioned counter-sorter as on the computer. And for this reason I consider that the Hollerith card is, generally, the most useful device for holding data for analysis.

2 Again I am restricting my discussion to some simple techniques for producing a set of punched cards which may be readily sorted by manual and mechanical methods but which can also be fed straight into the computer together with a few additional cards carrying the programme information.

3 Or, as we shall see, a small group of cards.

4 Bernard Berelson, *Content Analysis in Communication Research* (Chicago, Free Press, 1952), p. 17.

5 Cf. William H. Sewell, *The Construction and Standardization of a Scale for the Measurement of Socio-Economic Status of Oklahoma Farm Families* (Technical Bulletin of Oklahoma A and M College Agricultural Experiment Station, No. 9, 1940).

6 See above, especially chapter 14.

7 In fact, of course, one can programme the computer to read double-punched columns according to a predesigned cipher, but I am suggesting that restricting yourself in this way will make matters considerably easier when it comes to data analysis.

8 You might also want to leave something temporarily blank, i.e. not punch that column at all. (For example you might arrange various indicators of a variable P along columns 7–19 and leave column 20 blank intending to insert a compound index of P in that column after you have performed certain comparisons, and other jiggery pokery, amongst the indicators.)

9 The 'Hall-Jones' system of occupational classification is still well favoured for coding occupational information in the British Isles. This scale is based upon the occupational evaluations of a sample of the actual inhabitants. See above, p. 387.

10 Year group was a constant factor as a result of sampling strategy: all the children were in their fourth year at secondary school.

11 Johan Galtung, *Theory and Methods of Social Research* (London, Allen & Unwin, 1967), p. 68.

12 You will probably find that you will be sorting your data into sets or coding units in terms of several considerations at once. And some of the criteria determining these units will be dictated by your prior research design. For example, you will probably be dividing according to dimensions which you have already specified as variables to be controlled by selection.

13 See above pp. 184–5.

14 Of course some attention should be paid to sampling. For example, what would be a relevant sample of 'judges' for the coding of news-paper content? It might be a representative sample of readers, a sample of the journalists involved in the actual production of the material, or both, depending on the problem in hand.

15 It might also be fruitful to employ the Cloze procedure to˜this end. See in Ithiel De Sola Pool (ed.), *Trends in Content Analysis* (Urbana, Illinois University Press, 1959).

16 Galtung, op. cit., p. 137.

19 Statistricks!

1 See chapter 6.

2 This research design is rendered even more absurd when you consider that no theorist worth his salt would be expecting variations in the area of sports coverage to be accompanied by *immediate* fluctuations in popularity. Clearly it would take some ¿time? for readers to find out about the changes so the experiment would have to span a considerable period in ¿time?.

3 Or, as we shall see, vice versa.

4 If it did, we might refer to the data as 'normally distributed' with regard to this feature. See chapter 14.

5 To say that a hypothesis is 'perfectly true$_4$' is to say that, since no single contradicting instance has yet been observed, it has the temporary status of a unanimously acceptable empirical generalization, or fact. See chapter 5.

6 Perhaps, for example, those deriving from differentials in sample size.

7 Statisticians themselves believe that this prejudice is widespread amongst laymen, and, as we have seen, whatever is believed to be real is real in its consequences.

8 Indeed, where new developments in statistical theory *have* been imported into the analysis of social science hypotheses, these have very often involved a decidedly inductive and verificationist approach. A glaring example is the Bayesian school of thought which is already notorious in this respect.

9 John T. Roscoe, *Fundamental Research Statistics for the Behavioral Sciences* (New York, Holt, Rinehart & Winston, 1969), pp. 2–3 (pedantic parentheses added).

10 Even Sidney Siegel's useful *Nonparametric Statistics for the Behavioral Sciences* (New York, McGraw-Hill, 1956) treats the issue of 'statistical inference' entirely as a business of drawing conclusions about populations from data produced by measuring characteristics of samples. Sjoberg and Nett do note that 'different conceptions of the nature of reality lead to different conceptions of probability', and they stress that the notion of 'chance' as a hypothetical criterion against which to assess the plausibility of hypotheses 'differs somewhat from the idea that chance influences human action'. But they fail to follow this idea through. See Gideon Sjoberg and Roger Nett, *A Methodology for Social Research* (New York, Harper & Row, 1968), p. 284. And, though he has by no means maintained a coherently deductive approach, Blalock has suggested that sociologists should concentrate more upon *within* sample relationships, and that they should develop methods of examining these which do not pivot upon assumptions or estimations about the relationships between those samples and the populations from which they are supposed to have been drawn. See particularly H. M. Blalock, 'Some important methodological problems for sociology', *Sociology and Social Research*, 47 (1963), pp. 398–407.

11 See Voltaire, *Dictionnaire Philosophique* (1819, 36, p. 458).

12 The material in this section was compiled with the assistance of J. T. Evans, and will be expanded in L. T. Doyal, J. T. Evans and J. N. Lea, *Methods and Models of Enquiry in the Social Sciences* (in preparation).

13 It may have occurred to you that such a range of permissible values

could not have been coded on a single column of the computer card. Perhaps in these circumstances the researcher would have economized on columns by *grouping the data at the coding stage*, representing actual percentages in terms of the nine values 1–9 inclusive. But here we are pretending that the data have been left in the form of their initial presentation, and coded on two (presumably adjacent) columns.

14 If classes of *unequal* width are employed then, of course, our exemplary data can no longer be interpreted as forming a ratio, or even interval, scale.

15 Notice that, if these data were coded as suggested above (n. 13), this grouping could be effected simply by sorting the data on the first of the two columns representing 'examination performance'. This preparatory manipulation could be performed by hand, by a counter-sorter machine, or even with a computer.

16 You can find these easily in your haphazardly selected statistics textbook.

17 Herbert L. Costner, 'Criteria for measures of association', *American Sociological Review*, 30 (3) (1965), p. 341.

18 Such as tests of hypotheses about the social distribution of marked cards in a gaming house, or of loaded dice in Walthamstow!

19 Costner, op. cit., p. 343.

20 Again, refer to your textbook.

21 Siegel, op. cit., p. 33.

22 Ibid.

23 Op. cit., p. 344.

24 A 'P-R-E' interpretation has also been suggested for '*Spearman's rho*'. But I cannot follow it and remain suspicious of the extent to which this statistic can be shown to have any meaning except that which it acquires in the original derivation. See William H. Kruskal, 'Ordinal measures of association', *Journal of the American Statistical Association*, 53 (1958), pp. 825ff. and Costner, op. cit., p. 348. Another candidate, '*lambda-b*' was excluded in favour of '*the coefficient of predictability*' because the two formulae work in the same way and, after all, Guttman succeeded in thinking the idea first. I have also excluded '*phi-squared*' because, although this familiar statistic is formally equivalent to a 'P-R-E' measure for two-by-two comparisons, its traditional derivation is from the chi-squared distribution and this may cause confusion. As Costner says:

> In the special case of a 2 × 2 table, Goodman and Kruskal's tau-b is equal in value to phi squared. This can be readily shown algebraically by expressing tau-b in terms of the four cell frequencies and then simplifying the resulting expression. Thus phi squared, which may be computed either by applying a product-moment formula or by an appropriate 'norming' of the chi-square statistic, derives its clearest operational interpretation from neither of these features. On the contrary, it is interpretable in proportional-reduction-of-error terms only because it happens to be the equivalent of Goodman and Kruskal's tau (op. cit., pp. 351–2).

25 James A. Davis has made some suggestions for '*Yule's Q*', but these appear to me to be somewhat slanted in favour of the 'home team'. See *Elementary Survey Analysis* (Englewood Cliffs, New Jersey, Prentice-Hall, 1971), pp. 50–62.

26 The lines of thought behind Blalock's system of analysis for interval

scales and J. A. Davis's system for nominal dichotomies could be developed towards this end. Unfortunately, however, both of these writers fall short of adopting a stringently deductivist position. Davis's methods are unashamedly verificationist, and Blalock, though he is a proponent of deductive theorizing and has spoken of the possibility of de-emphasizing relations between samples and wider populations, is still hung up on 'statistical inference'. However I have a strong hunch that both these approaches could be adapted to the requirements of a falsificationist methodology if a suitably fearless heretic were to rewrite them 'outside-in'. see J. A. Davis, op. cit.; H. M. Blalock, *Causal Inferences in Non-Experimental Research* (University of North Carolina Press, 1961); and see also Bernard Burgoyne and Julienne Ford, 'Statistical risk-taking and the metaphysic of chance' (in preparation).

27 By 'unrepeatable' grouping procedures I mean those leaving room for choice in respect of the regrouping or collapsing of coded categories. An example would be the case of a five-point scale of measurement which suddenly makes an appearance as an ordinal dichotomy labelled 'high' versus 'low' with no attendant indication of how or why the original scale was compressed into these categories.

28 Davis, op. cit., pp. 59–60.

29 Or, if we were really fervently pessimistic, we might merely start getting paranoid about the extent to which these measures were really 'independent' after all!

30 Sometimes it may be possible to do a simple addition and division sum for each case, i.e. $(x_1+x_3+x_4)/3$ but difficulties must arise because of different types of scales and ranges of permissible values, and there may also be good theoretical reasons for attaching differential weightings to the various indicators. For scoring procedures and other technical issues involved in the construction of indices from indicators see J. A. Davis, *International Journal of Comparative Sociology*, 2 (1961), pp. 212–13; Louis Guttman, 'The quantification of a class of attributes', in P. Horst *et al.*, *The Prediction of Personal Adjustment* (New York, Social Science Research Council, 1941), pp. 319–48; Samuel A. Stouffer, 'Comparison of Guttman and latent structure scales', in S. A. Stouffer, E. A. Suchman, P. F. Lazarsfeld, S. A. Star and J. A. Clausen, *Measurement and Prediction* (Princeton University Press, 1950), chapter 1.

31 You will notice that this statement takes the form of a testable hypothesis. I have not actually subjected it to a genuinely risky test, so my opinion on the subject is about as boring as anyone else's. Coherent methods have certainly been developed, particularly by Lazarsfeld and by Guttman (see P. Horst *et al.*, op. cit.) but their standing as conventions is unknown.

32 See Bernard Burgoyne, *Spaced Out* (Thames & Hudson, forthcoming).

33 For example, Proctor and Loomis have suggested the following formula for estimating the 'cohesion' of a social group:

$$\text{Group cohesion} = \frac{\text{number of mutual choices}}{\text{total number of possible mutual choices}}$$

See C. H. Proctor and C. P. Loomis, 'Analysis of sociometric data', in M. Jahoda, M. Deutsch and S. W. Cook (eds), *Research Methods in*

Social Relations: With Especial Reference to Prejudice (New York, Dryden, 1951).

34 It has been common for writers to distinguish between 'quantitative' and 'qualitative' techniques of content analysis. But, on closer inspection it turns out that even such sophisticated 'qualitative' procedures as, say, the 'Cloze Procedure' are – at the last – reduced to simple 'quantitative' or frequency questions. In the case of 'Language correspondence' methods, such as Cloze, the final measure brought forward for comparison is an indicator of the average success with which a sample of other users of the language can replace items which have been deleted from the source's messages by the experimenter-analyst. See the articles by A. L. George, C. E. Osgood and Pool in Ithiel De Sola Pool (ed.), *Trends in Content Analysis* (Urbana, University of Illinois, 1959); J. Ruesch and G. Bateson, 'Structure and process in social relations', *Psychiatry*, 12 (1949), p. 123; C. E. Osgood, *Symbols of Democracy* (California University Press, 1952).

35 The efforts that have already been made in the fields of topological analysis are, without exception, conceived as routines of induction. See, for example, K. Lewin, *Principles of Topological Psychology*, translated by F. and G. Heider (New York, McGraw-Hill, 1966).

36 Because the only empirical anaglyph we have for the idea of cause is bound up with a very specific metaphysic of ¿time? and one which may by no means be regarded as a universal characteristic of human thinking and thought. Not only in the dark tales of ¿the past? but even today human beings exist who are happy to believe that effects may *precede* their own causes in ¿time?. Some of these sorts of thoughts are obscure to us because they are interwoven with world views which we find 'exotic' or 'primitive', others are inaccessible for quite different reasons.

37 Once this point is grasped it should be clear that the attempt to develop 'asymmetric' measures of association to 'reveal' the 'probable' causal sequence of a pair or group of variables is misguided. So it is not at all surprising to find that such a measure as Somers's '*dyx*', which was developed with this specific end in view, is necessarily derived from an unacceptable metaphysical assumption. This measure cannot be given a 'P-R-E' interpretation, and you will notice that it was not included in the Bag. See Robert H. Somers, 'A new asymmetric measure of association for ordinal variables', *American Sociological Review*, 27 (1962), pp. 799–811. *But*, notice that '*tau-b*', one of the measures which *was* included in the Bag, is also SKEW-IF in the sense that different results can be expected according to whether the analyst begins with one variable or the other, for example, whether he predicts Y from X or X from Y. Conventions centring around the use of this measure must therefore necessarily involve a suitable adjustment. See Costner, op. cit.

38 The first example which comes to my mind concerns the business of analysing 'compositional' or 'structural effects'. This should not present any intrinsic problems for the falsificationist, provided that he is careful not to make illegitimate transitions from one level of definition (say, school-classes-as-datum-units) to another (say individual-children-as-datum-units). On this issue see James A. Davis, Joe L. Spaeth and Carolyn Huson, 'A technique for analyzing the effects of group composition', *American Sociological Review*, 26 (1961),

pp. 215–26; W. S. Robinson, 'Ecological correlations and the be-
havior of individuals', *American Sociological Review*, 15 (1950); and
M. D. Hyman, 'Extending the ecological fallacy', *Sociology and Social
Research*, 55 (1) (1970).

20 What You Will!

1 Conservative MPs, supporters of the Black Paper position on secondary
   education and letter-writers to *The Times*, etc., have been only too
   ready to accept this 'evidence' that comprehensive schools don't
   work, and to use this to bolster up their arguments for the protection
   of grammar schools. And it is interesting to note that Ford's open
   declaration of her 'socialism' in the preface to her book only adds force
   to their rhetoric. Thus I fear that Shipman is misguided in his praise
   for Ford's honesty in that respect. M. D. Shipman, *The Limitations of
   Social Research* (London, Longman, 1972), p. 40.
2 And they paid you twenty quid for it – which didn't even cover the
   fine for your licence. All la glory, brother.
3 S. Andreski, *Social Sciences as Sorcery* (London, Deutsch, 1972).
4 See Howard Becker, 'Whose side are we on?', *Social Problems*, 14
   (4) (1967), pp. 239–48.
5 An ¿interesting? definition of alienation is given by the following: 'A
   man is in bondage to whatever he cannot part with that is less than
   himself.' George MacDonald, *Unspoken Sermons* (London, Geoffrey
   Bles, 1946), p. 41.
6 See for examples, Derek Price, *Little Science, Big Science* (New York,
   World Publishing Co., 1963), and Jacques Barzun, *Science: The
   Glorious Entertainment* (London, Secker & Warburg, 1964).
7 For good popular summaries of the Labelling-theoretic position see
   J. L. Simmons, *Deviants* (Berkeley, California, Glendessary, 1969),
   and Jock Young, *The Drug Takers* (London, Paladin, 1971).
8 Wendell Bell and James A. Mau, 'Images of the future', in J. C.
   McKinney and Edward A. Tiryakian, *Theoretical Sociology* (New
   York, Appleton-Century-Crofts, 1970), p. 233.
9 Ibid., pp. 207–9.
10 Hilary W. Putman reported in *The New York Times*, 30 January 1966,
   and cited in ibid., p. 209.
11 Ibid.
12 An interesting angle on this issue is provided by the perspective of the
   'Frankfurters'. See, for example, Jürgen Habermas, *Toward a Rational
   Society* (London, Heinemann, 1971), and the paper entitled 'Toward
   a critical theory for advanced industrial society' by Trent Schroyer in
   H. P. Dreitzel (ed.), *Recent Sociology* No. 2 (New York, Collier-
   Macmillan, 1970), pp. 209–31.
13 Frederik L. Polak, *The Image of the Future: Enlightening the Past,
   Orientating the Present, Forecasting the Future* (Dobbs Ferry, New
   York, Oceana, 1961), pp. 36–7. This passage is cited in Bell and Mau,
   op. cit., p. 213.
14 ('All things do move in three, but in four they merry be.')
15 Alvin Toffler, *Future Shock* (London, Pan, 1970), pp. 37–8.
16 The seminal discussion of the sociological concept of 'fatalism' is still
   David Matza's *Delinquency and Drift* (New York, Wiley, 1964), but
   see also the development of his ideas on the question of 'free will' in

Becoming Deviant (Englewood Cliffs, New Jersey, Prentice-Hall, 1969), particularly in the first chapter.

17 Toffler, op. cit., p. 183.

18 We are still grateful to Doris Lessing for jogging our memory on this point with her exceedingly timely novel, *Briefing for a Descent into Hell*. We know that there must be others who would enjoy the trip as much as we do!

19 At one moment Alvin Gouldner remembered it like this: 'Essentially the fate of objectivity in sociology is linked with, and its fortunes vary with, the changing hopes for a peace-bringing human unity. Some power-tempted social scientists are simply no longer able to hear this music. Others may withdraw because their hope is so vital that they cannot risk endangering it by an open confrontation. For some, an open admission would be dissonant with their conception of themselves as tough-minded and hard-headed. Still others have a genuine humility and feel that the pursuit of this high value is beyond their powers.' See 'The sociologist as partisan: sociology and the welfare state', *American Sociologist*, 3 (2) (May 1968): and notice also his final schizophrenic outburst in *The Coming Crisis of Western Sociology* (London, Heinemann, 1970), where Gouldner also remembers to attempt to destroy his own credibility with respect to Becker's famous question 'Whose side are we on?' Other interesting contributions to the Great Debate about the magic of sociological messages are: D. J. Gray, 'Value free sociology? A doctrine of hypocrisy and irresponsibility', *Sociological Quarterly*, 9 (2) (1968), pp. 176–85; Roger C. Buck, 'Reflexive predictions', *Philosophy of Science*, 30 (1963), pp. 359–69; J. H. Kultgen, 'The value of value judgements in sociology', *Sociological Quarterly*, 11 (2) (1970); Walter R. Gove, 'Should the sociology profession take moral stands on political issues?', *American Sociologist*, 5 (3) (1970); N. K. Denzin, 'Who leads: sociology or society?', *American Sociologist*, 5 (2) (1970), pp. 125–7; H. Becker, 'Whose side are we on?', *Social Problems*, 14 (4) (1967); George W. Fairweather, *Methods for Experimental Social Innovation* (New York, Wiley, 1967); James F. Short, 'Action research, collaboration and sociological evaluation', *Pacific Sociological Review*, 10 (2) (1967), pp. 47–53; S. S. Wolin, 'Paradigms and political theories', in P. King and J. Parekh (eds), *Politics And Experience* (Cambridge University Press, 1968), pp. 149–52; D. Dressler and W. Korber, 'A comment on the language of sociology', *Pacific Sociological Review*, 5 (1) (1962), pp. 36–9; R. A. Nisbet, 'Sociology as an art form', *Pacific Sociological Review*, 5 (2) (1962), pp. 64–74; A. M. Rose, 'Varieties of sociological imagination', *American Sociological Review*, 34 (5) (1969); William H. Friedland, 'Making sociology relevant: a teaching-research program for undergraduates', *American Sociologist*, 4 (2) (1969), pp. 104–10; Irving Horowitz, *Professing Sociology: Studies in the Life Cycle of Social Science* (University of Chicago Press, 1968); Clarence Schrag, 'Some demerits of contemporary sociology', *Pacific Sociological Review*, 4 (2) (1961), pp. 43–52; Scott Greer, *The Logic of Social Inquiry* (Chicago, Aldine, 1969); M. A. Weinstein, 'Hocking's existential sociology', *Sociology and Social Research*, 52 (4) (1968); W. P. McEwen, *The Problem of Social Scientific Knowledge* (Totowa, New Jersey, Bedminster Press, 1963); Richard Schmidt, 'In search of phenomenology', *Review of Metapsyhics*, 16 (1962), pp. 459–79;

Stephen Cole, 'Professional standing and the reception of scientific discoveries', *American Journal of Sociology*, 76 (2) (1970), pp. 286ff.; S. Wert, 'Scientist versus the ideology of science', *American Behavioral Scientist*, 35 (March 1961); B. S. Greenberg, *The Politics of American Science* (Harmondsworth, Penguin Books, 1969). But if I were to select one short article to take the place of all that reading, it would be A. J. Weigert, 'The immoral rhetoric of scientific sociology', *American Sociologist*, 5 (2) (1970), pp. 125–7. Let us not forget that we, too, issue from Crete!

Glossary of Fairy-Tale Words

AMAZING SERENDIPITY BUZZER   Transcendental flash.

BATHWATER *see* BATHWATER FALLACY

BATHWATER FALLACY   Fallacy of misplaced concreteness.

BRIDGE   Operationalization: the magical link between ideas and appearances.

CRICKET PITCH   Test ground for scientific theories.

DANCE *see* DERVISH DANCE

DERVISH DANCE   Formal choreography of testing rituals.

DIGGING   Knowing, feeling, understanding.

DIRTY LINEN *see* UNDERWEAR.

DO-IT-YOURSELF-MULTI-PURPOSE-DATA-MATRIX   Classification of modes of data stipulation which may be appropriate for social science purposes.

DWARVES   Operationalizers by appointment to the FAIRY courts.

FAIRIES   Ideas, potentially thoughts and/or images, manifestations or appearances.

FAIRY TALE   Connection of ideas in the form of an explanatory story, or theory.

FAIRYLAND   Land of ideas. Any realm of thought. Alternative universe.

GOLD STAR   Honorific title awarded for faithfulness to deductive methods in science.

GOLD-STAR BADGE   Mark of GOLD-STAR status.

GOLD-STAR RABBIT   One recognized as of GOLD-STAR merit.

GRYPHON   Chance.

LAUNDRY *see* UNDERWEAR.

LIBRARY   Storehouse of written thoughts kept as knowledge.

LIGHTS   Guides.

MAGICAL MOUNTAIN *see* MOUNTAIN.

MATRIX *see* DO-IT-YOURSELF-MULTI-PURPOSE-DATA-MATRIX.

MOCK TURTLE SOUP Positivistic inductivistic universe.

MOUNTAIN Solid conventions of academic scientific thought.

RABBIT Scientist.

RED Positivistic.

RED HERRING Red herring.

SAMPLING GAME Process of selecting 'representative' samples.

SOUP *see* MOCK TURTLE SOUP.

SPIDER Confusion or intimation thereof.

SPIDER BATTLE Philosophical brawl.

STATISTRICKS Statistical tricks.

THIRTY-NINE STIPS Contents of DO-IT-YOURSELF-MULTI-PURPOSE-DATA-MATRIX.

UMPIRE Philosopher of science.

UNDERWEAR Theory construction procedures.

WHITE Idealistic.

WHITE RABBIT Science teacher.

Index of Names

A

Abel, T., 211
Abell, P., 215
Agee, J., 453
al-Bitrogi, 95, 200
Alder, F., 206
Aldous, J., 447
Althauser, R. P., 443,
Anderson, R. T., 187
Andreski, S., 426, 460
Antoni, C., 157, 212
Aquinas, St T., 19, 82, 96, 200,
  207, 285, 330
Archimedes, 189
Aristotle, 19, 207
Arnold, D., 443
Averroes, 95, 200
Axelrod, D., 452

B

Bacon, Francis, 11, 39, 79, 186,
  197, 433
Baldwin, J. M., 196
Bales, R. F., 451
Barch, A. M. *et al.*, 347, 450
Barfield, O., 19, 23, 187, 192,
  195, 214
Barton, A. H., 211
Barzun, J., 188, 460
Becker, H. S., 158, 212, 427,
  429, 453, 460, 461
Beidelman, T. O., 212
Bell, W., 430, 431, 460
Bennet, J., 198

Bentham, J., 192
Berger, P., 186, 187, 197, 199,
  204, 207, 213, 214, 448
Bergson, H., 19, 187
Berkeley, Bishop, 188
Bernard of Verdun, 95, 200
Bierce, A., 443
Bingen, St Hildegarde of, 208
Bittner, E., 213
Blake, W., 74, 87, 199
Blalock, H., 155, 190, 205, 211,
  244, 416, 449, 456, 457, 458
Blau, P., 206, 207
Blauner, R., 440
Blomgren, G. W., 450
Blumberg, P., 441
Blumer, H., 451, 453
Bogart, L., 452
Bohannan, P., 189, 215
Bonjean, C. M. *et al.*, 201, 440
Borges, J. L., 132, 208
Bott, E., 447, 452
Bowman, P. H., 441
Box, S., 196, 202, 215
Bradbury, Ray, 448
Braithewaite, R. B., 155, 190
Braybrooke, D., 453
Briar, S., 103, 202
Bridgman, P. W., 149, 150, 156,
  204, 210
Brodbeck, M., 191, 204, 208
Bronowski, J., 187
Brook, R. *see* Thompson, H.
Brown, J. W., 344, 449
Bruno, G., 208
Bruyn, S. T., 191, 212, 380,
  447, 453

Buckley, K., 452
Buckley, W., 126–7, 205, 206
Bunge, M., 118, 204, 206
Burgoyne, B., 458
Burton, T. L., 450
Byrne, E. F., 273, 285, 444

C

Camilleri, S. F., 211
Campanella, T., 173
Campbell, R. T., 448, 449, 451, 452
Cannell, C. F., 452
Cardano, H., 274
Carey, A., 202, 441
Carlsmith, J. M., 441
Carnap, R., 285
Carroll, L., 2, 445
Cattell, R. B., 156, 208, 211
Cavendish, R., 197
Chapin, F. S., 149, 156, 210, 211
Chapman, L. J., 452
Chesterton, G. K., 87
Chomsky, N., 212, 213
Christiansen, R., 269
Cicourel, A. V., 159, 160–1, 187, 189, 191, 205, 212, 213, 451, 452, 453
Claster, D. S., 454
Clausen, J. A., 458
Cochran, W., 445
Cohen, P., 209
Cole, S., 462
Coleridge, S. T., 195
Comte, A., 189
Condorcet, J., Marquis de, 189
Cooley, C., 214
Coombs, C. H., 451
Copernicus, 96
Cornelius, Jerry, 434
Costner, H., 411–14, 457
Couch, C. J., 452
Cox, G. H., 348, 450
Crutchley, J. F., 189

D

Danto, A. C., 201
Darwin, C., 444

Davis, J. A., 416, 448, 457, 458, 459
Davitz, J. R., 441
Deming, W. E., 444
Denzin, N. K., 202, 348, 440, 445, 447, 450, 461
De Sola Pool, I., 455
Dewey, J., 187
Dickinson, R. E., 442
Dickson, W. J., 249
Dijksterhuis, E. J., 204
Dilthey, W., 150–1, 210
Disney, Walt, 41, 352
Dore, R. P., 206
Douglas, J., 187, 451
Doyal, L., 456
Dray, W., 203
Dreitzel, H. P., 210, 213
Dressler, D., 461
Dryden, J., 80
Dubin, R., 202
Du Bois, C. N., 344, 450
Duhem, P., 66, 97, 193, 200
Dunne, J. W., 187, 188
Durand, J., 345, 450
Durkheim, E., 20, 163–5, 172, 189, 205, 214, 215, 220, 447, 451
Duster, T., 187

E

Eddington, A. S., 440
Edwards, A. L., 448
Ellison, H., 429
Engels, F., 206
Erikson, K. T., 188, 189, 450
Evans, J. T., 456

F

Fairweather, G. W., 461
Fallding, H., 191, 192, 207
Father Christmas, 81, 197, 461
Fermat, P., 274
Feshbach, S., 441
Festinger, L., 187–8, 441, 451
Feyerabend, P., 100, 194, 201
Filmer, P. et al., 451, 453
Finnegan, Ruth, 200
Firey, W., 442

Fisher, J., 272, 277, 287, 451
Fisher, R., 271, 289, 443, 445
Flament, C., 205
Ford, J., 105–6, 196, 202, 211, 215, 424, 426, 448, 458, 460
Fort, C., 210
Frege, O., 41
Freedman, R., 443
Freidland, W. H., 461
Freidman, N., 449
Frost, David, 426

G

Gage, N. L., 449
Galilei, Galileo, 96–7, 200, 278, 330
Galton, F., 348, 450
Galtung, J., 205, 333, 391, 447, 449, 455
Gans, H., 454
Garfinkle, H., 159, 170, 187, 212, 213, 249, 250, 442, 453
Geertz, C., 442
George, A. L., 459
Gilbert, W. S., 435
Glaser, B., 209, 220, 320, 439, 447
Goethe, J. W., 19, 75, 120
Goffman, E., 157, 212, 453
Gold, R. L., 454
Goldman, L., 212
Goode, E., 187, 188
Goode, W. J., 208, 212, 325, 327, 446, 448, 451, 452
Goodman, L. A., 414, 416, 457
Gosnell, H. F., 353, 451
Gouldner, A., 79, 197, 208, 212, 461
Gray, D. J., 461
Greenberg, B. S., 462
Greer, Germaine, 431
Greer, S., 187, 188, 461
Gross, L., 208
Guetzkow, H. S., 441
Guttman, L., 184, 393, 416, 458

H

Habermas, J., 147, 186, 460
Hacking, I., 198

Hall, J., 440–1
Hartland, H. S., 195, 197
Hatt, P., 208, 212, 325, 327, 446, 448, 451, 452
Hegel, G. F., 98, 206, 214
Hempel, C., 51, 83, 86, 155, 190, 191, 193, 198, 203, 208, 209, 288, 444
Heraclitus, 319, 324
Hesse, H., 193
Hirschi, T., 290, 444
Ho, Ping ti, see Ping ti Ho
Hollingshead, A., 442
Homans, G. C., 105–6, 130, 155, 190, 193, 199, 207, 211
Hook, S., 203
Horobin, G., 443
Horowitz, I., 198, 461
Horton, R., 200
Hubbard, L. R., 192
Hughes, C. S., 157, 210
Humpty Dumpty, 247, 435–6
Husserl, E., 18, 186
Huxley, J., 29, 94
Hyman, H., 453
Hyman, M. D., 460
Hypatia, 406

I

Ibn Tofail, 95
Illersic, A. R., 444
Isajiw, W., 205

J

Jahoda, M., 458
James, W., 19, 39, 214
Janes, R. W., 453
Jones, C., 440–1
Juergens, R. E., 210
Junker, B., 454

K

Kahan, M. et al., 441
Kahn, R. L., 452
Kant, I., 19, 66, 198
Kaplan, B., 206, 212, 451
Katz, E., 446, 451

Keats, J., 82
Kellner, H., 199, 448
Kellner, J., 452
Kish, L., 439
Kitsuse, 451
Kolb, W. L., 442
Kolmogorov, A. N., 274, 445
Korber, W., 461
Krishnamurti, J. K., 192
Kruskal, W. H., 414, 416, 457
Kuhn, M. H., 452
Kuhn, T. S., 1, 39-40, 63, 66,
    69, 73-4, 99-100, 186, 189,
    190, 193, 194, 198, 200, 201
Kultgen, J. H., 461

L

Laing, R. D., 43, 87, 132, 187,
    199, 208
Lakatos, I., 64-7, 100, 186, 189,
    192, 193, 194, 200, 448
La Piere, R. T., 448
Laplace, P. S., 193, 274, 286,
    287, 444
Lastrucci, C. L., 331
Lazarsfeld, P. F., 211, 439, 446,
    447, 458
Lee, R. S., 444
Leibniz, G. W., 274
Lenski, G. E., 452
Le Roy, E., 66
Lessing, Doris, 461
Lev, J., 416
Lévi-Strauss, C., 212
Levy, M., 203
Lévy-Bruhl, L., 20
Lewin, K., 459
Lewis, C. S., 87, 453
Littlewood, S. R., 197
Lockwood, D., 441
Lombrosa, C., 441
Longford, Lord, 260, 261
Loomis, C. P., 458
Loomis, W. C. and R. K., 192,
    204
Luckman, D., 186, 187, 199, 207,
    213, 214
Lukács, G., 75, 195
Lundberg, G. A., 149, 156, 210,
    211
Lunt, P. S., 442

Lyman, S., 196, 214
Lynd, R. S. and H., 442

M

Mabley, J., 451
MacAndrew, C., 213
McCall, G. J., 187, 191, 199
McClelland, D. C., 344, 450,
    451
MacDonald, G., 460
McEwan, W. P., 461
McHugh, P., 213
MacIver, R. M., 128, 205, 213
MacKenzie, D. A., 199
McKinney, J. C., 187, 203, 212,
    214, 460
Madge, J., 452
Maharaj Ji, Guru, 192
Manning, P. K., 452
Marley, E., 348, 450
Marsh, R. M., 451
Marx, K., 19, 87, 157, 163-5,
    189, 199, 214, 215, 220, 243
Masterman, M., 186
Matza, D., 202, 204, 443, 460
Mau, J. A., 430, 431, 460
Mead, G. H., 214
Merleau-Ponty, M., 187
Merton, R. K., 192, 201, 207
Mill, J. S., 139, 192, 203, 208,
    439
Milton, J., 36, 87
Mohanty, C. N., 186
Monod, J., 444
Morrison, P., 22, 188
Moser, C. A., 451
Mosteller, F., 344, 450
Musgrave, A., 186
Myrdal, G., 208

N

Nadel, S. F., 102, 202
Nagel, E., 206
Narroll, R., 344, 450
Nett, R., 201, 209, 442, 443, 444,
    456
Nettl, J. P., 210
Nettler, G., 206
Newson. J. and E., 189

Newton, I., 274
Nisbet, R. A., 461
Northrop, F. S. C., 440

O

Oleson, V. C., 453
Omar Khayyam, 55
Osgood, C. E., 459

P

Pandora, 343
Park, P., 204
Park, R., 442
Parsons, T., 55, 195, 203, 209, 211
Pascal, B., 274
Peake, M., 45, 190
Pearson, K., 156, 211
Perelman, C., 445
Phillips, B. S., 208, 211
Pierce, A., 205
Pierce, C. S., 444, 447
Piliavin, I., 103, 202
Ping ti Ho, 451
Plutarch, 200
Poincaré, M., 66, 75, 275
Polak, F. C., 432, 433, 460
Polanyi, M., 445
Polsky, N., 187
Pope, A., 1, 275
Popper, K., 63, 66, 74, 97–9, 140, 155, 189, 193, 195, 201, 209, 211, 274, 275, 285, 331, 403, 449
Potter, Beatrix, 443
Prezelecki, M., 209
Price, D., 188, 194
Proctor, C. H., 458
Prosser, W. L., 449
Ptolemy, 95, 96, 200
Putman, H. W., 460

R

Raphael, 88
Record, J. C., 202
Redfield, R., 382, 454
Reisman, J. M., 347

Richards, I. A., 186
Rickert, H., 210
Robinson, W. S., 460
Roethlisberger, F. J., 441
Roscoe, J. T., 456
Rose, A. M., 461
Rosenberg, M., 211, 212
Rosenthal, R., 202
Roszack, T., 188
Rousseau, J.-J., 189
Rubin, D., 443
Rudner, R., 198
Ruesch, J., 459
Runciman, W. G., 207
Russell, B., 82, 445
Ryan, A., 198
Ryle, G., 254

S

Sachs, H., 187, 213
Santayana, G., 443
Sartre, J.-P., 87
Schachter, S. et al., 441
Scheff, T., 126–7, 205, 207
Schmidt, A., 212
Schmidt, R., 461
Schrag, C., 137, 208, 461
Schroyer, T., 209, 460
Schulman, J. L., 347
Schutz, A., 3, 169, 186, 187, 189, 199, 209, 212, 214
Schwartz, D., 215
Schwartz, H., 453
Schwartz, M. and C., 453
Scott, M. B., 196, 214
Sechrest, L., 344, 450
Seeman, M., 242, 440
Sellitz, C. et al., 448
Selvin, H., 289, 290, 444
Servien, P., 444
Sewell, W. H., 455
Sherif, M. and C. W., 441
Shipman, M. D., 460
Short, J. F., 202, 461
Sicinski, A., 452
Siegel, S., 413, 456
Simmel, G., 163–5, 213–15, 220
Simmons, J. L., 187, 191, 199, 460
Simms, J. C., 448
Singer, R. D., 441

Sio, A., 443
Sjoberg, G., 201, 202, 209, 215,
    251, 252, 253, 255, 256, 442–
    444, 456
Skolnick, J. H., 453
Somers, R. H., 414, 458
Sorokin, P., 41
Spearman, C., 414
Spektor, A. J., 207
Spencer, H., 29
Squire, C., 199
Stacey, M., 452
Stecchini, C. C., 201
Stein, G., 40
Stouffer, S. A., 207, 216, 458
Strauss, A., 209, 220, 320, 447
Strauss, M. A., 447
Sturtevant, W. C., 212
Sudnow, D., 213
Swinburne, A. C., 25
Szasz, T., 188, 191

T

Tawney, R. H., 203
Theobald, R. and E., 212
Thompson, H., 187, 429
Thorndike, R. L., 443
Tillich, P., 199
Tiryakian, E. A., 187, 203, 212,
    213, 460
Toffler, A., 433, 460, 461
Tolman, E. C., 207
Tolman, S., 439
Toulmin, S., 7, 9, 188, 197
Trevor Roper, H., 203
Turbeyne, C., 191
Turner, R., 442, 452
Tweedledee, 80, 148
Tweedledum, 80–1, 148

U

Urban VIII, 173, 174

V

Van den Berghe, P. L., 206
Velikovsky, I., 210

Venn, J., 275
Vernon, J., 202
Vierkandt, 41
Viteles, M. S., 441
Voltaire, 456

W

Wagner, H. R., 192
Walker, H., 416
Wallace, W., 190, 192, 198
Walsh, W. H., 442
Warner, W. C., 442, 450
Washburne, C., 451
Watkins, J. W. N., 99, 201
Webb, E. et al., 215, 338, 344,
    440, 447, 449, 450, 451
Webberman, E., 345, 450
Weber, M., 109, 163, 164, 165,
    203, 210, 211, 214, 215, 220
Weigert, A. J., 200, 462
Weil, A., 195
Weinstein, M. A., 461
Weiss, S., 443, 444
Weyl, H., 215
Whitehead, A. N., 184, 187
Whitehouse, Mrs Mary, 260,
    261, 433
Willer, D., 98, 207, 265, 443
Willmot, D., 441
Winch, P., 157, 200, 212
Winston, S., 451
Wirth, L., 442
Wittgenstein, L., 189, 211
Wolin, W. S., 461
Wrong, D., 190

Y

Young, M., 441
Young, W. S. (Jock), 460
Yules, G. H., 414, 416

Z

Zarathustra, 433
Zelditch, M., 443
Znaniecki, F., 443

Index of Subjects

A

Abstraction, 130, 164–5
Academic success, 173–4
Acceptability, 74
Accident, 275, 280
Accidentalism, 121
Accounting, 195, 213–14
Accretion measures, 343
Acne, 176
Acquiescence response set, 366
Actometers, 347
Advance (of knowledge), 11–12, 22, 27, 35, *and see* Progress (of knowledge)
Age, 244–5, 295
Alchemy, 2, 21
Alcohol, 195
Alienation, 150, 175, 195, 241–3, 430, 440, 460
Altered states of consciousness, 73, 195, 440
Ambition, 150
Analogy, 41
Analytical theory, 51, 54, 57, 116, 133, 134, 209, 223–5, 233, 235, 244–5, 252, 256–257
Analytic induction, 443
Angels, 195
Anomalies, 99, 194
Anonymity, 364
Antecedent variables, 141, 229, 230, 252
Anthropology, 20
Appearances, 16, 17, 21, 23–5, 96, 98–100, 105, 116, 120, 129, 137, 140, 144, 146, 155, 166–9, 172, 175, 185, 219, 221, 226, 244, 247, 250, 294, 322, 331, 341, 418, 421, 430, 439
Area sampling, 309–10
Arithmetic, 179, 181, 215
Assumptions, 349, 352, 356, 400, 405
Astronomers, 96
Attention, 7–9
Attribute(s), 116, 407
Attrition, 269–71, 294, 301
Autobiographies, 110
Aversion therapy, 202

B

Basic beliefs, 16, 25, 40, 86, 90, 169, 316, 322
Bathwater fallacy, 54–6, 127–8, 134, 137, 427, 432
BB *see* Basic beliefs
Because, 117
Becomings, 121, 123, 132, 158, 165, 253
Beings, 121, 132, 158, 165, 253
Belief, 9, 17, 21, 24, 86, 88, 90–91, 93, 107, 146, 163, 276
Bias, 269–71, 273, 291, 294, 301–302, 308–9, 313, 336, 352, 356, 370
Big bang theory, 22
Biographies, 110
Birth rate, 130
Black hole(s), 21–2, 429

Blancmange, 14, 19, 57, 64, 67, 130
Blue moon, 71, 291, 308
Bongy Wongy, 151, 249, 316, 349, 397, 399, 401
Boojum, 3, 21, 56
Bracketing, 4–5, 186
Breaking (data), 389, 397, 400
Breathalyser test, 351
Bricolage, 163, 430
Bridge principles, 145, 209–10
British Museum, 52–3, 57, 58, 191
Bucket theories of the mind, 40

C

Calculus of probability, 274–5, 277, 283, 285–7, 288, 290–1, 403, 405, 415
Cameo, 343
Cannabis, 195
Capitalism, 109
Case studies, 109–10, 251, 254, 256, 267
Casual causality, 133, 233, 283
Categorical causality, 133, 233, 283
Caterpillar, 58, 61
Causality, 122, 125, 133, 202, 205, 233, 421, 429
Causal model, 225
Causal sketch, 126, 129
Causation see Causality
Cause(s), 32, 106, 110, 117–19, 122, 125–8, 130, 141, 220, 224–5, 244, 253, 314, 315, 430, 459
Census, 306, 308, 352
Central tendency (measurement of), 409
Chance, 114, 118, 272–3, 275–7, 279–80, 282–3, 286–7, 290, 405, 412, 414–15, 444, 456
Change, 123–4
Chi-squared, 290, 405, 414
Clean Air Research, 350
Cloning, 434
Cloze procedure, 455, 459
Cluster sampling, 309
Coding, 336, 339, 341, 356, 383–95, 400, 409

Coding frame, 384, 386, 392, 394
Coding units, 384, 391, 455
Coefficient of concordance, 328, 369, 448
Coefficient of determination, 412–16
Coefficient of predictability, 415–416
Cognition, 86
Coincidence, 275
Collective falsificationism, 233, 245, 259, 401
Collective representations, 18, 23, 177
Collective solipsism, 163, 213
Columns (on computer cards), 385
Commensurability, 43, 190
Common sense, 1–3, 6, 8–10, 13, 16, 21, 24, 26, 29, 32, 34–7, 41–4, 50–1, 56, 60, 81, 83, 91, 97, 117–19, 129, 161, 167, 169, 184–5, 215, 219, 372, 374, 396
Communication, 124, 169, 256, 424, 427, 429
Community studies, 306
Comparative method, 139
Completeness, 205
Compositional effects see Structural effects
Computer, 40, 53, 55, 273, 290, 383, 387, 400, 424, 437, 455, 457
Computer cards, 111, 383, 385, 389, 391, 400, 420, 454–5
Concepts, 9, 19, 50, 172
Conclusions, 13
Cone, 25
Confounding variables, 237, 239, 253, 289
Confusion, 48, 51, 119, 250
Consciousness, 378–80, 382
Consequentiality (of beliefs), 88
Consistency, 205
Constant(s), 114, 253, 295–6, 314
Content analysis, 180, 351, 421
Contingency, 51, 83, 86, 91, 94, 98, 101, 190, 196
Contradiction, 51
Control, 92, 108, 113, 258, 267, 270, 344, 353, 432, 453

Conundrum, 21, 72, 79, 137, 194–5, 308, 341, 342
Conventionalist stratagem, 196, 274
Cooling the mark out, 55
Correctness, 198
Cosmology, 22–3
Cosmos, 16
Cricket pitch, 97
Culture, 43, 103, 170
Cumulative frequency, 409
Curiosity, 221

D

d (Somers's), 414
Data, 7, 40, 106, 147, 160, 168, 177, 184, 209, 251, 253, 259, 275, 281, 289, 312–15, 319, 322, 324, 328–30, 333, 337, 339, 343–83, 386, 393, 396
Data analysis, 322, 384, 387, 395, 400–1, 425
Data preparation procedures, 406–11
Data stipulation, 331–82, 384
Datum unit *see* Unit datum
Datum universe, 337–8, 374, 380, 393–4
Decision rules, 406, 411–22
Deduction, 64, 136–7, 142
Deductive nomological explanation, 45–6, 48–51, 57, 101, 117, 119, 129, 138–9, 151, 156, 209, 224–5, 233, 256–7, 283–4
Deductivism, 153, 156, 158
Deferred gratification, 175
Delusion, 27
Demographic data, 350, 353
Demographic transition, 55, 207
Dependent variable(s), 110, 128, 141, 223, 225–6, 233, 239, 252, 254, 259, 260, 266, 396, 414
Dervish dance, 256–7, 312
Description, 40
Descriptive statistics, 404, 407–411
Deviance, 126, 150
Diaries, 110
¿Direction?, 121–5, 178, 216, 302, 333, 413, 416, 420, 421, 427

Discovery, 35, 60, 76, 168, 169, 233, 281, 323
Dispersion (measure of), 410–11
Doctrine of observational proof, 65
Do-it-yourself-multi-purpose data-matrix, 334–82
Domain assumptions, 208, 253
Dramaturgical model, 55
Dream(s), 5, 14, 18, 71, 81–2, 166, 383
d-statistics, 410–11
Dustbins, 243–4, 324
dyx (Somers's), 459

E

Eating habits, 103
Ecological fallacy, 447, 460
Economics, 78
Educational policy, 130
Effect(s), 32, 110, 125, 127–8, 130, 141, 220, 221, 225, 268, 314, 315, 459
Elgin Marbles, 52
Empirical import, 83, 86, 274
Empirical theory, 139
Enlightenment, the so-called, 10
Epidemiology, 284
Epistemic correlate(s), 243, 245, 351
Epistemological alienation, 428
Epistemology, 9, 56, 63, 120, 186
Equivalence classes, 181
Erosion measures, 343
Erotic stratification, 55, 175
Errors, 47, 141, 152, 224, 253, 294
Esemplastic, 75
eta-squared, 415–16
Ethnomethodological encounter, 249–50
Ethnomethodological experiment, 371–2, 373, 384
Ethnomethodology, 157–9, 192, 212, 213, 371
Ethnoscience, 158
Evidence, 82–4, 91–4, 97, 101, 109, 189, 323, 341, 343, 376, 420, 426, 428
Evidential density, 339–41
Exact percipient fancy, 75

Expectations, 169
Experiment, 66, 107, 109, 110,
  112, 202, 248, 249, 251, 254,
  255, 257, 260, 267, 337, 352,
  353, 355, 371
Experimental method, 108
Experimental variables, 237,
  238, 239–66, 295
Expert, 10, 35, 93, 428
Explanandum, 45, 47–8, 105,
  117, 134, 225, 284
Explanans, 45, 47, 50, 105, 117,
  134, 284
Explanation, 42–3, 45, 47, 49–50,
  53–4, 81, 116, 118, 119, 122,
  129, 130, 152, 178, 225, 227,
  284
Explanatory sketches, 51
Explanatory theories, 51, 54, 57,
  116, 133, 134, 137, 141, 224,
  233, 235, 284, 425
Exploratory research, 233
External measurement, 337, 339,
  340, 346
Extraneous variables, 141, 226,
  229, 238, 239, 248, 249, 251,
  260, 261, 270, 271–2, 289, 295,
  313, 314, 439
Extraordinary science, 59
Extraordinary theory, 71

F

Fact(s), 3, 4, 7, 9, 27, 34, 40,
  63, 65, 76, 77, 82, 102, 119,
  139, 146–7, 194, 253, 323, 350,
  424, 430
Fairies, 77, 79, 133, 430, 438
Fairyland, 385
Fairy tales, 2, 14, 26, 75–6, 81,
  82, 91–5, 98, 101–12, 115, 116,
  120, 124, 125, 128, 130, 131,
  139, 141, 143, 145, 169, 172,
  173–5, 195, 219, 223, 230, 239,
  244, 247, 252, 282, 284, 315,
  331, 417–18, 434
Falsification, 140, 309, 317,
  331
Falsificationism, 99, 101, 102,
  105, 193, 254, 311, 318–19,
  329, 405, 411, 414, 416, 417,
  427, 457

Falsificationist attitude of mind,
  100, 185, 219, 234, 317
¿Falsity? 9, 51, 82, 84, 86
Falsity₁, 191
Falsity₂, 88, 91, 254, 417, 429
Falsity₃, 88, 429
Falsity₄, 88, 91, 95, 98, 104, 106,
  115, 233, 405, 429
Fashion (in science), 66–7
Fatalism, 433–4, 460
Feather, 97
Feedback, 125, 126, 132
FF see Figuration of facts
Figuration of facts, 17, 19, 20–5,
  36, 38, 61, 69, 316, 322, 341
First-order meanings, 168, 171,
  172, 177, 178, 183, 304, 305,
  307, 314, 320, 327, 328, 341,
  349, 351, 352, 356, 364, 365,
  369, 374, 378, 382, 392, 394,
  407
First-order theories, 169, 173,
  179
Forbid, 98–9
Forms, 166, 195
Fortune, 121
Frequency distribution, 279–80,
  283, 393, 399, 408, 419, 422
Frequency polygon, 409
Friendship, 150, 155
Frog's leg, 97
Function, 128
Functionalism, 47, 203, 205, 212
Future, 102, 103, 129, 431, 432,
  433–5

G

Game, 60
gamma (Goodman and Krus-
  kal's), 414, 415–16
Gatekeepers, 306
Gemeinschaft, 434
Generalization(s), 42, 43, 52,
  117, 137, 140, 163, 166, 233,
  281, 404, 422, 423
Gestalt switch, 7, 196
Glossing, 4, 5
Gnosticism, 212
Graffiti, 393
Graph theory, 205
Grimoire, 185

Grounded theory, 139, 209, 320
Grouped frequency table, 408
Guttman scaling, 184–5

H

Hall-Jones scale, 387
Happenings, 118, 120, 124, 125,
129, 132, 141, 146, 150, 152,
156, 160, 165, 166, 168, 171,
175, 182, 183, 283, 284, 286,
295, 331, 347, 352, 374, 384,
392, 393
Hawthorne experiments, 248–9,
442
Head-counting, 346
Hell's Angels, 10
Heretics, 187
Heroism (methodological), 66
Heterogeneous sampling, 226,
299
Hierarchy of credibility, 428
Hippies, 10, 16
Histogram, 397, 404, 408
Holism (methodological), 66
Hollerith cards see Computer
cards
Homogeneous sampling, 266,
299
Honesty, 84, 91
Hope, 461
Hunch, 257, and see Implicit
theory
Hustlers, 10
Hypotheses, 42, 82, 83, 97, 98,
102–10, 113, 131, 138, 146,
161, 173, 174, 185, 224, 233,
235, 237, 251, 253, 256–7, 264,
283, 309, 313, 330–2, 341, 355,
374, 396, 399, 401–6, 416, 419,
421, 422, 424, 425

I

I Ching, 275
Idealism, 16, 142, 144, 146, 147,
152–6, 158, 159, 163, 173, 177,
198, 212, 282, 372
Idealization, 170
Idiotic idiography, 141
Illusion, 20, 37, 140

Imagination, 60, 73–5, 78, 79,
134, 136, 137, 139, 140, 147,
165, 175, 177, 195, 209, 214,
220, 221, 261, 282, 397
Imminent migrant, 382
Implicit theory, 51, 57, 116, 133,
161, 220, 224, 226, 252, 256,
368, 425
Inadmissible evidence, 341 278,
Income, 103, 150
Independent variables, 110, 141,
223, 225, 229–33, 239, 248,
252, 254, 259, 266, 396
Index construction, 247, 326,
418, 420, 427, 457
Indicators, 174, 175, 240, 241,
243–5, 248, 254, 258–9, 264,
270–1, 326, 330, 345, 357, 363,
366, 386, 393, 418, 419, 457
Individualism (methodological),
207
Induction, 64, 136, 137, 139,
140, 147, 165, 167, 175, 177,
195, 209, 214, 220, 221, 256,
287, 406, 414, 446, 459
Inductivism, 152, 153, 156, 158,
192, 196, 283, 285, 288, 293,
320, 372, 404, 416
In-group preference, 116
Initial data see Raw data
Inspiration, 72–4, 111, 195, 316,
368, 373
Institutionalization, 204
Instrument design, 357, 363–4
Instrument presentation, 357, 364
Intaglio, 343
Intelligence, 130, 149, 150, 182,
226, 243, 244
Interactional sampling, 301, 305–
307, 445
Interactive sampling see Inter-
actional sampling
Interiorization, 166
Internal measurement, 337–40,
370
Interpersonal behaviour, 87
Interpersonal trust, 90
Interrogative brackets, 4
Interval scales, 182, 183, 336,
408, 409, 413, 415, 420
Intervening variables, 141, 223,
225–7, 229–33, 237, 252–4,
259, 260, 266

Interviews, 247, 250, 323–4, 338, 352, 355–7, 363–4, 368
Intrusive measurement, 337–40, 370
Invalidity, 85, 332
Invention, 29, 35, 60, 169, 323
Inventory of variables to be measured, 235, 239, 240, 245, 257–8, 357, 383, 425, 441
Isomorph(s), 52, 172, 175, 413
Isomorphism, 52, 55, 183, 264, 269, 294, 299, 302, 305, 307, 331
Isomorphizing, 52

J

Jelly pie, 158, 161, 212, 373
Judgments, 36, 48, 50, 52, 83, 84, 88, 91, 98, 117, 121, 130, 133, 139, 140–1, 158, 165, 189, 220, 224, 230, 234, 237, 283, 288, 291, 402, 425

K

Kept knowledge, 24–7, 32, 33, 36, 51, 54, 61, 91, 131, 169, 171, 221, 316, 322
Key location sampling, 306, 446
Kitchen-sink category, 336, 363
KK *see* Kept knowledge
Knickerbocker glory, 249, 259
Knowledge, 1, 2, 4, 11, 12, 18, 22, 24, 32, 35, 39, 41, 62, 63, 66, 74, 77, 115, 130, 144, 188, 245, 250, 282, 399, 428, 433

L

lambda-b, 457
Language, 10, 14, 32, 129, 244, 250, 331, 382, 383, 432, 435
Law, 139
Law of Nature, 192
Letters, 110
Level of analysis, 90, 133, 136, 196, 231, 291, 335, 338, 340, 347, 349, 351
Level of meaning, 9, 178
Library, 26, 54, 56, 57, 102, 109,

126, 164, 191, 241, 251, 253, 256, 258, 263, 293, 334, 355–357, 372, 403
Logic, 47, 85, 86, 90, 134, 148, 198, 281, 291, 427, 432
Logical theory of probability, 276, 288, 445
Logic-in-use, 212
Logico-deductive method, 46
Longitudinal studies, 314
Loosely structured data, 336, 338, 340, 344, 348, 356, 374, 386
Love, 86, 375–6, 434

M

Mad Hatter, 71
Magic, 2, 7, 8, 79, 118, 139, 173, 422, 424, 429
Man, 132, 164, 165, 376, 431, 433
Manipulation (of variables), 248, 261, 331
Martian(s), 6, 187
Match sampling, 267, 269, 299
Mathematical measurement, 180, 181
Mathematics, 84, 128, 194, 328
Mean (arithmetic), 283, 404, 409–10, 411, 414, 443; regression to mean, 443
Meanings, 8, 13, 74, 78, 122, 166, 167, 168, 170, 171, 175, 183, 219, 220, 292, 323, 332, 345, 351, 374, 375, 393, 394, 416, 428, 430, 431, 435
Measurement, 35, 102, 112, 114, 142, 155, 157, 158, 173, 175, 176, 177, 178, 183, 184, 239, 240, 241, 244, 247, 258, 260, 264, 266, 270, 315, 324, 328, 330, 332, 336, 338, 339, 345, 350, 352, 355, 369, 370, 380, 382, 383, 386, 396, 399, 400, 401, 407, 409, 419, 424
Memory, 15, 124, 134, 137
Mental experiment, 248, 251, 253, 255, 256, 258, 266
Metaphor(s), 52, 54, 60, 134
Metaphysics, 16, 18, 21–3, 87, 275, 286, 289, 414, 433

Method of agreement, 220
Method of concomitant varia-
tions, 220
Method of difference, 220
Method of residues, 221
Methodology, 9, 90, 156, 224
Middle range theories, 55, 192,
207
Middlers, 409–10
Mistake(s), 24, 141, 199
Mnemonic(s), 256
Mock Turtle see Soup
Mode, 409, 410
Model(s), 51–3, 55, 57, 122, 127,
134, 139, 190, 399, 422
Moment, 22, 84, 130, 254, 260,
435
Monads, 195
Monocausality, 121
Mopping-up operations, 201
m-statistics, 409–10, 414
Multicausality, 121, 123
Multiple-form measures, 325–
327
Mushroom, 59, 61, 170, 373

N

Naturalistic doctrine of observa-
tion, 65
Naturalistic fallacy, 197
Nature, 22, 23, 63
Neo-idealism, 147, 210, 213
Newcomer, 381
Newts, 116
Nimbleness of limb, 238
Nominal dichotomy, 407, 415
Nominal scales, 392, 407, 409,
413, 414, 415, 420, 181,
183
Non-grouped frequency table,
408
Non-parametric statistics, 413
Non-response, 356
Non-Specific Unrethritis, 284
Normal curve, 280, 283, 422
Normality, 5, 170, 171
Normal science, 62, 63, 99, 102,
104, 107, 115, 155, 221, 224,
276, 279, 281
Number(s), 177–80, 279, 285,
286, 287, 290, 302, 446

O

Objectifiability, 177, 248
Objectification, 166
Objective mind, 151
Objectivity, 92, 146, 189, 461
Observation(s), 100, 110, 139,
140, 152, 161, 169, 176, 177,
287, 331, 333, 372, 386, 404
Observatory, 95, 119, 120, 330
Obtrusive measurement, 337,
339, 340, 370
Occultism, 78
Official statistics, 160, 351
Olber's paradox, 22
One-way mirrors, 353
Ontological assumptions, 16, 120
Operationalism see Operationism
Operationalization, 146, 147,
149, 152, 158, 159, 196, 244,
245, 247, 330, 357, 409
Operationism, 151–3
Opinio, 285, 287, 424, 426, 428,
430
Opinion(s), see Opinio
Opium, 195, 383
Ordinal scales, 182, 183, 328,
336, 359, 408, 409, 411, 413,
420
Organic systems, 55
Os intermaxillare, 76
Oyster eating, 42, 46
Oyster-gut-saga, 46
Oysters, 162

P

Panel studies, 314
Parachute, 151, 346
Paradigm, 2, 14, 16–17, 21, 24,
29, 32, 35, 37–8, 40, 60, 62–3,
65, 77, 82–3, 90, 94, 99, 100,
105, 116, 118, 130, 131, 136,
146, 147, 155, 161, 186, 188,
189, 196, 204, 316, 322, 331,
375, 380, 381
Paradox, 77, 137, 308
Parametric statistics, 413
Paranoia, 431
Parity of esteem, 181
Participant observation, 251,
313, 314, 374, 376–82

Passing, 375
Passivism (as epistemology), 64
Past, 253, 431, 432, 433, 434, 435
Patent Elastic Summerhouse, 276
Penisometer, 260–1
Perception, 340
Percepts, 19, 172
Permutation, 275
Phantasy, 2, 17, 54, 67, 77–8,
  82, 144
Phenomenology, 3, 158
Phenomenon, 4, 7–8, 18, 43, 56,
  95, 103, 220, 221, 225
Phewangulation see Principle of
  phewangulation
phi, 414
Philosophers' stone, 21
Physical manipulation (of vari-
  ables), 115
Physics, 96
Pilot survey, 368
Ping-pong balls, 53
Plausibility, 106
Poetic intuition, 74
Point biserial r squared, 415, 416
Police, 103
Political attitudes, 125
Political involvement, 173
Politics of science, 428
Pornography, 260, 433
Positivism, 142, 144, 146, 147,
  152–6, 158, 163, 173, 221, 281,
  285, 288, 289, 293, 320, 404
Power, 252, 428, 432, 433
Pragmatism, 40
Praxis, 90
Prediction, 92, 103, 107, 204, 254
Prehistoric thought, 118
Prejudice, 140
Present, 254, 431, 433, 434, 435
Primitive mentality, 118
Principle of data reliability, 324,
  329, 435
Principle of data validity, 324,
  333
Principle of insufficient reason,
  286
Principle of the moving observer,
  346
Principle of phewangulation, 259,
  261
Principle of replicability, 245,
  311, 319, 324, 329

Principle of triangulation, 245,
  259, 319, 345, 418
Prison records, 110
Probability, 12, 105, 139, 275,
  277, 283, 284, 287, 288, 289,
  416, 423, 443, 456
Probability sampling, 273, 276,
  279, 291, 294, 295, 308–10,
  404, 447
Probability statements, 13, 274
Probability statistics, 282, 285,
  291
Probability theory, 13, 60
Problem, 34, 35, 41, 100, 114
Professional criminals, 10
Progress (of knowledge), 11–12,
  29, 48, 56, 200, 432, 434, 437
Progressive problem shifts, 67,
  194, 201
Project Camelot, 198
Proof, 82, 98, 101–2
Propaganda, 432
Prophecy, 103, 254
Proportional reduction in error,
  412, 414
Propositions, 9, 42, 82, 83, 94,
  130, 131, 404
Protestant Ethic, 109
Psychotropic drugs, 1
Punching (computer cards), 386,
  391, 394
Pure measurement, 179
Purposive sampling, 26, 267,
  268, 269, 270, 271, 291, 294,
  295, 299, 308, 310
Puzzles, 35, 41, 44, 52, 99, 118,
  119, 167, 171, 194, 195, 221,
  223, 234, 257, 340, 425
Pyramid, 25, 29

Q

Q (Yule's), 414, 415–16, 457
Quadratic regression equations,
  413
Quantification, 179, 180, 241,
  325, 446
Quantum theory, 283
Quartile deviation, 410
Questionnaires, 247, 302, 314,
  323, 336, 338, 353, 355–7, 363,
  364, 368, 369, 384, 386, 427

Quota sampling, 268, 269, 270, 301, 307

R

Radii of reasoning, 46, 50, 57, 60, 61, 76, 90, 94, 133, 169, 316
Randomization, 60, 114, 238, 239, 258, 276, 288, 453
Random sampling, 272, 273, 279, 289, 309
Range (statistical), 410
Rational reconstruction, 432
Ratio scales, 180, 183, 336, 408, 409, 413, 415
Raw data, 334, 339, 341, 384, 386, 425
Reality, 2–7, 9, 11, 17, 19, 20, 21, 27, 29, 41, 44, 56, 63, 77, 78, 81, 105, 106, 146, 147, 149, 152, 153, 157, 158, 159, 160, 161, 165, 169, 171, 175, 177, 178, 187, 209, 223, 244, 264, 282–3, 338, 349, 364, 371, 378, 426, 428, 444
Reason, 32, 40, 56, 61, 62
Reasonableness, 41, 48
Reasoning, 9, 51
Recognition, 86, 146, 323
Reconstructed logic, 212
Regression (statistical), 413, 414
Reification, 167
Relative deprivation, 116, 207
Reliability, 245, 325, 327–31, 340, 341, 345, 346, 348, 363, 365, 367, 368, 393, 394
Religious maniacs, 10
Representations, 172, 177
Representativeness, 264–5, 306, 318, 332
Research inventory see Inventory of variables to be measured
Research programme, 244, 255, 293, 330, 369
Research strategy, 248, 253, 257, 259, 266, 425
Residual rule breaking, 126
Respondent fatigue, 365
Retrodiction, 254
Retroduction, 137, 140, 163, 224

Revolution (in science), 100, 195
Revolution (social), 131
Revolutionary conventionalism, 66
Rhetoric, 427, 429
rho (Spearman's), 414, 457
Rice, 111
Rigidly structured data, 335, 338, 340, 343, 374, 386
Riskiness (of tests), 99, 106, 109, 111, 274, 372, 383, 404, 449, 458
Rituals, 219, 224, 248, 264
Role-playing, 374, 375, 376, 381
Roominess (of theories), 65, 67, 71, 100, 131, 201
Rorschach inkblot, 8
Rotten teeth, 13
RR see Radii of reasoning and Rules of reasonableness
Rules, 12, 24, 44, 65, 137, 140, 146
Rules of reasonableness, 24, 25, 27, 35, 36, 42, 43, 50, 54, 57, 60, 76, 133, 169, 322
Run-of-the-mill see Normal science

S

Sample, 239, 243, 248, 262, 264, 273, 277, 281, 293–321, 322, 330, 356, 366, 367, 369, 392, 393, 394, 400, 405, 413, 419, 423
Sampling, 238, 248, 255, 263–4, 265, 281–2, 286, 289, 293, 321, 384, 424, 425, 427
Sampling frame, 267, 270, 271, 295, 296, 308, 314, 315
Scales, 175, 176, 178, 179, 181, 184, 191, 247, 327, 328, 335, 336, 338, 340, 347, 386–7, 393, 415
Schizophrenic outburst, 435
Science, 1, 2, 4, 6, 9, 11–12, 17, 21, 29, 32, 43–4, 56, 60, 62, 65, 66, 76, 79, 83–4, 91, 93, 94, 105, 107, 117, 119, 134, 140, 147, 149, 150, 169, 188, 193, 219, 224, 429, 432

Scientia, 285
Scientific attitude, 17
Scientism, 60, 78, 83, 428, 432
Scrambling rituals, 271; *and see*
　　Randomization
Second-order happenings, 168,
　　254
Second-order meanings, 243,
　　245, 306, 307, 319, 332, 337,
　　338, 339, 341, 365, 376, 378,
　　382, 392, 394
Second-order theory, 169, 171–2,
　　173, 177, 178, 179, 220, 233,
　　250, 349
Selection, 113, 130, 169, 239,
　　258, 266, 267, 295, 370, 389
Self-fulfilling, 87
Serendipity, 194–209
Set theory, 275, 284, 294
Sexual behaviour, 129, 250
Significance tests, 283, 289, 290
Situationism, 120, 373
Snark, 3, 80
Snowball sampling, 301–5, 357
Social class, 116, 125, 130, 150,
　　155, 175, 226, 227, 238, 246–7,
　　278, 281–3, 286, 291, 293, 387,
　　388
Social journalism, 429
Sociology, 6, 38, 55, 79, 143,
　　150, 161, 163, 164, 168, 189,
　　204
Sociometry, 304, 421
Sophisticated falsificationism, 67
Sorting procedures, 399
Soup, 264, 277, 278, 281–3, 286,
　　291, 293, 401, 427
Space, 1, 7, 22, 53, 89, 166, 213,
　　413, 421
Specialization, 29
Split half, 327
Standard deviation, 410
Stars, 21, 95, 96, 132
Statistical induction, 204, 208,
　　283–4
Statistical inference, 404, 405,
　　406, 412, 414, 422, 457
Statistical manipulation of vari-
　　ables, 111, 115, 248, 251, 254,
　　255, 258, 260, 261, 383, 396,
　　399, 400, 403, 405, 406, 416,
　　421
Statistical significance, 416

Statistical theory, 400–3
Statistics, 204, 265, 320
Statistricks, 417, 423
Status crystallization, 55
Status inconsistency, 116
Steady state theory, 22
Stoicism, 118
Structural effects, 447, 459
Structural sampling, 268, 269,
　　301–2, 307
Subjectifiability, 177, 248
Subjectivity, 75, 147
Subsamples, 294, 309, 310, 312,
　　318, 396, 404, 446
Suicide rates, 351
Sums, 13, 128, 285, 400
Surprise, 250
Symbolic data, 383, 384, 385,
　　394, 425, 454
Symmetry, 127, 409, 421, 459
System, 128
Systematic cutting, 113
Systematic sampling, 309

T

Table, 111–12
Tabula rasa, 60
Taken-for-granted, 3, 8, 25, 32,
　　36, 57, 65, 74–5, 77, 79, 103,
　　136, 151, 157, 159, 161, 163,
　　168, 171, 172, 188, 196, 205,
　　264, 289, 291, 301, 322, 323,
　　331, 337, 372, 375, 380, 428,
　　430, 432, 433, 435, 437
Tape-recorder, 38, 40, 348, 356,
　　374
Tarot, 281
Tattooing, 127
tau-b, 415–16
Taxonomy, 211, 413
Technology, 428
Temporary member, 381
Test, 42, 77, 82, 86, 91–4, 97,
　　101, 102, 107, 109, 111, 134,
　　138, 139, 140, 141, 142, 146,
　　152, 153, 159, 169, 172, 173,
　　174, 177, 178, 185, 197, 198,
　　199, 224, 237, 247, 248, 251,
　　254, 256, 258, 260, 264, 283,
　　309, 313, 316, 330–1, 336,
　　341, 355, 373–4, 383, 396,

400, 403, 405, 406, 411, 421, 446
Thematic Apperception Tests, 8
Theoretical sampling, 320
Theories, 34, 38, 47, 50, 61, 66, 67, 77, 82, 94, 98, 102, 104, 105, 106, 118, 138, 139, 140, 141, 142, 146, 152, 153, 159, 172, 221, 227, 232, 239, 240, 243, 249, 254, 265, 274, 296, 303, 321, 323, 331, 368, 383, 400, 402, 422, 423
Theory construction, 142, 153, 163, 220, 221, 256, 284, 285
Thing, 4
Thinking, 5, 12, 14–15, 21–3, 60, 72–4, 77–8, 129, 133, 134, 137, 141, 188, 195, 196, 427, 431
Thirty-nine stips *see* Do-it-your-self-multi-purpose-data-matrix
Thought(s), 2, 12, 14, 15, 17, 19, 20–2, 24, 27, 29, 36, 56, 59, 60–2, 73, 78, 86, 120, 133, 134, 137, 140, 186, 195, 196, 370
Thrush, 167
¿Time? 21, 32, 53, 56, 59, 61, 62, 73, 78, 86, 89, 95, 108, 123, 128, 137, 141, 159, 166, 205, 213, 245, 254, 259, 260, 281, 304, 314, 315, 318–19, 320, 324, 332, 334, 340, 346, 355, 375, 376, 377, 382
Time machines, 432
Timing, 437
Topological measurement, 180–2
Totemism, 20
Traits, 116
Transcend(ence), 15, 21, 37, 60–61, 66, 81, 89, 100, 119, 133, 159, 163, 178, 229, 276
Triangulation *see* Principle of triangulation
True₂ learner, 381
¿Truth?, 1, 9–12, 14, 32, 38, 54, 61, 63, 65, 76–7, 82–4, 86, 88, 190, 330, 424, 427, 428, 429, 437
Truth₁, 88, 89, 93, 97, 105, 106, 134, 157, 165, 198, 199, 426, 427, 435

Truth₂, 88, 89, 91, 93, 100, 106, 134, 243, 264, 276, 304, 323, 381, 416, 420, 430, 446
Truth₃, 88, 89, 91, 93, 102, 106, 134, 291, 411, 430
Truth₄, 88, 89, 91, 92, 93–5, 98, 101, 106, 107, 115, 134, 138, 139, 157, 161, 173, 178, 233, 234, 254, 256, 284, 285, 290, 313, 315, 318, 372, 398, 400, 401, 426, 430
Tychism, 121
Typification, 38, 168, 169
Typological sampling, 266, 299
Typology, 122, 155, 191, 211, 215, 267

U

Ultimate causes, 131
Uncertainty principle, 449
Underpants, 161
Understanding, 21, 29, 52, 92, 166
Uninterpreted axiomatic system, 406
Unit datum, 334–6, 351, 384
Universe, 264, 269, 310
Unobtrusive measurement, 332, 344
Unstructured data, 335, 338, 340, 345, 374, 386, 394
Unthinkable, 73–6, 78
Urbanization, 251
Urphänomene, 75
Utility (of a theory), 107

V

Validity, 50, 51, 54, 57, 134, 161, 329, 330, 331, 332, 333, 338, 340, 343, 345, 356, 363, 367, 369, 370, 404, 427, 448
Values, 176
Variables, 35, 103, 104, 106, 107, 108, 109, 112, 113, 114, 116, 120, 127, 130, 141, 143, 169, 173, 175, 185, 221, 240, 250, 261, 264, 282, 295, 315, 330, 355, 359, 365, 376, 385–6, 393, 397, 399, 400, 411, 415, 417–18

Vectors, 127
Verification, 102, 140, 416
Verificationism, 193, 196, 254
    289, 318, 333, 372, 405, 417,
    418
Verisimilitude, 193
Verstehende, 151, 152, 210
Video-tape, 339, 341, 348, 373
Vocabulary of intervention, 129

Vortex, 57
Voting behaviour, 125, 353

W

Wellington boots, 14, 57, 322
Witchcraft, 107
Working universe, 255

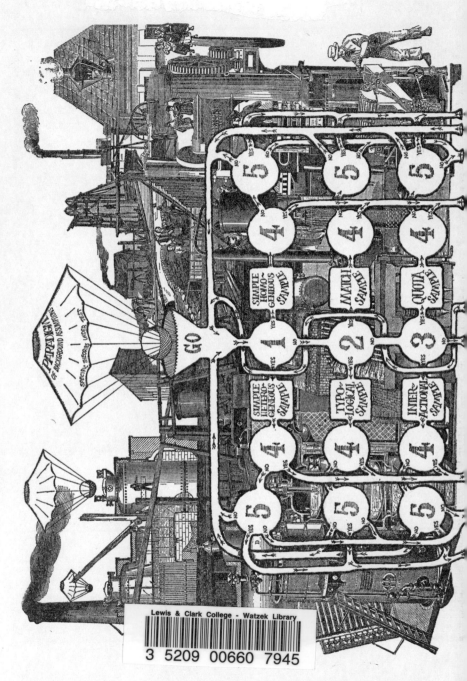